Analysing Sentences

An Introduction to English Syntax

Second Edition

NOEL BURTON-ROBERTS

LONGMAN
LONDON AND NEW YORK

Pearson Education Limited
Edinburgh Gate, Harlow,
Essex CM20 2JE, England

and Associated Companies throughout the world

Visit us on the world wide web at:
http://www.pearsoneduc.com

First edition © Longman Group Ltd 1986
Second edition © Addison Wesley Longman Limited 1997

First published 1986
Third edition 1998

ISBN 0 582 24876–0 Paper

British Library Cataloguing-in-Publication Data
A catalogue record for this book is available from the British Library

Library of Congress Cataloging-in-Publication Data
Burton-Roberts, Noel, 1948–
    Analysing sentences : an introduction to English syntax / Noel Burton-Roberts. –
2nd ed.
        p.   cm. – (Learning about language)
    Includes bibliographical references and index.
    ISBN 0-582-24876-0 (pbk.)
    1. English language—Sentences. 2. English language—Syntax.
    I. Title.   II. Series.
    PE1375.B87 1997
    428.2—dc21   96-48575
                                                                            CIP

10 9 8 7 6
06   05   04   03

Set by 8 in 10/12 pt Palatino
Printed in Malaysia, VVP

Contents

Preface to the Second Edition

When I first wrote *Analysing Sentences*, I had in mind the kind of mixed audience that I taught (and still teach) in an introductory course at Newcastle. This included first-year undergraduates in linguistics and English language who would be going on to find out more about English syntax, syntactic theory, and argumentation in syntactic theory, in later years. It also included many others who probably would not continue and whose purposes were different and quite varied. For these, the book had to provide a self-contained, systematic, and coherent, introductory picture of English in its own right. They were less interested, perhaps, in syntactic theory than in forming a reasonably informed impression of the structural range of the language and a grasp of the vocabulary and concepts needed to describe it. So the aim was to strike a balance between providing both descriptive range and descriptive convenience on the one hand while, on the other, offering something of genuine use to someone about to embark more seriously on syntactic theory and argumentation.

Many of the changes in this second edition have been made with this balance in mind. Occasionally, in the first edition, I made decisions which, while pedagogically convenient, have come over the years to seem less and less defensible or useful in an introduction to syntax. So I have done something about them. For teachers familiar with the first edition who want an overview of more important changes, I have listed them below.

A more general change concerns the exercises. There are more of them and there are now 'Further Exercises'. These come without answers and can be used for seminar work. Some are designed (as before) to test comprehension, others to give practice in handling new data and to encourage thought. More than in the first edition, rather than give a phrase-marker in the text, I set the drawing of the phrase-marker as an exercise. It is always given in a 'Discussion' at the end of the chapter. This, I think, makes for more worthwhile and enjoyable reading, and it builds confidence. It seems essential the reader be encouraged to do these before consulting the Discussion.

One thing that has not changed is the 'Verb Group'. Much though I feel inclined to, I won't apologise for retaining this! I grant the evidence which suggests there is no such thing (and its incompatibility with X-bar). But there is less agreement on how verbs in English *are* to be treated. Some textbooks simply avoid the issues, by restricting their coverage of the possibilities I have gathered up under 'Vgrp'. I have kept it because it is convenient: it provides a way of covering those possibilities (and introducing needed vocabulary, in a way beginners find intuitive) without immediately embroiling them in problems, lengthy explanations, and excuses. Besides, I have found it useful as an illustrative starting point in later courses on argumentation.

The following major changes of detail have been made, not only in aid of bringing the analysis a little more into line with common current practice, but also in the light of my own experience of teaching the first edition. This has made me think that I was sometimes a little over-cautious as regards what is teachable at this stage. Even so, many of the changes have actually had a simplifying effect.

(i) Chapter 2. Governors (first edition) are now explicitly referred to as 'heads' (not as 'governors').

(ii) Chapter 5. Adjunct adverbials are now, in addition, explicitly referred to as 'VP-adverbials'. This is more helpful, in my view. And, while the distinction between the 'conjunct adverbials' and 'disjunct adverbials' of the first edition is alluded to, this detail has been played down. Both are now explicitly referred to as 'Sentence-adverbials' ('S-adverbials').

(iii) Chapter 6. What in the first edition was called 'Subject-Auxiliary Inversion' is now more accurately 'Auxiliary fronting'. More importantly, the auxiliary is now fronted to the complementiser position (daughter of S-bar, sister of S). This is a major change and involves changes elsewhere – see below. It means that 'S-bar' is now introduced in Chapter 6 rather than Chapter 8. Auxiliary-fronting leaves a gap under AUX.

(iv) Chapter 6. It is more helpful to the student (to remember that passive verbs are not intransitive) to have a gap in the object position following a passive verb. Some students do this spontaneously, anyway. And it provides a better preparation for what is to follow, both in the book and elsewhere. So I now insist on a gap in object position.

(v) Chapter 7. The term 'zero article' has been abandoned in favour of 'unfilled DET'.

(vi) Chapter 7. The discussion of *one* in the first edition was unsatisfactory. It was not used to motivate any distinction, within NP, between complements and adjuncts and so never really worked. I have simplified here by postponing all mention of *one* to an Appendix in Chapter 7, where it *is* associated with the distinction beween adjuncts ('NOM-modifiers') and complements ('N-modifiers'). The chapter can be read quite independently of that appendix, however (in my experience, beginners find the distinction between adjunct and complement difficult in the context of NP). Tutors can decide for themselves whether to insist that the distinction be respected in Chapter 7. Other changes (in Chapters 8 and 9) anyway mean that it does now eventually emerge, clearly and naturally, when really necessary.

(vii) Chapter 8. I now introduce the complementiser *whether* (and hence subordinate *yes/no* interrogative clauses) here, along with *that*.

(viii) Chapter 8. The representation of noun-complement clauses in the first edition was unsatisfactory. As complements, these are now more simply and accurately represented as sisters of N within NOM. See below for a consequent change to the structural position of restrictive relative clauses.

(ix) Chapter 9. The order of presentation has changed: the chapter now moves from wh-interrogative clauses (main and subordinate) to relative clauses. This is convenient if, as I do, one spends two separate weeks on this chapter (one on interrogatives, one on relatives). A further minor change from the first edition is that subject constituent questions are now presented as having a fronted auxiliary. (There is a 'Further Exercise' on this.)

(x) Chapter 9. Since auxiliaries are now fronted to the (S-bar) complementiser position (Ch. 6), which cannot be filled twice over, Wh-expressions are now fronted to a higher Comp position (Comp-2). Comp-2 is here defined as daughter of S-double bar, sister of S-bar.

(xi) Chapter 9. Since noun complement clauses are now sisters of N (Ch. 8), relative clauses are now represented as sisters of

NOM. As explained there, this distinction between N-modifier (complement clause) and NOM-modifier (relative clause) parallels that between complement and adjunct in the VP. If interested (or required!), the student is now in a position to generalise this to all modifiers in NP, by turning back to the Appendix in Chapter 7.

(xii) Chapter 10 remains largely unchanged (apart from changes consequent on those in earlier chapters) though there is slightly more detail and discussion.

In preparing this second edition, I have benefited from the comments and advice of many people. They are too numerous to mention and thank individually here, but I must mention the help of Phil Carr and Siobhan Chapman. The students at Newcastle (whose responses have invariably been interesting and instructive) have taught me more than they know. I am especially grateful to Georgette Ioup, who I met in Morocco in 1983 when I had just started writing the first edition. Her detailed and insightful comments on it over the last ten years have been of great help, not to say indispensible. My wife Tessa has born with grace my probings of her linguistic competence and Julia, my daughter, has made the rewriting much more enjoyable by joining me in vandalising copies of the first edition, pasting, and stapling.

I would like to dedicate this second edition to my mother and the memory of my father.

Preface to the First Edition

This book grew out of a longish pamphlet used with first year undergraduates in the University of Newcastle upon Tyne, which I wrote in 1979. I'd like to acknowledge the late Barbara Strang's encouragement when I wrote that pamphlet. Thanks, too, to Geoff Leech and Mick Short (the series editors) for their help and encouragement in producing the book as it now stands. Valerie Adams, painstakingly and to good effect, went through each chapter as it was completed and for this I am very grateful. This book has also benefited from comments made by Ewan Klein, Maggie Cooper, Rodney Huddleston, Michael Anthony, Phil Carr, Liz Smith, and Lesley Milroy. Herman Moisl's arbitrations between myself and the word processor are gratefully acknowledged. I owe a general debt of gratitude to Sir Randolph Quirk, who introduced me to the study of the English language in the first place. Finally, my thanks to Tessa for her support and patience.

Introduction

Attempting to describe the language you speak is about as difficult as attempting to describe yourself as a person. Your language is very much part of you and your thinking. You use your language so instinctively that it is difficult to stand outside yourself and think of it as something that is independent of you, something which you know and which can be described. You may even feel inclined to say that your language is not something you know, you just speak it, and that's all there is to it. But as the native speaker of a language, there is an important sense in which you do know all that there is to know about that language. This is not to deny that there are almost certainly words with which you are not familiar. Perhaps you don't know the meaning of the word *lagophthalmic*. If so, your (understandable) ignorance of this is more medical ignorance than ignorance about the English language, and is anyway quickly remedied with the help of a dictionary. But there is much more to a language than its words. There is much more that you do know about your language which cannot so conveniently be looked up, and which you were never explicitly taught. And this is knowledge of a more fundamental and systematic kind than knowledge of the meanings of individual words. The more fundamental such knowledge is, the more difficult it is to become consciously aware of it.

We are brought up sharply against our own knowledge of the language when, for example, we hear a foreigner make a mistake. You may have had the frustrating experience of knowing that something is wrong but not being able to say precisely what it is, beyond saying 'We just don't say it like that.' The very deep-seated character of speakers' knowledge of their language makes it extremely difficult for them to explain what it is they know.

Here are some examples to illustrate the point. As a speaker of English, you will agree that [1] and [2] are good English sentences:

[1] Dick believes himself to be a genius.
[2] Dick believes he is a genius.

but that there is something wrong with [3] and [4]:

[3] Dick believes he to be a genius.
[4] Dick believes himself is a genius.

It is interesting that, simply on the basis of assuming you speak English, and knowing nothing else about you, I can predict that you will judge [1] and [2] to be good and [3] and [4] to be odd, even though these sentences are something you may never have considered before.

In attempting to answer the question 'Is this an example of a good English sentence or not?' we are obliged to go to speakers of the language and ask them whether they would accept it as such. (If we ourselves speak the language, then we may ask ourselves.) It is difficult to see how else we could decide what is and what is not a sentence of English. Yet, if this is so, our agreement about [1]–[4] constitutes a fact about the English language. In a real sense, then, all the facts about the language lie inside the heads of its speakers.

But can you give an explanation for the oddity of [3] and [4] – beyond saying that we just don't say it like that?

Here is another example. If the negative of [5] is [6],

[5] They were jumping on it.
[6] They weren't jumping on it.

why isn't [8] the negative of [7]?

[7] They tried jumping on it.
[8] They triedn't jumping on it.

And another example: Since [9] is a good English sentence, why aren't [10] and [11]?

[9] Bevis mended his car in the garage and Max did so in the lay-by.
[10] Bevis put his car in the garage and Max did so in the lay-by.
[11] Bevis went to the circus and Max did so to the zoo.

Finally, compare [12] and [13]:

[12] The fact that I communicated to Mona is irrelevant.

[13] The fact that I communicated with Mona is irrelevant.

Superficially, the only difference between these might seem to be that between the prepositions *with* and *to*. So we might expect the difference to be exactly the same as that between *I went with Max* and *I went to Max*. Your understanding of the difference between [12] and [13], however, goes way beyond your understanding of the difference between *with* and *to*. You can demonstrate this for yourself: try replacing the *that* in each sentence by *which*. How do you react? Do you agree that you can do it with [12] but not [13]? What is going on here? Why should the choice of preposition in one part of a sentence affect the choice of *that* or *which* in another part? You know it does, but what exactly is it that you know? What exactly is wrong with *The fact which I communicated with Mona is irrelevant*? In a quite literal sense, there is more going on here than meets the eye.

These are just a tiny sample of a large body of facts, mysteries, and puzzles offered by the English language. Some of the puzzles have been solved (to our present satisfaction, at least). Others remain puzzles, or there is disagreement as to what the most appropriate explanation might be. And, as we find out more about the language, we should expect to discover further puzzles, and perhaps even find things puzzling which we thought we had understood.

The aim of this book is to encourage you to stand outside yourself and confront just one aspect of your largely unconscious knowledge of English. It does not discuss, let alone offer solutions to, all the puzzles known to exist, nor even to give very detailed accounts of intricacies like those above. But it will introduce you to a method of describing the language, and provide you with a vocabulary with which to start thinking about the language in terms of which the puzzles can be identified and solutions sought.

The chapters that follow are concerned with English SYNTAX. *Syntax* is traditionally the name given to the study of the form, positioning, and grouping, of the elements that go to make up sentences. In a word, it is about the STRUCTURE of sentences. In studying a language, there is of course a lot else to talk about besides its syntax. For example, we can investigate the form and grouping of the elements within words themselves. The systematic study of word-structure is called MORPHOLOGY. Or we can concentrate on the meaning of sentences and how their meaning is related to the meaning of the words they contain. This is called SEMANTICS. Or we can concentrate on how linguistic expressions are connected with the sounds of speech. This is called PHONOLOGY.

I shall say nothing about the phonology of English, and very little about morphology or semantics. It should become clear, though, just how closely the form (syntax) and the meaning (semantics) of English sentences are related.

The book is an introduction to the practical analysis of English sentences rather than an introduction to linguistic theory. But since we will be concerned with a language and its syntax, some of the concepts, aims and methods of linguistics are relevant. If you are interested in discovering more about linguistic theory, finding out something of the syntax of a language you know well seems an appropriate (indeed indispensible) way to start. Chapter 11 is included with such readers in mind. It is designed to place the description of English offered in the previous chapters in a wider context and raise some questions about the general aims and principles of syntactic analysis.

Finally, a word or two about the description offered here. In a book of this length, it hardly needs pointing out that the description is not exhaustive. Nevertheless, the range of structures covered is intended to be comprehensive enough for the book to serve not only as the basis for more exhaustive and specialised study but as a self-contained description for non-specialists who need a practical, and appliable, system of analysis for the major structures.

Since this last aim is important, I have concentrated on presenting a single, more or less traditional, analysis of each structure considered, without overburdening the reader with too much discussion of how that analysis might or might not be justified in the light of further evidence. This might give the misleading impression that there is just one possible analysis and that there is universal agreement that it is the one in this book! This is far from being the case. But sometimes the evidence that might support an alternative analysis is complex and indirect and its discussion would be inappropriate in such an introduction. The reader should bear in mind, then, that we are never irrevocably committed to a particular analysis but are free to amend it in the light of further evidence. Finding that evidence, and deciding between competing analyses on the basis of such evidence is, in the end, what 'doing syntax' is all about.

The organisation of the chapters

Chapters 1, 2, and 3 have a dual purpose: they introduce general ideas relevant to the analysis of sentences while simultaneously beginning the analysis itself.

Chapters 4 and 5 complete the general overview of the simple sentence.

Chapters 6 and 7 each go into more detail on certain aspects of the structure of simple sentences.

Chapters 8, 9, and 10 deal with different kinds of subordinate clause in the complex sentence.

Chapter 11 is a more general discussion of the background to and purpose of the kind of analysis presented in Chapters 1 to 10.

A note on how to read this book

There are several kinds of exercises. The end-of-chapter 'Exercises' are followed immediately by answer/discussion sections. These should form an important part of your reading of each chapter. Most of these are designed to give you practice in applying the analyses discussed in the chapter, but some develop the discussion further.

In addition, there are end-of-chapter 'Further Exercises'. These come without answers or discussion. If you are using the book as part of a taught course, you may be asked to write these up for marking and discussion by your tutor.

There are also numerous small exercises within the text of each chapter, forming an integral part of the discussion. Try doing these as and when they occur, before reading further. As often as not, the discussion that follows depends on your having done the exercise. A line has been ruled at the point where it is suggested you stop and do it. You will find it helpful to have pencil and paper to hand. Doing these exercises should make your reading of the book more productive and interesting than simply attempting to absorb the material passively.

Chapter 1

Sentence Structure: Constituents

Structure

The concept of STRUCTURE is fundamental to the study of syntax. But it is a very general concept that can be applied to any complex thing, whether it be a bicycle, a commercial company, or a carbon molecule. When we say of a thing that it is COMPLEX we mean, not that it is complicated (though of course it may be), but that

(a) it is divisible into parts (called CONSTITUENTS),
(b) there are different kinds of parts (different CATEGORIES of constituents),
(c) the constituents are ARRANGED in a specifiable way,
(d) that each constituent has a certain specifiable FUNCTION in the structure of the thing as a whole.

When anything can be analysed in this way, we say that it has structure. And in considering structure it is important to note that, more often than not, the constituents of a complex thing are themselves complex. In other words, the parts themselves consist of parts which may in turn consist of further parts. When this is so we may speak of a HIERARCHY of parts and HIERARCHICAL STRUCTURE.

It is obvious, for example, that a complex thing like a bicycle is not just a collection of randomly assembled bits and pieces. Suppose you gathered together all the components of a bicycle: metal tubes, hubs, spokes, chain, cable, and so on. Now try to imagine all the possible objects you could construct by fixing these components together. Would they all be bicycles? Surely not. Some of them would no doubt be excellent bicycles, while others wouldn't remotely resemble a bicycle (though they might make interesting sculptures). And, of course, there would be intermediate cases, things which we would probably want to say were bicycles, if only because they resembled bicycles more than anything else.

So, only some of the possible ways of fitting bicycle components together produce a bicycle. A bicycle consists not just of its components but, much more importantly, in **the STRUCTURE that results from fitting them together in a particular way**.

When we turn to linguistic expressions, we find a similar state of affairs. Suppose you have a collection of words, say all the words in a dictionary. Can you imagine all the possible word-sequences you could construct by putting these words together? The possibilities are endless. Clearly not all the sequences would be acceptable expressions or sentences of English. And again, some would be odder than others. When a sequence of words fails to constitute a good expression in the language, I shall describe it as being UNGRAMMATICAL (or ILL-FORMED) and mark it with an asterisk (*). Here are some examples:

[1a] *the nevertheless procrastinate in foxtrot
[1b] *and and if
[1c] *disappears none girls of the students
[1d] *put Mary
[1e] *Max will bought a frying pans.

More subtle examples of ungrammatical sentences were given in the introduction.

Ultimately, a full syntactic description of the English language (indeed, of any language) consists in explaining why some strings of words of the language are well-formed expressions and why others are not. Just how this ultimate (and very ambitious) goal might be attempted is discussed in Chapter 11. For the moment it is enough to say that it could not be achieved without recognising the importance of structure. Just as the concept of structure was required in distinguishing between the bicycles and the would-be bicycles, so the concept of structure is essential in distinguishing between the strings of words that are well-formed expressions in the language and those that are not.

We can use diagrams to show how things can be analysed into their constituent parts. For instance, [2] says that a bicycle can be analysed into two wheels, a frame, a chain, handlebars, among other things (the dots mean 'and other things'):

Such diagrams are called TREE-DIAGRAMS; as conventionally represented, however, the trees are upside-down.

[2]

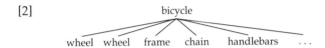

I have mentioned that the constituents of a complex thing can themselves be complex. An example of this is a bicycle wheel. It is itself a constituent of the bicycle, but in turn consists of hub, spokes, rim, tyre, etc. Although it is true that spokes are constituents of bicycles, it is more important to note that they are constituents of bicycles only because they are constituents of the wheel which, in turn, is a constituent of the bicycle. The relation between spoke and bicycle is indirect, mediated by wheel. We might express this by saying that, though the spoke is a constituent of the bicycle, it is not an IMMEDIATE CONSTITUENT of it. It is important to recognise the indirectness of the relationship between bicycle and spoke because, in giving a description of the structure of bicycles, we need to be able to say that wheels are parts of bicycles. But if we were to allow that spokes were immediate constituents of bicycles rather than of wheels this would leave wheels rather out of the picture. It would imply that bicycles could have spokes independently of the fact that they have wheels, and that spokes were not a necessary part of the structure of wheels.

As mentioned, specifying the FUNCTION of constituents is an important part of structural analysis. Notice that if we were to represent spokes as immediate constituents of bicycles, it would be impossible to specify correctly what the function of the spokes is – for the spokes don't have a function in respect of the bicycle directly, but only in respect of the wheels of which they are part. In talking of the function of the spokes, then, we are going to have to mention the wheels anyway.

Which of the following tree-diagrams best represents the structural relationship between bicycle and spoke just discussed?

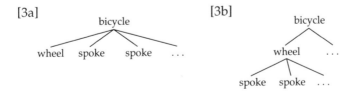

Although each tree-diagram is incomplete, [3b] more accurately reflects the structural relationship between bicycle and spoke, since it says that spokes are constituents of wheel which, in turn, is a constituent of bicycle. It correctly describes the relationship between bicycle, wheel, and spoke as being a hierarchical relation. [3a], on the other hand, in having a line directly joining spoke to bicycle, says that spokes are immediate constituents of bicycles, independently of the fact that wheels are constituents of bicycles.

This book is concerned with SYNTACTIC STRUCTURE, that is, with analysing linguistic expressions into their constituent parts, identifying the categories of those constituents, and determining their functions. But what kind of expressions should we begin with? I shall take the SENTENCE as the starting point for analysis. I shall assume (and in fact already have assumed) that you have an intuitive idea of what counts as a sentence of English.

The first question to be asked is 'What do sentences consist of?' The answer might appear to be blindingly obvious: 'Sentences consist of words.' In the rest of this chapter (and, for that matter, the rest of the book) I shall try to convince you that this apparently natural answer is not the most appropriate one. In fact, the discussion of hierarchical structure and the importance of recognising that sentences have such structure forces us very quickly to abandon the idea that sentences consist, in any simple way, of words.

This can be shown by asking whether the relationship between a sentence and its words is direct, or whether it is indirect, mediated by parts of intermediate complexity. This amounts to asking the question 'Are words the IMMEDIATE CONSTITUENTS of the sentences that contain them?' It is only if the words contained in a sentence are its immediate constituents that we can allow that sentences actually consist of words. As an aid to thinking about this question – and to gain practice in getting such diagrams to say what you want them to say – draw a tree-diagram, starting with 'Sentence' at the top, which says of sentence [4] that its words are its immediate constituents, that it consists directly of the words it contains.

[4] Old Sam sunbathed beside a stream.

Having done that, consider whether the diagram you have drawn gives an accurate representation of the structure of the sentence as you feel it to be.

The diagram that says of sentence [4] that its words are its immediate constituents looks like this:

[5]

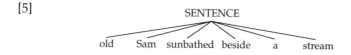

Do you feel that the diagram is wrong or unhelpful as a description of sentence [4]? How much does it tell us? Certainly it tells us what words appear in the sentence. And it tells us in what order they appear. But it tells us nothing more. In addition to being uninformative the diagram is actually wrong as a description of the structure of the sentence. In essence, it says of sentence [4] that it has no structure – or no more structure than a sequence of numbers (1–2–3–4–5) or an ordered string of beads. This is surely wrong.

In not allowing that the sentence has constituents that mediate between it and its words, the diagram does not allow that certain of the words seem to belong with others, that the words seem to work in groups. It says that the words have no relationship to each other except the relationship of being in a certain order in the same sentence. And, although the diagram tells us in what order the words occur, in failing to assign any but the simplest possible structure to the sentence, it fails to give any explanation of why they occur in that order to form a sentence, and why the orders in [6] and [7], for example, do not form sentences of English.

[6] *Stream old Sam sunbathed beside a
[7] *Sunbathed old beside stream a Sam

We need to say that sentence [4] is more highly structured than [5] says it is. After all, as we saw in the discussion of bicycles earlier, what position a spoke occupies in the structure of a bicycle is determined by its being a constituent of wheel, which itself has a certain specifiable position within the bicycle. If you attempt to reposition the spokes from out of their structural position within the wheel, you land up with an unworkable bicycle. A very similar thing has happened in [6] and [7]. The arrangement of words in a sentence is largely determined by the fact that the words are not immediate constituents of the sentence, but belong with other words to form groups which have their own specifiable position in the structure of the sentence. It is these groups (or further groups made up of these groups) that function as immediate constituents of the sentence. In short, while sentences CONTAIN words, they don't CONSIST (just of) words.

In addition, we need to be able to say what kinds (or CATEGORIES) of words can combine to form structural groups. What is wrong with [6] and [7] is that words have been displaced from positions in which they are capable of forming groups with the words next to them to positions where they are not, given the kinds of words they are. But the diagram gives no information of this sort. Such information is not only needed to account for the ungrammaticality of [6] and [7]; it is also needed if we want to explain why replacing *stream* with *road* yields another good sentence of English:

[8]   Old Sam sunbathed beside a road.

but replacing *stream* with *laughing* or *surreptitiously* does not.

[9a] *Old Sam sunbathed beside a laughing.
[9b] *Old Sam sunbathed beside a surreptitiously.

Road can replace *stream* in [4] because *road* and *stream* belong to the same category: they are both nouns. *Laughing* (a verb) and *surreptitiously* (an adverb) cannot replace *stream* because they belong to different categories.

So we need to include information about GRAMMATICAL CATE-GORIES in our diagrams and this is something I shall consider in later chapters. This, together with information on how the words group together to form intermediate constituents, will help to explain not only the facts about [6]–[9], but also facts about the functions of words (and groups of words) in sentences.

The discussion so far suggests that diagram [5] is not just unhelpful, but actually wrong as a structural description of sentence [4]. As soon as we want to explain even the simplest things about sentences, it becomes necessary to go beyond the idea that sentences simply consist of words strung together in a line. We need to acknowledge that sentences have hierarchical structure.

Establishing constituents

I have been complaining in a rather general way about diagram [5]. What is needed now is a more specific demonstration of just how it is wrong. I shall not attempt here to give a comprehensive or systematic analysis of sentence [4], but to give a general introduction to the identification of constituents larger than the word.

One way of clearly establishing that [5] is wrong is as follows. If the sentence had the same (lack of) structure as an ordered sequence of numbers, we should be able to lop words off the end of the sentence and still be left with a good sentence every time we did so. We can lop numbers off the end of a number sequence and still be left with a good (though shorter) number sequence: 1–2–3–4–5, 1–2–3–4, 1–2–3, 1–2, 1. Begin by removing first one word and then another from the end of sentence [4] until you are left with just one word. Each time write down the string that remains. In front of every string of words that seems to you *not* to constitute a COMPLETE AND GRAMMATICAL SENTENCE, put an asterisk.

Assuming we all speak the same language, you should have a list of five strings marked in the following way:

[10] *Old Sam sunbathed beside a
[11] *Old Sam sunbathed beside
[12] Old Sam sunbathed
[13] *Old Sam
[14] *Old

Of the strings, only [12] could stand as a complete and well-formed sentence. [13] may not seem quite as odd as [10], [11] and [14] do, for reasons which will become apparent shortly. Nevertheless, it should still be asterisked since it is not a complete sentence. What needs to be explained is why string [12] is a good sentence while none of the others are.

In the first place, you should note that not all parts of a sentence are necessary in order for that sentence to be complete and well-formed. For simplicity, consider [15].

[15] Martha smiled.

[15] is a good sentence as it stands. But notice that we could add to it. For example, we could add the word *invitingly*, to produce another good sentence [16]:

[16] Martha smiled invitingly.

In [16], then, we may say that *invitingly* is an OPTIONAL part of the sentence: leaving it out gives us another complete and perfectly grammatical sentence, namely [15]. (By contrast, *Martha*, and *smiled* are OBLIGATORY.)

The importance of this in the present context is that I have referred to *invitingly* as a part, as a constituent, of sentence [16]; I have said that it is an optional part. Now it is obvious that *invitingly* must be a constituent part (a structural unit) in sentence [16], since it is a single word. Now, to go back to sentence [4], we saw in [10]–[14] that we could omit the SEQUENCE OF WORDS *beside* plus *a* plus *stream* and be left with a good sentence. In other words, that SEQUENCE is optional. Notice, however, that it is only the sequence as a whole, as a single unit, that is optional. None of the words in the sequence can be omitted individually. So, just as I needed to refer to the single word *invitingly* and say that it was an optional constituent in the structure of sentence [16], so I need to be able to refer to the sequence of words *beside* plus *a* plus *stream* as a unit, and say of it that, as a unit, it is optional in the structure of sentence [4]. In doing so, I acknowledge that word-sequence as an identifiable part, as a constituent, of that sentence.

Sequences of words that can function as constituents in the structure of sentences are called PHRASES. And since our tree diagrams are intended to represent structure by marking which sequences of words in a sentence are its constituent phrases, such diagrams are called PHRASE-MARKERS.

I have shown that the sequence of words *beside a stream* is a constituent of sentence [4]. It is, therefore, a phrase. And once we have recognised it as a phrase, we must treat the words within it as parts, not so much of the sentence, but of the phrase itself. This phrase is intermediate between the sentence and the words, rather in the way that wheel is intermediate between bicycle and spoke. Since we cannot omit any of the words individually, it appears that, while the phrase as a whole is optional in the structure of the sentence, the words themselves are not optional, but necessary in the structure of the phrase.

In sentence [17] below, there are two separate sequences of words which can be omitted without affecting the grammaticality of the sentence. Can you identify them?

[17] The very muscular gentleman next to me lit a cigar.

Since [18], [19], and [20] are all perfectly good, complete sentences

[18] The (…) gentleman next to me lit a cigar.

[19] The very muscular gentleman (…) lit a cigar.
[20] The (…) gentleman (…) lit a cigar.

we need to be able to say that *very muscular* (omitted in [18] and [20]) and *next to me* (omitted in [19] and [20]) are PHRASES which are optional constituents in the structure of sentence [17]. In saying this, I am not necessarily saying that they are immediate constituents of the sentence itself: we may (and in this case will) find that they are immediate constituents, not of the sentence, but of yet further phrases within the sentence.

If a sequence of words can be omitted from a sentence leaving another good sentence, this is a good indication that the sequence is a phrase functioning as a constituent in the structure of the sentence. However, not all phrases are omissible. We must therefore find a more general and systematic way of demonstrating that a given sequence of words is a phrase.

There are several different ways of doing this. You will recall that we were never in doubt that *invitingly* was a constituent in [16]: it is a single word, after all. And we wanted to say of the sequence of words *beside a stream* that it had the same unitary character as a single word. This suggests that **if you can replace a SEQUENCE OF WORDS in a sentence with a SINGLE WORD without changing the overall structure of the sentence, then that sequence functions as a constituent of the sentence and is therefore a phrase.** This test will confirm that *beside a stream* is functioning as a constituent in sentence [4]. For example, if the speaker of sentence [4] were in a position to point to the spot where Sam sunbathed, he could quite easily replace *beside a stream* by *here* or *there*:

[21a] Old Sam sunbathed here.
[21b] Old Sam sunbathed there.

Or he could be vague about where Sam sunbathed, replacing *beside a stream* with *somewhere*.

[22] Old Sam sunbathed somewhere.

If we consider questions and their answers, we find a very clear example of this. We can form a question from sentence [4] by replacing *beside a stream* with the single question word *where* as in [23] and [24]:

[23] Old Sam sunbathed where?
[24] Where did old Sam sunbathe?

Since we have used *where* to replace *beside a stream*, it is natural that *beside a stream* should be a possible answer to the question, since answering such questions is a matter of replacing the question word with an informative phrase. So, **answers to 'WH' questions (that is, questions that contain one of the question words** *who, which, what, why, where, when, whose,* **and** *how*) **are phrases.**

So, it seems that we are justified in taking *beside a stream* as a phrase. The question that arises now is, How should we represent this phrase in terms of a phrase-marker? As with the whole sentence, we need to know whether the words of the phrase are its immediate constituents, or whether it contains further phrases. There are just three phrase-markers that could possibly represent the structure of *beside a stream*:

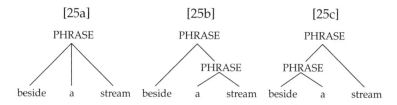

[25a]   [25b]   [25c]

Each gives a different analysis. Which do you think is the best representation of the structure of the phrase? In coming to a decision on this, you should ask yourself whether *a* belongs more with *beside* than with *stream*, more with *stream* than with *beside*, or whether it doesn't seem to belong more with one than the other. It may be useful to note that if it seems very definitely not to belong with one (i.e. if [b] or [c] seems more definitely wrong than the other), then it will almost certainly belong with the other. [a] is right, therefore, only if [b] and [c] seem equally bad.

Now check that the tests mentioned above, replacement by a single word and the question test, confirm the analysis you have chosen.

Phrase-marker [25a] says that the phrase does not contain any further phrases. It says that *a* does not belong more with either of the other words, that the words themselves are the immediate constituents of the phrase. As mentioned, if [25a] is correct, then

[b] and [c] should seem equally bad as representations of the structure. But [c] is surely much worse than [b]. [c] suggests that we should be able to find a single word to replace the supposed phrase *beside a*. It is difficult to start thinking of what kind of word could replace that sequence. Not only does it seem incomplete as it stands, but it is impossible to say what it is supposed to mean. On the other hand, *a stream* does seem complete, it is fairly clear what it means, and we don't have to rack our brains too much to discover that there are several single words that we could use to replace it. For example, *it*, *something*, or *one*, yield perfectly good phrases: *beside it*, *beside something*, and *beside one*.

Notice, too, that if we were to change the singular *stream* to the plural *streams*, we would get the ungrammatical word-sequence **beside a streams* – unless we also omit *a* (to give *beside streams*). This suggests rather strongly that *a* belongs definitely with *stream* rather than with *beside*, that *a* is DEPENDENT on *stream*. This piece of evidence is similar to that produced by the test of replacement by a single word, since it shows that we are obliged to use the single word *streams* to replace the sequence *a stream*.

The question test confirms that *a stream* is a phrase:

[26] Question: [a] Old Sam sunbathed beside what?
  [b] What did old Sam sunbathe beside?
 Answer: A stream.

And notice that there is no question to which **beside a* would be a suitable answer.

[27] provides further evidence that *a stream* forms a phrase, since it has been moved as a unit in forming a new construction.

[27] *A stream* is what old Sam sunbathed *beside*.

It is worth noting, then, that **the MOVEMENT of a sequence of words in forming a construction indicates that the sequence is a phrase**. As a further example, note the acceptability of moving *beside a stream* to the beginning of sentence [4]:

[28] Beside a stream, old Sam sunbathed.

In short, the various kinds of evidence discussed confirm that [25b] is the correct representation of the structure of our phrase.

As an exercise, think of some other possible answers to the question represented in [26]. They can be as different as you like from the answer already given, and they can be as long as you like. Provided they do not sound ungrammatical, every sequence of words you choose will be a phrase.

Here are some suggestions:

[29a] his magnolia bush
[29b] a large pile of Bokhara rugs
[29c] the most beautiful olive grove I've ever laid eyes on
[29d] an unreliable alsatian that was taking the occasional nip at his toes.

All these are phrases. They could all serve as answers to the question, and they are all replaceable by a single word. Furthermore, they all contain further phrases.

Earlier, when we were considering whether there was a single word that could be used to replace the sequence *beside a*, I mentioned meaning and implied that **phrases form not only SYNTACTIC UNITS (constituents in the structural form of sentences) but also SEMANTIC UNITS. By this I mean that they form identifiable parts of the MEANING of sentences; they form coherent units of sense.** While it may be reasonable to ask what *beside a stream* and *a stream* mean, it does not seem reasonable to ask what *beside a* means; it would be impossible to answer such a question.

Does the discussion so far suggest any explanation why the sequence of words in [13] on page 13 seems more acceptable than those in [10], [11] and [14]? How, exactly?

I put an asterisk in front of [13] because it was not a complete sentence. However, it is a complete phrase, and in this it contrasts with the other strings. *Old Sam* could be replaced by a single word – *he, someone,* or even just *Sam* – making no difference to the overall structure of the sentence. Furthermore, *old Sam* could be used as an answer to the question *Who sunbathed beside a stream?*, where I have replaced the sequence *old Sam* with the single 'WH' word *who*.

'Phrase' and 'constituent'

I have said that a PHRASE is a sequence of words that can function as a CONSTITUENT in the structure of sentences. The important word here is 'can'.

We have seen that *beside a stream*, *a stream*, and *old Sam* can function as constituents in sentence-structure (and do function as constituents in sentence [4] and many other sentences). They are therefore phrases. The fact that those WORD-SEQUENCES are constituents in sentence [4], however, does not mean that they function as constituents of every sentence in which they appear. Here, as an obvious example of this, is a sentence in which the sequence consisting of *old* and *Sam* is not a constituent:

[30] Though he was old Sam did regular press-ups.

This is immediately clear when we try to replace that sequence with a single word:

[31] *Though he was *someone* did regular press-ups.

and when we apply the question test:

[32a] *Though he was who did regular press-ups?
[32b] *Who though he was did regular press-ups?

Out of the context of any particular sentence, *old Sam* is a phrase. It is a phrase because it *can* be a constituent of a sentence. But it does not have to be. *Old Sam* is not a constituent of sentence [30].

You should now be able to make sense of the following statement. Although the WORD SEQUENCE *old + Sam* appears in sentence [30], and although *old Sam* is indeed a PHRASE, it is not a CONSTITUENT of sentence [30]. This means that, although *old Sam* is indeed a phrase, it is not a phrase that figures in the structure of [30]! As mentioned in the Introduction, in a quite literal sense there is more to syntax, and to your own understanding of sentences, than meets the eye. Hierarchical sentence structure is really quite abstract. That is why it is worth investigating, and why we need to construct concrete phrase-markers to represent this abstract structure.

If all this seems unnecessarily complicated and paradoxical, consider this. You don't need me to tell you that words such as *catastrophic*, *cattle*, and *scatter* have nothing to do with cats and do not contain the word *cat*, despite containing the letter sequence *c+a+t*. What is true at the level of words is true at the level of phrases and sentences.

Consider now sentence [33]:

[33] Sam sunbathed beside a stream that had dried up.

and decide whether the sequence *a* + *stream* + *that* + *had* + *dried* + *up* is a constituent or not.

Since that sequence of words would constitute a perfectly good answer to the question 'What did old Sam sunbathe beside?' and since (like the sequence *a stream* in sentence [4]) it is replaceable by a single word while preserving the overall structure of the sentence, it is a constituent. And, just as with *a stream* in sentence [4], it forms a further phrase with *beside*. This further phrase can be represented as in [34]:

[34]

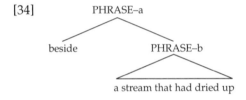

a stream that had dried up

In [34] I have adopted the useful convention of using a TRIANGLE to represent a constituent when I am not concerned with its internal structure. And for ease of reference I have distinguished the phrases by letter.

The question I want you to consider now is this: Do the words *beside* and *a* and *stream*, which formed a constituent in sentence [4], form a constituent in sentence [33]? And if not, why not? (The phrase-marker [34] should help you to answer this.)

You have probably guessed that the answer is 'No'. But why not? Well, we agreed that in [33]/[34] *a* + *stream* is part of a larger phrase, but that larger phrase is not *beside a stream* but *a stream that had dried up*. *Beside* forms a phrase, not with *a stream*, but with the whole sequence *a stream that had dried up*. The words *a* and *stream* are part of PHRASE–b. If an element is part of a phrase, it can only relate to other elements within that same phrase. If we wanted to say that *beside a stream* formed a phrase in [33], we would be forced to represent the complete phrase *beside a stream that had dried up* as in [35]:

[35]

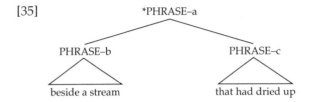

But [35] is wrong, since it does not represent *a stream that had dried up* as a phrase. The moral is that an element can belong directly only to one phrase at a time. I say 'directly' since in [34], for example, *a stream* belongs both to PHRASE–b (directly) and to PHRASE–a (indirectly). It is, in fact, impossible to draw a phrase-marker that says of *a stream* that it simultaneously forms a phrase directly with *beside* AND with *that had dried up*.

In case you are uncertain whether or not a given sequence of elements is represented as a phrase by a phrase-marker, the following discussion should help to clarify matters. **Any point in a phrase-marker that could branch and bear a label is called a** NODE. In phrase-marker [34] there are two nodes. I have labelled them 'PHRASE–a' and 'PHRASE–b'. A node is said to DOMINATE everything that appears below it and joined to it by a line. Thus the node labelled 'PHRASE–a' dominates all the following elements: *beside*, PHRASE–b, *a*, *stream*, *that*, *had*, *dried*, and *up*. A node is said to IMMEDIATELY DOMINATE another element when there are no intervening elements, Thus PHRASE–a immediately dominates just *beside* and PHRASE–b. Though PHRASE–a dominates *stream*, it does not immediately dominate it, because the node labelled 'PHRASE–b' intervenes.

Using this convenient terminology, I can now show how to decide whether a sequence of elements is represented as a constituent in a phrase-marker. **A sequence of elements is represented as a constituent in a phrase-marker if there is a node that dominates all those elements and no others**. In other words, if you can trace just the elements under consideration (i.e. all those elements and only those elements) back to a single node, then those elements are represented as a constituent.

Look at the phrase-marker given in [34]. The sequence *a + stream + that + had + dried + up* is represented as a constituent because the elements (words, in this case) can all be traced back to a single node that does not dominate any other element, namely, PHRASE–b. The sequence *beside + a*, on the other hand, is not

represented as a constituent because the only node that dominates both of the elements within that sequence (PHRASE–a)
dominates other elements as well (namely, *stream, that, had, dried,*
and *up*). Similarly, in the incorrect phrase-marker [35], *a stream
that had dried up* is not represented as a constituent because there
is no node that dominates all and only those words. The only
node that dominates all of them is PHRASE–a, but PHRASE–a
does not dominate only those words, it also dominates *beside*.

I have given two examples in which a sequence of words functioning as a constituent in one sentence does not function as a
constituent in another. Here, as a final example, is what is known
as a STRUCTURALLY AMBIGUOUS sentence. On one interpretation, the
sequence *old + Sam* does function as a constituent, while on the
other interpretation it doesn't:

[36] Hazeltine asked how old Sam was.

Try to identify the two meanings of [36]. A good way of doing
this is to decide on the exact question which Hazeltine is
reported in [36] to have asked. You may find it helpful to make a
written note of the two questions.

Having identified the two meanings in the way suggested, you
should not have much difficulty in deciding which interpretation
demands that the sequence does form a constituent and which
demands that it does not.

The two quite different questions that could have been asked
by Hazeltine are [a] 'How old is Sam?' and [b] 'How is old Sam?'.
As the different questions show, on the first interpretation [a] *old*
belongs with *how* to form the phrase *how old*. In this question, the
phrase as a unit has been moved from its position at the end of
the sentence (*Sam is how old?*). On this interpretation, since *old*
forms a constituent with *how*, it cannot also form a constituent
with *Sam*. It is on the second interpretation [b] that *old* and *Sam*
go together to form a phrase. This example illustrates how deciding what phrases there are in the sentence is necessary in order to
decide what the sentence actually means.

Most people, when presented with a sequence of words out of
the context of any sentence, have quite definite feelings as to
whether that sequence could function as a constituent in a sentence
(i.e. whether it is a phrase). As mentioned, it is usually simply a
matter of deciding whether it seems to form a unit of sense. In the

main, this is a reliable guide as to whether that sequence actually is a constituent in a given sentence to be analysed, though, as we have seen from the last three examples, not one hundred per cent reliable. And, even in the context of a sentence, you will find that you do have an intuitive feeling as to which sequences are functioning as its constituents. In this chapter I have considered various kinds of evidence for constituents – omission, replacement by a single word, the question test, movement, the sense test. These are useful in confirming your intuitions, and in checking on cases where you are in doubt – one's first intuitions are not always strong and not always reliable.

Exercises

1.   On the basis of tree-diagram (a) below, say which of the following sequences are constituents of A.
     (i) c + d   (ii) a + b + c   (iii) c + d + e + f   (iv) e + f
     (v) e + f + g + h   (vi) g + h   (vii) E + C   (viii) D + E
     (ix) F + g + h.

(a)

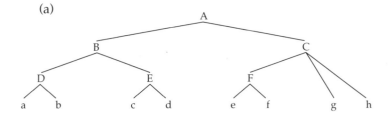

2.   In tree-diagram (a) above, what are the *immediate* constituents of: (i) A?   (ii) B?   (iii) C?

3.(a) Draw a phrase-marker for the phrase *their rather dubious jokes*, showing that it contains the further phrase *rather dubious jokes*, which in turn contains *rather dubious* as a phrase.
(b) *Men from the Ministry* is a phrase, which contains *from the Ministry* and *the Ministry* as phrases. Draw a phrase-marker for the whole phrase.

4.   Decide whether the italicised strings in the following sentences are constituents of those sentences or not. N.B. one of

the sentences is ambiguous; as with the ambiguous example discussed in this chapter, you should identify the two interpretations and be quite clear in your mind on which interpretation the italicised sequence forms a constituent.

(a) John considered *visiting his great aunt*.
(b) Maria retreated from *the bollard she had just demolished*.
(c) Maria retreated *from the bollard* she had just demolished.
(d) *In the machine* the gremlin could be heard juggling with ball-bearings.
(e) *In the machine the gremlin* could be heard juggling with ball-bearings.
(f) Sam managed to touch *the man with the umbrella*.
(g) Rory put *a silencer on the gun*.

5.   In the light of the discussion of this chapter, how many constituents can you identify in sentence (a) given that the much shorter (b) is a grammatical sentence? (Do not attempt a complete analysis of sentence (a) – the fact that sentence (b) is well-formed does not provide enough information for this.)

(a) Being of a cautious disposition, Timothy very wisely avoided the heavily built man whenever he drank at the Wrestler's Arms.
(b) Timothy avoided the man.

6.   I have not yet provided a complete analysis of sentence [4]. We have agreed that *old Sam*, *beside a stream*, and *a stream* are among its constituent phrases. We may therefore draw an incomplete phrase-marker as in (a):

(a)

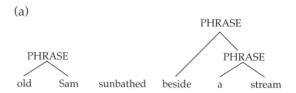

We know that the complete string constitutes a sentence. In order to complete the phrase-marker, then, all the elements must finally be joined up to a single (SENTENCE) node in some way. The question is How? There are three ways in which this could be done. Each way offers a different analysis of the sentence (in particular, each way offers a different analysis of how *sunbathed* fits into the structure). Draw the three complete phrase-markers and explain in words what different claims are made about the structure of the sentence by each phrase-marker. (You should take care that the phrases we have already acknowledged remain represented as phrases in your complete phrase-markers.) You are not asked here to choose which you think is the most appropriate phrase-marker (though you will almost certainly have views on the matter). In fact, all three analyses have been proposed at one time or another, though one of them is more common than the others, and it is this that I shall adopt in the next chapter.

Discussion of exercises

1. (i) Yes. Both *c* and *d* (and only *c* and *d*) can be traced back to the node labelled *E*.   (ii) No. *D* dominates *a* and *b* but it does not dominate *c*; and while node *B* dominates *a* and *b* and *c*, it also dominates *d*; so there is no node that dominates all of *a* and *b* and *c*, and only *a* and *b* and *c*.   (iii) No. There is no single node that dominates all of *c*, *d*, *e*, and *f* and only them. Only *A* dominates them all, but *A* dominates *a*, *b*, *g*, and *h* too.   (iv) Yes. *e* and *f* (and only *e* and *f*) can be traced back to the single node *F*.   (v) Yes. They alone can be traced back to *C*.   (vi) No.   (vii) No.   (viii) Yes.   (ix) Yes.

2. (i) *B* and *C*.   (ii) *D* and *E*.   (iii) *F*, *g*, and *h*.

3. (a)   (b)

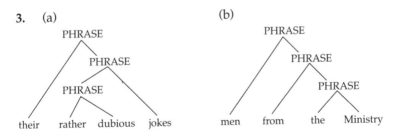

4.(a) Yes. It could be replaced by *it* and by *what* in forming the question *What did he consider?*, to which *visiting his great aunt*

is a possible answer. (Note also that the sequence needs to be treated as a unit in forming the construction *visiting his great aunt is what he considered*.)

(b)   Yes. (cf. *she retreated from it; what did she retreat from?* Answer: *the bollard she had just demolished*.)

(c)   No. In (b) the sequence *the + bollard* was shown to be part of the phrase *the bollard she had just demolished*; it cannot then form a constituent with *from*. (See the discussion of *beside a stream that had dried up* [33] in the chapter, pp. 20–21.)

(d)   Yes. It could be replaced by *there* or *somewhere*; *in the machine* is a good answer to the question *Where could the gremlin be heard juggling with ball-bearings?* Notice that the sequence could be omitted leaving a well-formed sentence.

(e)   No. This is most easily demonstrated by trying to imagine what question *In the machine the gremlin* could be an answer to. There is no single question word that would cover the sequence. *Who/What could be heard ...?* could receive *the gremlin* as a possible answer; *Where could the gremlin be heard ...* could receive *In the machine*. Each of these, then, are phrases. But there is no single question word that covers both *where* and *what*. So here we have a sequence of phrases that do not between them form a larger phrase.

(f)   This is the ambiguous sentence. On one interpretation the sequence is a constituent, cf. *Sam managed to touch HIM* and *WHO did Sam manage to touch?* (Answer: *The man with the umbrella*). On the other interpretation, it is not a single phrase but a sequence of two phrases. Cf. *Sam managed to touch HIM with an umbrella, WHO did Sam manage to touch with an umbrella?* (Answer: *the man*).

(g)   No. Consider the oddity of **Rory put IT/*Rory put SOMETHING, *What did Rory put?* (Answer: **A silencer on the gun*).

5.   The fact that (b) is a well-formed sentence allows us to infer that every sequence of words omitted from (a) in order to form (b) can be counted as a constituent of (a), viz.

Being of a cautious disposition
very wisely
heavily built
whenever he drank at the Wrestler's Arms.

There are other constituents, of course, and the constituents listed here themselves contain further phrases.

6. The three complete phrase-markers are:

(a)

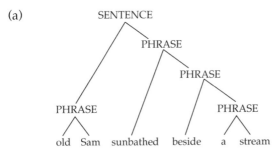

(b)

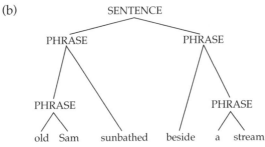

(c)

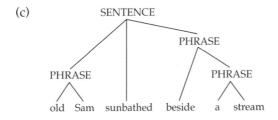

Phrase-marker (a) represents *sunbathed* as forming a constituent with *beside a stream*, and divides the sentence into just two immediate constituents: *old Sam* and *sunbathed beside a stream*. Phrase-marker (b) again divides the sentence into two, but this time the two parts are *old Sam sunbathed* and *beside a stream*. Phrase-marker (c) represents the sentence as having three immediate constituents, *old Sam* and *sunbathed* and *beside a stream*; it says that *sunbathed* forms a constituent neither with *old Sam* nor with *beside a stream*.

In attempting to represent what phrase-marker (a) represents, you may have been tempted simply to draw an extra line out from the phrase node dominating *beside a stream* as in phrase-marker (d):

(d)

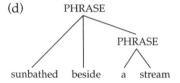

(d), in fact, is incorrect. Can you see why? (Check the discussion on page 21.) Although it associates *sunbathed* with *beside a stream*, it fails to represent *beside a stream* as a phrase in its own right, independently of *sunbathed*. It fails to do this because there is no node that dominates all and only *beside + a + stream*. (The only node that dominates them all dominates *sunbathed* as well). Check that you have not succumbed to a similar temptation in connection with (b).

Further exercises

1. The structural ambiguity of [36] in the text is a matter of whether *old Sam* or *how old* is a constituent. All the following are structurally ambiguous. In each case, identify the source of the ambiguity in terms of two different constituent analyses, as I have just done with [36].

    (i) This story shows what evil men can do.
    (ii) They only sell rotten fruit and vegetables.
    (iii) She returned early that evening.
    (iv) More interesting meals would have been appreciated.
    (v) We need an agreement between workers on overtime.
    (vi) Bill asked the man who he had seen.
    (vii) She was at the window, the street atlas in her hand, looking up the street.

2. This is a more general (and open-ended) exercise, designed to get you to think about the nature of sentences in general in the light of the discussion of this chapter.

In the text, I referred to [36] as 'an ambiguous sentence'. But there is another way of looking at things. It could be argued that [36] is not a single ambiguous sentence, but the (printed) representation of two quite distinct sentences, one of which includes the phrase *old Sam*, while the other does not, neither of which is ambiguous. Rightly or wrongly, linguists often talk of 'ambiguous sentences', and in this book I shall follow that practice. But the question is, are they (am I) strictly right to do so? Think about this in the light of the Introduction and the discussion of structure and 'sentence' in this chapter.

Chapter 2

Sentence Structure: Functions

As I pointed out at the beginning of Chapter 1, understanding the structure of a sentence involves more than knowing what its CONSTITUENTS are. It involves knowing the CATEGORY and the FUNCTION of those constituents. As you will see in this and the next chapter, these three aspects of syntactic analysis are closely bound up with one another. This chapter is mainly about syntactic functions, and about how function relates to category and constituency.

A systematic analysis is best begun, not by immediately considering the words contained in the sentence, but by first identifying the very largest phrases – those phrases which are immediate constituents, not of any other phrase, but of the sentence itself. So my first illustration of the relationship between constituents, their categories, and their functions, will concern **the immediate constituents of the sentence itself**.

Subject and predicate

In order to be sure of identifying only the very largest (immediate) constituents of the sentence I shall, wherever possible, divide the sentence into the fewest possible parts, i.e. into two. Take the simplest possible complete sentence structure, as exemplified in [1]:

[1] Ducks paddle.

(*Blenkinsop coughed, Pigs fly, Empires decline*, and *Martha retaliated* would do just as well.) In this case, it is clear that we have no option but to analyse the sentence as consisting of two parts, as in [2]:

[2]

But what about more complicated sentences? A speaker's ability to recognise the structure of the sentences of his language is largely a matter of being able to perceive a similar pattern across a wide range of apparently different sentences. Take [3] as an example:

[3] The ducks are paddling away.

We want to say that [3] has **the same general structure** as [1]. By this I mean that **it is divisible into two** CONSTITUENTS **in exactly the same way, that the two constituents are of the same general kind (or** CATEGORY**) as the corresponding constituents of [1], and that they have the same syntactic** FUNCTIONS **as those in [1]**.

Notice that, in asking which sequence of words in [3] corresponds to *ducks* in [1], I am again asking which sequence of words in [3] could be replaced by the single word *ducks* while leaving a grammatical sentence. The answer can only be *The ducks*. Replacing that sequence by *ducks* yields the well-formed sentence *Ducks are paddling away*. In each of these sentences, both *ducks* and *the ducks* could be replaced by the same single word *they*. And the rest of [3] – *are paddling away* – can be replaced by the single word *paddle* (from [1]), giving the well-formed sentence *The ducks paddle*.

This exhaustively divides [3] into two parts, as in [4]:

[4] [The ducks] [are paddling away].

The same division is shown in [5] and [6]:

[5] [Those gigantic ducks] [were paddling away furiously].
[6] [The mouth-watering duck on the table] [won't be paddling away again].

In making this first division I have divided these sentences into two constituents, the first of which is traditionally said to function as SUBJECT, **and the second as** PREDICATE. One way of thinking of these functions is to think of the subject as being used to mention something and the predicate as used to say something true or false about the subject. The general structure of [1], [3], [5], and [6] is identical. Those sentences only differ at a lower (more detailed) level in the hierarchical structure.

In exercise 6 of Chapter 1, I raised the question of how *sunbathed* fitted into the structure of *Old Sam sunbathed beside a stream*, and offered three alternative analyses. Each analysis makes a different claim as to what the immediate constituents of that sentence are. On the basis of the discussion so far, can you decide which of those analyses is being adopted here?

It is analysis (a): [*Old Sam*] (subject) and [*sunbathed beside a stream*] (predicate).

It will have occurred to you that sentences can be a good deal more complicated than those that we have looked at here. In fact, theoretically, there is no limit to the degree of complexity. If, when presented with a more complicated sentence, you are in doubt as to the correct subject-predicate division, a simple test can be applied:

Question test for subject:
Turn the sentence into a question that can be answered by 'yes' or 'no' (a *yes/no* question). The phrase functioning as subject is the one that requires to change its position when the sentence is so changed.

You will recall from Chapter 1 that the movement of a sequence of words in forming a construction shows that it is a constituent. This particular movement test will confirm not only that *the ducks, those gigantic ducks* and *that mouth-watering duck on the table* are constituents, but that those constituents are functioning as the subjects of the sentences in which they appear:

[7] ⌐Are⌐ [the ducks] paddling away?

Now form the yes/no questions that correspond to [5] and [6].

---

[8] ⌐Were⌐ [those gigantic ducks] paddling away furiously?

[9] ⌐Won't⌐ [the mouth-watering duck on the table] be paddling away again?

You may find that you intuitively know what the correct subject-predicate division is without having to apply the test. However, the question movement test is important because it is actually part of the definition of what a 'subject' is that it changes its position in such questions. The test is particularly useful in cases like the following:

[10] It is snowing again.

In [10] it is rather difficult to view the predicate (*is snowing again*) as being used to say something true or false of *It* (the subject). *It* does not mention anything. (Notice that [10] is not really an answer to the question 'What is snowing again?' which is itself an odd question.) Nevertheless, *It* is the subject of [10] precisely because it changes position in the yes/no question:

[11] $\overrightarrow{\text{Is [it]}}$ snowing again?

Using this test, identify the subjects of the following sentences:

[12] Some nasty accident could have occurred.
[13] The clown in the make-up room doesn't want to perform.
[14] Elizabeth and Leicester are rowing on the river.
[15] None of her attempts to give up chocolate were really serious.
[16] As a matter of fact, the man you paid to do it has been arrested.

Examples [12]–[15] can be analysed as having a subject-predicate structure as follows:

[12] [Some nasty accident] [could have occurred].
   (Could some nasty accident have occurred?)
[13] [The clown in the make-up room] [doesn't want to perform].
   (Doesn't the clown in the make-up room want to perform?)
[14] [Elizabeth and Leicester] [are rowing on the river].
   (Are Elizabeth and Leicester rowing on the river?)
[15] [None of her attempts to give up chocolate] [were really serious].
   (Were none of her attempts to give up chocolate really serious?)

Example [16] illustrates the fact that the constituent functioning as subject does not always begin the sentence. The question that corresponds to this example is:

[16] As a matter of fact, has the man you paid to do it been arrested?

This question form identifies *the man you paid to do it* as the subject. The phrase *as a matter of fact* has not moved in forming the question and is therefore not part of the subject. Since *as a matter of fact* belongs neither within subject nor within predicate, [16] is one sentence that cannot be exhaustively analysed into a two-part, subject-predicate structure. For the moment, however, I shall concentrate on those that can.

A temptation that the question movement test will help you avoid is that of taking the first string of words that could be the subject as actually being the subject of the sentence in which it appears. Look again at [13], [14], and [15]. [13] begins with the sequence *the clown*, [14] with *Elizabeth*, and [15] with *none of her attempts*. All these could be subjects (see [17]–[19] below), but not in the sentences we have considered.

[17] The clown refuses to perform.
[18] Elizabeth excels at Real Tennis.
[19] None of her attempts were really serious.

The temptation to identify less than the whole of the relevant phrase crops up in all constituent analysis. In the case of subjects, the question movement test helps. For example, if the subjects of [17]–[19] are taken to be the subjects of [13]–[15], it is not clear how to form the appropriate questions, and all attempts to do so will result in ungrammatical sentences. (Why not check this for yourself?)

In general, you will usually find that taking less than the whole of the phrase leaves you with a residue that is not easily accounted for in structural terms. For instance, in the above cases, if *the clown*, *Elizabeth* and *none of her attempts* are taken to be the subjects of [13]–[15] respectively, the following strings are left as residues:

[20] in the make-up room doesn't want to perform
[21] and Leicester are rowing on the river
[22] to give up chocolate were really serious.

But none of these strings seems to hang together as a phrase, they do not form units of sense, and it is difficult to see what their function could be. They cannot be predicates; we couldn't say, for example, that *to give up chocolate were really serious* is predicated as being true of *none of her attempts*.

In applying the question movement test to the following examples, you will find that you have to modify it slightly.

[23] My new duck lays lightly boiled eggs.
[24] Elizabeth and Leicester excel at Real Tennis.
[25] The chiropodist fell in love with most of his patients.

Form the yes/no questions that correspond to these examples.

As you will have discovered, the appropriate questions are formed by introducing a form of the verb *do*. For the purposes of this test, it is convenient to assume that *do* is introduced as in [26]–[28].

[26] My new duck *does* lay lightly boiled eggs.
[27] Elizabeth and Leicester *do* excel at Real Tennis.
[28] The chiropodist *did* fall in love with most of his patients.

and that the questions are formed from [26]–[28] by the now familiar movement of the subject, giving

[29] Does [my new duck] lay lightly boiled eggs?
[30] Do [Elizabeth and Leicester] excel at Real Tennis?
[31] Did [the chiropodist] fall in love with most of his patients?

(This difference between [12]–[16] and [23]–[25] is explained in Chapter 6.)

Noun Phrase and Verb Phrase

So much, then, for the functions (subject and predicate) of the immediate constituents of the sentence. I will return to the functions of constituents, in a more general way, later in the chapter. The question that now arises is: **What KINDS of phrases function as subjects and predicates?** We have seen that such phrases can vary widely in their form and complexity. Nevertheless, all the SUBJECTS we have looked at have one thing in common: they all contain, and are centred on, the same CATEGORY of word, a NOUN. They are all NOUN PHRASES (NP). The single words that can replace them are all NOUNS or PRONOUNS. The phrases functioning as PREDICATES, on the other hand, all contain, and are centred on, a VERB. They are all VERB PHRASES (VP). Predictably, they are all replaceable by single-word VERBS.

Any phrase that can function as a subject is a Noun Phrase. You might ask why we need to distinguish between the category and the function of a constituent. We need to do this because most categories of phrase have a variety of different functions. Although subjects are always Noun Phrases, this does not mean that all Noun Phrases function as subject. For example, we saw that the Noun Phrase *the chiropodist* was functioning as subject in [25]. In [32], though, it is not:

[32] The pianist has rejected the chiropodist.

Notice that it does not change position in the yes/no question (*Has the pianist rejected the chiropodist?*). In this sentence it is *the pianist* that has moved. *The chiropodist* is here part of the predicate *rejected the chiropodist*. It is a constituent of the Verb Phrase and has another function (discussed in Chapter 4).

Here is a list of phrases. Some are Noun Phrases, some are Verb Phrases, and some are phrases belonging to categories not yet introduced. Identify the phrases (as Noun Phrase, Verb Phrase, or 'other') by combining them (just two at a time) and seeing which combinations make well-formed subject-predicate sentences.

(a) remind me of you
(b) as quickly as he could
(c) soggy chips
(d) pamphlets advertising new syntactic theories
(e) at the latter end of the day
(f) were raining from the sky
(g) are in demand.

The only well-formed subject-predicate combinations are: (c) + (a), (c) + (f), (c) + (g), (d) + (a), (d) + (f), and (d) + (g). Since (c) and (d) function as subjects they are NPs. (a), (f), and (g), which function as predicates, are VPs. Since (b) and (e) don't combine, in any order, with any of the other phrases nor with each other, they belong to categories other than NP and VP.

Information about the categories of the immediate constituents of the sentence can now be included in a phrase-marker, by labelling the appropriate nodes, as in [33]:

[33]

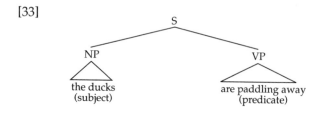

The diagram has the obvious interpretation: the sequence *the + ducks* is (or forms) a constituent belonging to the category Noun Phrase; the sequence *are paddling away* is (or forms) a constituent belonging to the category Verb Phrase; the NP and the VP together form a sentence (S).

Since I have been concerned only with the general structure of the sentence (that is, just the immediate constituents of the sentence itself) I have used the triangle notation for NP and VP to avoid having to give further details about their internal structure. And because I have not entered into any detail beyond identifying the subject and the predicate, the phrase-marker in [33] serves as a partial analysis of all the sentences considered in this chapter – with the exception of [16], which, for reasons already given, is a special case.

A point to note about [33] – and phrase-markers in general – is that a specification of the functions of the constituents (given in brackets in [33]) is not strictly part of the phrase-marker, and is not normally included. This is because it is possible to determine the functions of constituents from other information already contained in the phrase-marker – information about category and position.

For example, **the SUBJECT of a sentence can be defined as that NP which is immediately dominated by S. A PREDICATE is a VP immediately dominated by S**.

This definition of subject in terms of the phrase-marker will confirm that *the chiropodist* is not the subject of [32]. Draw the phrase-marker for that sentence.

---

[34]

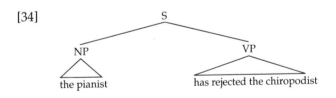

In [34] there are two NPs, *the pianist* and *the chiropodist*, but only one of those NPs is immediately dominated by S (*the pianist*). So *the pianist* is the subject. *The chiropodist* is not immediately dominated by S because the VP node intervenes between it and S. Hence it is not the subject by that definition.

As yet I have said nothing about how to identify nouns, verbs or other categories of words. This is discussed in the next chapter. What is important here is for you to be able to perceive how the various parts of a sentence can be expected to function in relation to each other. Without the idea of subject function and predicate function, it would be difficult to know where to begin the analysis of a sentence. In giving an analysis of a sentence, you should always satisfy yourself that any constituent you wish to say is contained in the sentence has a well-defined function and meaning. This goes not only for the immediate constituents of S but for all constituents. So I will generalise the discussion a little.

Dependency and function

Since I am discussing the functions of constituents, it will help if I introduce some terminology to describe relationships between them. When two constituent nodes are immediately dominated by the same single node, as is the case with B and C in [35],

[35]

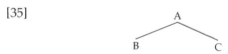

they are said to be SISTERS. As you might guess, since B and C are sisters in [35], they are also the DAUGHTERS of A, the node that immediately dominates them; and A is the MOTHER of B and C. Fanciful perhaps – but easily remembered!

It is the relationship of sister that concerns us here. SISTER constituents are usually represented at the same level of structure in phrase-markers. In general, **constituents have their functions in respect of their sister constituents**. Thus, in each of the sentences that we have considered so far, the subject NP and the predicate VP are sisters represented at the same level of structure, and the NP (e.g. *the ducks*) has its subject's function in respect of its sister, the predicate VP (e.g. *are paddling away*); and the VP has its predicate's function in respect of the subject NP. Notice that subject and predicate are dependent on each other (mutually dependent) in the sense that an NP only functions as a subject in the presence of a sister VP, and a VP only functions as predicate in the presence of a sister NP. The two of them together are required to form a complete sentence; neither can be omitted in a well-formed sentence.

Anticipating later chapters, let us take an initial look at the other main functions. There are three general concepts here. These are HEAD, and the functions that other elements have in relation to heads, namely MODIFIER and COMPLEMENT.

Modifier and head

Consider the structure I assigned to *their rather dubious jokes* in Exercise 3 of Chapter 1. (Since I am concentrating on the relationship between constituency and function, I have omitted the category labels which would be required for a complete analysis of the phrase.)

[36]

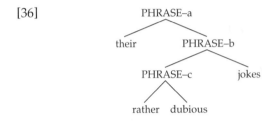

Make a list of all the sister relationships in that phrase.

There are three sister relationships: (1) *their* and PHRASE–b (*rather dubious jokes*), (2) PHRASE–c (*rather dubious*) and *jokes*, (3) *rather* and *dubious*. The relation that holds between these sister constituents is of the same general kind, that of MODIFICATION.

To begin at the lowest level of structure, *rather* has its function in respect of its sister *dubious*. It specifies the extent of the dubiousness, telling us how dubious the jokes are. *Rather* is DEPENDENT on *dubious*, in the sense that it is only present because *dubious* is. If we were to omit *dubious*, *rather* would be left without a function, and the omission would result in an ill-formed string (**their rather jokes*). Notice, however, that *dubious* is in no way dependent on *rather*. We can omit *rather* and still be left with a perfectly good phrase (*their dubious jokes*). This, then, is a ONE-WAY FUNCTION/ DEPENDENCY. *Rather* depends on *dubious* but not vice-versa. This function is called MODIFICATION. The function of *rather* is to modify *dubious*.

What about the function of *dubious* itself? **In a phrase containing a modifier, the element that is modified forms the essential**

centre of the phrase and is said to be the HEAD of the phrase. In this case, then, *dubious* functions as the head of the phrase *rather dubious*. I shall say more about heads of phrases in the next chapter.

A MODIFIER–HEAD relationship also holds, at the next (higher) level of structure, between the whole phrase *rather dubious* and the word *jokes*. *Rather dubious* specifies the character of the jokes. Again, *rather dubious* as a whole is a dependent modifier of *jokes* but not vice-versa. *Rather dubious* could be omitted (giving *their jokes*), but *jokes* (the head of the phrase) could not (**their rather dubious*).

Rather dubious jokes, then, forms a phrase but it does not tell us which rather dubious jokes are being referred to. It is the function of *their* to specify this. At this highest level of structure in the phrase, *their* is dependent on *rather dubious jokes*. Since *their* is dependent on *rather dubious jokes* but not vice versa, I shall treat the relation as another example of the modifier-head relation.

You might find it useful to picture the functional relations as in [37], where the direction of the dependencies is indicated by an arrow, and the functions by M (modifier) and H (head):

[37]

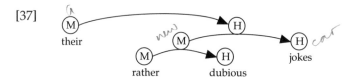

Now that the functions of these constituents have been specified, [36] should appear as a natural and obvious analysis. Compare it with some alternative analyses, [38] and [39]:

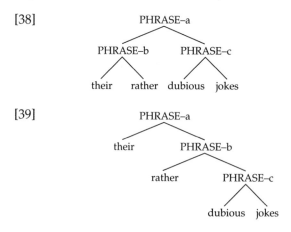

Both these analyses should now strike you as odd. *Their* and *rather* both belong to categories that can only have modifying functions; they cannot themselves function as the head of a phrase. So they cannot have their functions in respect of each other. But in [38] they are represented as sisters, forming a phrase. The fact that this supposed phrase does not seem to have a well-defined meaning is thus quite predictable. Notice that, since constituents function in respect of their sister constituents, *rather* is completely 'cut off' from the element (*dubious*) that it wants to modify.

[39] is marginally better, but still wrong. Before reading further, you might like to decide for yourself in the light of the preceding discussion exactly how it is better than [38], and exactly how it is still not so good as the analysis given in [36].

---

[39] is better than [38] in that *their* is correctly represented as a (modifying) sister of PHRASE–b (*rather dubious jokes*). It is still wrong, though, because it represents *rather* and *dubious jokes* as sisters, so that *rather* is now modifying, not just *dubious*, but the phrase *dubious jokes*. But we saw earlier that rather is dependent on (and belongs with) just *dubious*. It has to do with the dubious-ness of the jokes, not the jokes themselves. The original analysis of PHRASE–b (given in [36]) rightly predicts that the string *rather dubious jokes* corresponds in meaning with the phrase given as [40]:

[40] *jokes* which are *rather dubious*.

By contrast, the oddity of the analysis of PHRASE–b given in [39] is brought out by the fact that it predicts that PHRASE–b corresponds in meaning with the ungrammatical [41]:

[41] **dubious jokes* which are *rather*.

Dubious and *jokes* is another example of a sequence of words that forms a phrasal constituent in some contexts but not in others. We have seen that, in the context of *rather*, we need to relate *rather* and *dubious* before relating the whole phrase *rather dubious* to *jokes*. So *dubious* and *jokes* do not form a constituent in the context of *rather*. In the absence of *rather* (or any other modi-fier of *dubious*), on the other hand, there is no reason why *dubious* and *jokes* should not form a constituent, as in the phrase *their dubious jokes*:

[42]

Head and complement

We have now looked at **the two-way function/dependency of subject and predicate** and several examples of the **one-way function/dependency of modifier and head**. Now look again at the phrase *beside a stream* (from the sentence *Old Sam sunbathed beside a stream*) in the light of the discussion in this chapter. Do you recall the structure of the phrase? Draw the phrase-marker. How many sister relationships are there in the phrase?

[43]

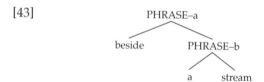

There are two sister relationships: (1) at the lowest level of structure, that between *a* and *stream* and (2) at the next level up, that between *beside* and PHRASE–b (*a stream*). The relationship between *a* and *stream* is the same kind of relationship as that between *their* and *rather dubious jokes*. In the last chapter I showed that *a* is dependent on *stream* and has its function only in respect of *stream*. *Beside* and *a* do not relate to each other either syntactically (that is to say, in terms of constituency or function) or semantically (they do not form a unit of sense). But what kind of relationship holds between *beside* and PHRASE–b (*a stream*)? Try to determine whether the relationship is a TWO-WAY DEPENDENCY or whether it is an example of the ONE-WAY DEPENDENCY OF MODIFIER AND HEAD. (You will need to consider the phrase in the context of its sentence.)

The way to do this is to see if either of the constituents of the phrase can be omitted individually in the context of the sentence. Can they?

Both [44] (with *beside* omitted) and [45] (with *a stream* omitted) are ungrammatical:

[44] *Old Sam sunbathed a stream
[45] *Old Sam sunbathed beside

Although the whole phrase could be omitted, neither of its constituents can be omitted individually. It appears that *beside* calls for the presence of a phrase such as *a stream* and that *a stream* depends on the presence of *beside*. It is therefore a two-way dependency.

The phrase *beside a stream* is telling us WHERE the sunbathing took place. It specifies a LOCATION. The location of a thing or an activity is usually expressed by orientating it in space (or in time: *after the storm, before seven o'clock*) in relation to some other thing, activity, event, or time. Although *beside* and *a stream* are both needed to express the spatial orientation in this case, it is clearly the word *beside* that is giving the phrase as a whole its locational character. So **beside is the head of the phrase**. And, just as Noun Phrases are named after, and have the same category as, their heads (nouns), the whole phrase *beside a stream* will be named after the category of the word *beside*. I discuss this more systematically in the next chapter.

We have seen that, unlike the modifier-head relations considered earlier, the relation between *beside* and *a stream* is a two-way dependency. Notice also that *a stream* does not tell us something about the head (*beside*) in the way that the modifiers considered in the last section do. So we distinguish between the function of elements that relate to a head in a one-way dependency from the function of elements that relate to a head in a two-way dependency. *Beside* demands a following phrase like *a stream*. **When a head DEMANDS a further expression in this way, that other (OBLIGATORY) expression is said to COMPLEMENT the head.** *A stream* functions as the complement of *beside*. What we have here, then, is not the functional relation of MODIFICATION, but the functional relation of COMPLEMENTATION.

Complements typically follow their heads in English. Modifiers, by contrast, can precede or follow their heads, though so far I have only given examples of modifiers preceding their heads.

Beside a stream illustrates both these general kinds of dependencies. If we were to give a graphic representation of the functional dependencies in that phrase, the mutual dependency of head (H) and complement (C) could be represented by a double arrow as in [46]:

[46]

$$\underset{\text{beside}}{\textcircled{H}} \overset{}{\Longleftarrow\!\!=\!\!=\!\!=\!\!=\!\!\Longrightarrow} \underset{a}{\textcircled{M}} \;-\; \overset{\textcircled{C}}{} \;-\;\!\!\blacktriangleright\underset{\text{stream}}{\textcircled{H}}$$

Look now at [47].

[47] Phil dreads affectionate cats.

It is a sentence so, overall, it is an example of the subject-predicate relation. But its predicate includes both a relation of modification and a relation of complementation. Before reading further, try to identify the modifier-head relation and the head-complement relation.

Phil is the subject and [*dreads affectionate cats*] is the predicate. Within the predicate, *affectionate* can be omitted (cf. *Phil dreads cats*), so it must be a modifier. It is clearly telling us about the cats. So it is modifying *cats*. *Cats*, then, is the (modified) head of the phrase [*affectionate cats*]. All that remains is to decide the relation between *dreads* and [*affectionate cats*]. Neither can be omitted (neither **Phil affectionate cats* nor **Phil dreads* is a well-formed sentence). This suggests that the relation between *dreads* and [*affectionate cats*] is a (two-way) head-complement dependency. Since heads precede their complements, *dreads* must be the head and [*affectionate cats*] the complement. There is a further, and more important, reason for thinking that *dreads* is the head. You now know that, as the predicate of the sentence, [*dreads affectionate cats*] is a Verb Phrase and must therefore have a verb as its head. If you did not already know, *dreads* is a verb (this is discussed properly in Chapter 4).

The functional dependencies exemplified in [47] can be represented as in [48]:

[48]

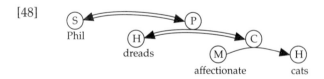

With this example, and throughout the chapter, I have aimed to show how constituency, function, and meaning are interrelated. Giving appropriate analyses of sentences in terms of their constituents depends on how you actually understand those sentences. Constructing the phrase-marker of a sentence involves giving an explicit graphic representation of what you, as a speaker of the language, know about that sentence. The meaning of a sentence depends not just on the meaning of its words, but on how those words are structured into phrases, and on the functions of those words and phrases. If you insist that each sequence of words which you want to say forms a constituent has a well-defined meaning and function (is a phrase), you will find that an appropriate analysis will suggest itself naturally.

Exercises

1. Identify the subjects and predicates of the following sentences.

(a) Her memory for names and dates was a constant source of amazement to him.
(b) The prune fritters left something to be desired.
(c) There are too many uninvited guests here.
(d) Only six of the thirty domino-toppling contestants came properly equipped.
(e) It was Lydia who finally trapped the pig.
(f) The fact that you received no birthday greetings from Mars doesn't mean that it is uninhabited.
(g) In the machine, the gremlin could be heard juggling with ball-bearings.

2. Identify the category of the following phrases (as Noun Phrase, Verb Phrase, or 'other').

(a) installed for only £199.95
(b) were being given away
(c) too far to drive in a day
(d) obsolescent washing machines
(e) ten long holidays at the Hotel Mortification
(f) which I had bought only the day before
(g) have made me realise that 'cheap' does indeed mean 'nasty'.

3.(a) The phrase *more exciting ideas* is ambiguous and needs a different structural analysis for each of its two interpretations. Draw the phrase-markers, giving an indication of which interpretation goes with which analysis.

(b)   Draw the phrase-markers for the following phrases:
  (i) young car salesmen   (ii) second-hand car salesmen.

4.   The phrase *the old Rumanian history teacher* has several different interpretations. Here are three structural analyses.

(a)

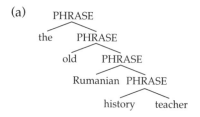

(b)

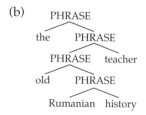

(c)

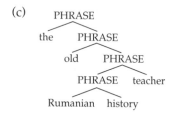

  (i) Which analysis corresponds with the interpretation 'the old teacher of Rumanian history'?
 (ii) Give the interpretations that correspond with the other analyses.
(iii) 'The history teacher from Old Rumania' is perhaps a less likely interpretation. Nevertheless it is possible to construct

a phrase-marker that would impose that interpretation on the phrase. Draw the phrase-marker.

5. Decide on the functions of the bracketed constituents in the following sentences.

(a) Old Sam sunbathed [beside a stream].
(b) The [well-built] gentleman offered me a cigar.
(c) People [in running kit] are popping up from under the table.
(d) People in [running kit] are popping up from under the table.

To answer this properly, you should not only state the function of the constituent but also indicate in respect of what other constituent it has that function. As mentioned in this chapter, you will find this much easier if you first satisfy yourself that you know the general structure of each sentence (i.e. that you can identify the subject NP and the predicate VP). First decide whether the bracketted constituent belongs within the subject or the predicate. Since constituents have their functions in respect of SISTER constituents, a constituent within the subject can only relate to other constituents within the subject, and a constituent within the predicate to other constituents within that predicate.

6. We have now looked at several of the dependencies in the sentence *Old Sam sunbathed beside a stream*. From exercise 5 above you should have discovered the function of *beside a stream*. All that remains is to decide on the function of *old*. Do that and then give a complete representation of all the dependencies in that sentence, using single and double arrows, and M for modifier, H for head, C for complement, S for subject, and P for predicate.

Discussion of exercises

1.(a) [Her memory for names and dates] [was a constant source of amazement to him].

(b) [The prune fritters] [left something to be desired]. A form of the verb *do* would have been required in applying the question test here.

(c) [There] [are too many uninvited guests here]. This subject-predicate division is probably not very obvious, since *there* (like *it* in *it is raining*) does not mention anything. Nevertheless, the question movement test gives a clear result: cf. *Are there too many uninvited guests here?*

(d)   [Only six of the thirty domino-toppling contestants] [came properly equipped].

(e)   [It] [was Lydia who finally trapped the pig]. Again, *it* is an empty subject, but it undergoes movement in the question (cf. *Was it Lydia who finally trapped the pig?*).

(f)   [The fact that you received no greetings from Mars] [doesn't mean that it is uninhabited].

(g)   This is an example where the subject does not begin the sentence; *in the machine* is not part of the subject. *The gremlin* is subject and *could be heard juggling with ball-bearings* is the predicate.

2.   The following are the only well-formed subject-predicate combinations: (d) + (b);   (d) + (g);   (e) + (b);   (e) + (g). Since they can function as subjects, (d) and (e) are the NPs; (b) and (g), functioning as predicates, are the VPs. (a), (c), and (f) belong to other categories.

3.(a) One interpretation (i) is equivalent to that of 'more ideas that are exciting'. The other (ii) corresponds with 'ideas that are more exciting'. On both interpretations, the syntactic function of *more* is that of a modifier (notice that it can be omitted). The difference in interpretation is a matter of whether *more* modifies just *exciting*, as in (ii) or *exciting ideas* (that is, *ideas*, which happens to be modified by *exciting*), as in (i). The two phrase-markers are:

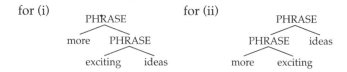

(b)   (i) Since people (salesmen, for example), but not things (cars, for example) can be described as 'young', *young* must modify a constituent of which *salesmen* is the head. It cannot modify *car* and hence cannot form a constituent with *car*. The natural phrase-marker, then, is:

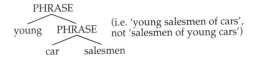

PHRASE
young   PHRASE   (i.e. 'young salesmen of cars',
         car   salesmen   not 'salesmen of young cars')

(ii) Things, but not people can be second-hand, so *second-hand* must modify (and hence form a constituent with) *car*, rather than any constituent having *salesmen* as its head.

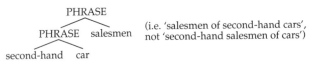

PHRASE
PHRASE   salesmen   (i.e. 'salesmen of second-hand cars',
second-hand   car   not 'second-hand salesmen of cars')

4.(i) Phrase-marker (c). This should be clearer after the following discussion.

(ii) In diagram (a) *Rumanian* modifies a phrase (*history teacher*) which has *teacher* (modified by *history*) as its head, so it is the (history) teacher that is Rumanian, not the history. The same goes for *old*: it modifies a phrase (*Rumanian history teacher*) which has *teacher* as its head. So, again, it is the teacher who is old. The interpretation can be expressed as 'the old teacher of history who comes from Rumania'. In diagram (b), *Rumanian* is the sister, and hence the modifier, of *history*. Here it is the history that is Rumanian rather than the teacher. And *old* modifies a phrase that has *history* as head, so again it is the (Rumanian) history that is old, not the teacher. So the interpretation is 'the teacher of old Rumanian history'.

(iii)

PHRASE
the   PHRASE
    PHRASE   PHRASE
  old Rumanian   history teacher

5.(a) You know that the sentence is divided into subject and predicate as follows: [Old Sam] [sunbathed beside a stream], so *beside a stream* must have its function in respect of its sister within the predicate, *sunbathed*. We have already noted that it is optional and that it specifies something about the sunbathing, namely its location. Therefore the function of *beside a stream* is that of modifier of *sunbathed*. This is our first example in which the modifier follows the head.

(b)   *Well-built* is a constituent in the structure of the subject NP
       the well-built gentleman, so it must have its function in respect
       of either *the* or *gentleman*. *Well-built gentleman* seems to form
       a unit of sense, in contrast to *the well-built*. In fact, the struc-
       ture of this phrase is almost identical to that of *their rather
       dubious jokes* (which, incidentally, is also a Noun Phrase – as
       you may have already noticed). *Well-built* corresponds struc-
       turally with *rather dubious*. So the function of *well-built* is that
       of modifier of *gentleman*.

(c)   It is clear that *people in running kit* is the subject NP. *In run-
       ning kit* must therefore have its function in respect of *people*.
       It is also optional. It seems natural then that *people* is the
       head of that NP, and that *in running kit* is the modifier of that
       head. Another example of the modifier following the head
       of the phrase.

(d)   Notice that neither *in* nor *running kit* can be omitted indi-
       vidually: **people running kit are popping up from under the
       table*; **people in are popping up from under the table*. This indic-
       ates that *running kit* is required to complete the meaning of
       in and that *running kit* is only present because *in* is. We
       have here the mutual dependency of complementation,
       and – as usual in complementations – the second constitu-
       ent (*running kit*) is said to complement the first (*in*), which
       is the head. This is the same category of phrase as *beside a
       stream*.

6.   It has already been shown that *old Sam* is the subject NP in
       this sentence and that *old* is omissible. Furthermore, *old*
       gives us further information about Sam. The function of *old*
       is as a modifier of *Sam*, the head of the NP. In addition, as
       you discovered in Exercise 5, the function of *beside a stream* is
       to modify *sunbathed*. Integrating these, and the other depen-
       dencies into a single representation yields:

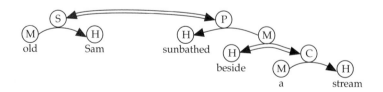

Further exercises

1. For each of the following sentences, identify the subject NP and the predicate VP by drawing phrase-markers like that in [33] on page 36. In cases where the sentence is *not* exhaustively divisible into NP followed by VP, list the extra constituents separately.

   (i) I am accepting your invitation.
   (ii) The income received from fines can't be taken into account.
   (iii) Grishkin and the man in brown are in league.
   (iv) One day, my boy, all this will be yours.
   (v) One day will be enough for this job.
   (vi) A gorilla swinging about in the trees above our heads interrupted this already lengthy story.
   (vii) Next Sunday or the Sunday after that would be convenient dates.
   (viii) Last week it rained solidly.
   (ix) The existence of stars of such extreme density that not even light can escape them has not been doubted recently.
   (x) The temptation to identify less than the whole of the relevant phrase crops up in all constituent analysis.
   (xi) Not everyone who accepted that afternoon's invitation to visit the slaughterhouse found it quite as edifying as you.
   (xii) The many meetings in Downing Street and elsewhere between the Prime Minister and other leaders involved in the crisis have failed to yield any solution acceptable to them or to the United Nations.

2. Below are five phrases and four phrase-markers. On the basis of your understanding of them, assign each phrase to the appropriate phrase-marker. One of the phrase-markers is appropriate for two of the phrases. If you have problems, re-read the discussion of the 'sister' relation in the chapter.

   (i) Refurbished citrus fruit markets
   (ii) New central fruit markets
   (iii) Animals from the zoo
   (iv) Gas appliances from Italy
   (v) Free-range egg packagers

(a)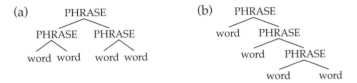

(b)

(c)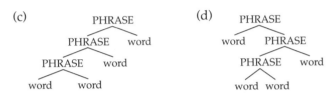

(d)

3. Having discovered which phrase should be assigned to phrase-marker (d), explain why phrase-marker (c) would not provide an appropriate analysis of that phrase.

4. For phrase-markers (a) and (b) above, think up one further phrase that would fit those structures.

5. Using just 'phrase' and 'word' (as in Exercise 2) above draw phrase-markers for the following phrases.

   (i) Students doing chemistry.
  (ii) Students doing chemistry in September.
 (iii) Students with long hair doing chemistry.
  (iv) Several very noisy newspaper vendors.
   (v) Ten fully automatic deluxe hair driers.

6. For each sister relation in the phrase-marker you have drawn for (iii) in Exercise 5, decide whether it is a head-complement relation or a modifier-head relation. In each case, which element is the head?

Chapter 3

Sentence Structure: Categories

I have explained the oddity of *their rather jokes* as being due to the fact that *rather* had a function only in respect of *dubious* and that, if you omit *dubious, rather* is left without a function. But why is *rather* left without a function? In the absence of *dubious,* why can't *rather* modify *jokes* instead? Or couldn't we say that *rather* modifies (or is modified by) *their*?

In a sense, you already know the answers to these questions. You already know that *rather* just isn't the *kind* of word that can modify (and thereby form a constituent with) *jokes* – nor is *jokes* the kind of word that can be modified by *rather.* You already know that *dubious* differs from *rather* in being the kind of word that can modify *jokes,* and differs from *jokes* in being the kind of word that can be modified by *rather.*

It is a brute fact about the way speakers understand their language that they recognise several different kinds of word – in other words, they assign the words of their language to several distinct CATEGORIES. In doing so, they recognise that each word has a restricted range of possible functions and that there are restrictions on how the words can combine to form phrases. In illustration of the fact that you yourself do this, try the following exercise. Decide which of the following words belongs to the same category as *rather,* which to the same category as *dubious,* and which to the same category as *joke.* One of the words is of a category distinct from all three.

tactics, extremely, could, subtle

Consider the following strings:

[1a] their tactics
[1b] their dubious tactics
[1c] *their rather tactics
[1d] *their tactics dubious jokes
[1e] *their rather tactics jokes

[2a] *their extremely
[2b] *their dubious extremely
[2c] *their extremely jokes
[2d] their extremely dubious jokes
[2e] *their rather extremely jokes

The strings in [1] show that *tactics* **has the same** DISTRIBUTION **as** *jokes*. **By this I mean that** *tactics* **has the same range of functions, can combine with the same other elements, and can occupy the same positions as** *jokes*. Like *jokes*, it can be modified by *their* [1a] and by *dubious* [1b]. Like *jokes*, it cannot be modified by *rather* [1c]. [1d] and [1e] show that it cannot occupy the positions or assume the functions of either *rather* [1d] or *dubious* [1c]. **In short,** *tactics* **and** *jokes* **belong to the same category**, which is probably the decision you came to by intuition.

Now check list [2], making a note of what each string tells you about *extremely*.

In contrast to *jokes* and *tactics*, *extremely* cannot be modified by either *their* [2a] or *dubious* [2b]. And in contrast to *dubious*, it can neither modify *jokes* [2c], nor be modified by *rather* [2e]. *Extremely* has all this in common with *rather*. More positively, in common with *rather*, when it appears in a position in which it can be interpreted as modifying *dubious* [2d], it is acceptable. *Extremely* and *rather*, then, have the same distribution and so belong to the same category. They both specify the degree of the dubiousness of the jokes.

The same considerations would lead you to assign *subtle* to the same category as *dubious*. They both specify some characteristic of the jokes. The odd one out is *could*. Every attempt to incorporate *could* into the structure of the phrase results in ill-formed strings, so it must belong to yet another category.

I have mentioned only the category of SINGLE WORDS. Categories of single words are called LEXICAL CATEGORIES. 'Noun' is an example of a lexical category. But you know from Chapter 2 that PHRASES have categories too. These are called PHRASAL CATEGORIES (e.g. 'Noun Phrase'). Notice that, since *their rather dubious jokes* is a well-formed phrase, and since *rather* and *extremely*, *dubious* and *subtle*, and *jokes* and *tactics* belong to the same categories, it is predictable that *their extremely subtle tactics* should be a well-formed phrase as well. It is also predictable that the two phrases should belong to the same phrasal category, and that they should have the same internal structure. As at the word level, this allows us to predict that, as whole phrases, they have the same DISTRIBUTION – they will be able to occupy the same positions in sentence structure and have the same range of functions.

It is clear that, instead of talking about individual words and phrases, we need to make more general statements about what does and what does not constitute a well-formed expression in the language in terms of the CATEGORIES involved. But first of all, we need to name these categories. In the rest of this chapter, then, I shall introduce some lexical categories by name and give hints on how to identify their members. I shall also discuss the category of phrases and how this relates to the category of the words that they contain. The notion of head is important here.

Nouns

For the purposes of identification, it is perhaps best to start with a very traditional definition of what a noun is: **a noun is the name of a person, place, or thing**. There are problems with this definition. For example, 'thing' has to be interpreted very broadly, to include substances like butter and foam (since *butter* and *foam* are nouns), abstract concepts like honesty and multiplication (since *honesty* and *multiplication* are nouns), collections of things like federations, crowds, and cutlery, and phenomena like gravity and time (for the same reason). Suspicions, accidents, refusals, and facts are not obviously things, yet *suspicion*, *accident*, *refusal*, and *fact* are all nouns. On the other hand, while *behind* and *ahead* might be said to stand for places, they are not normally taken to be nouns. Nevertheless the definition is useful as a starting point. Here are some further examples of nouns:

January, Frankenstein, Bugsy, Jessica, Java, Portsmouth, gorilla, university, jam, theory, inspector, nationalisation, gremlin, joke, tactic, gallon, furniture, year, couple.

You might well ask why I so confidently insist that *suspicion*, *honesty* and *January* are nouns when suspicions, honesty, and January are not strictly either people, places or things. In answer to this, you need to recall what the point of categorising words was in the first place. **By assigning a word to a particular category, we make a general statement about its distribution** – i.e. about its possible syntactic positions and functions. *Honesty, suspicions,* and *January* are nouns because they occupy the same range of positions and have the same range of functions as other words that obviously are nouns by that traditional definition. In the final analysis, then, it is the syntactic criterion of distribution that decides the matter. So I shall supplement the traditional account of nouns with some distributional clues to their identification.

In addition, every category of words has its own range of possible WORD FORMS (its MORPHOLOGICAL possibilities). Nouns are no exception. As we shall see, this too can be useful in identifying them.

A morphological identifying feature of all nouns is that they have a GENITIVE (or POSSESSIVE) form. For example, *Bill's* (as in *Bill's pancakes* or *those are Bill's*), *mud's* (as in *the mud's consistency*).

Other features are shared by some nouns and not by others (in other words, there are several SUB-CATEGORIES of the noun category).

To begin with PROPER NOUNS – these are NAMES (with an initial capital). Examples from the above list are: *January, Frankenstein, Bugsy, Jessica, Java, Portsmouth*.

All other nouns are COMMON NOUNS. Most of what follows normally applies only to common nouns.

All common nouns can be preceded by *the* (THE DEFINITE ARTICLE) to form a Noun Phrase (e.g. *the accident, the mud, the cutlery*).

Common nouns that refer to 'things' that can be counted (COUNT NOUNS)

(a) can be preceded by the definite article or *a/an* (THE INDEFINITE ARTICLE) (e.g. *a stream, an accident*) to form a Noun Phrase;
(b) can be preceded by NUMERALS (*one, two, three* ...) to form a Noun Phrase, and by expressions like *several, many,* etc.;
(c) regularly appear in a PLURAL FORM in addition to a SINGULAR form:

SINGULAR	PLURAL
accident, man,	*accidents,* men,
foot, analysis.	*feet, analyses.*

This morphological possibility readily identifies a word as a noun.

Nouns that refer to 'things' that cannot be counted (NON-COUNT NOUNS, sometimes called MASS NOUNS – e.g. *butter, foam, cutlery,*

furniture, honesty, grace) do not normally display any of these possibilities. They cannot normally be preceded by *a/an* (*a foam, **a
butter*, *a furniture) nor by numerals or similar expressions (**two
foams*, *nine furnitures, *several muds). Nor can they normally
appear in a PLURAL form (*foams, *butters, *honesties). But they can
be preceded by *some* (*some foam, some furniture, some honesty*).

The above remarks have been qualified by 'normally' because
it is in fact often possible to turn a non-count noun into a count
noun precisely by modifying it by *a/an*, or a numeral, and/or
giving it a plural form. This usually involves a change of meaning: *a mud, two butters* (a kind of mud, two kinds of butter); *a beer,
three beers* (a kind of beer, or a drink of beer). (See also *with an
honesty that surprised me*.)

Many nouns are both count and non-count. For example,
theory can stand alone or with *some* (cf. *some theory*) as a non-
count noun, but it can also be preceded by *a* and by numerals
and have a plural form as a count noun (*a theory, theories, three
theories*). Other examples that are both count and non-count are
suspicion, egg, cake, and *charity*.

Proper nouns, because they anyway stand for single, identifiable individuals, do not normally have any modifiers at all or
appear in a plural form. However, in special circumstances, they
can be modified by *the* or *a* and appear in a plural form: *the
Ewings* (= the Ewing family), *the Borg of Wimbledon fame, the
Einsteins of this world, a pensive Holmes*.

There is more one could say about these various sub-categories
of nouns, but the above should suffice for the purposes of identification.

Now identify all the nouns in the following passage:

> As Max and Adrian were talking, the daylight was fading from
> the West. Clouds were gathering and there was a chill in the air.
> They decided to end their conversation. Lights were shining from
> a passing steamer. Pessimistic thoughts filled the minds of both
> men, but Adrian pushed them aside as being merely the result of
> his tiredness. Besides, he had sand in his shoes.

The nouns in the passage are: *Max, Adrian, daylight, West, clouds,
chill, air, conversation, lights, steamer, thoughts, minds, men, Adrian,
result, tiredness, sand, shoes.*

If you included *they, them* and *he* on the grounds that they
stood for persons and things, this is perfectly reasonable. They

are pronouns. PRONOUNS **are used to stand in place of complete Noun Phrases (NPs).** In the above passage, *they* stands for *Max and Adrian*, *them* stands for *pessimistic thoughts*, and *he* stands for *Adrian*. As you saw in Chapter 1, substituting single words like these is an important test for whether a sequence of words constitutes a phrase or not. In substituting a pronoun, we test more specifically whether the phrase is a Noun Phrase or not.

Here are some further examples of pronouns:

DEFINITE PRONOUNS: *she/her, it, I/me, we/us, you, they/them*
INDEFINITE PRONOUNS: *some, something, someone, anything, anyone*
DEMONSTRATIVE PRONOUNS: *this, that, these, those*
INTERROGATIVE (QUESTION) PRONOUNS: *who, which, what, whose*
POSSESSIVE PRONOUNS: *mine, yours, his, hers, ours, yours, theirs,*
whose

Lexical and phrasal categories (noun and Noun Phrase)

Before introducing further lexical categories, I shall look at the relation between lexical and phrasal categories, using nouns and Noun Phrases as an example. In Chapter 2 I said that an NP is a phrase that contains, and is centred on, a noun. *Their rather dubious jokes* is an NP and it contains the noun *jokes*. But it contains words of other categories as well. Why does the phrase as a whole have to be of the same category as *jokes*? Why can't it be of the same category as *their* or *rather* or *dubious*? The answer crucially involves the notion of HEAD introduced in Chapter 2.

In Chapter 2 I showed how *rather* modified *dubious*, *rather dubious* modified *jokes*, and *their* modified *rather dubious jokes*. At every level of structure in the phrase, it is *jokes* that functions as head. **In a modifier-head relation it is the category of the HEAD word that determines the category of the phrase a whole.** The other words are present only because of the function they (directly or indirectly) have in respect of the head noun. In a sense, then, *their rather dubious jokes* and *their extremely subtle tactics* can be seen as expansions of *jokes* and *tactics* respectively.

It is the head noun that determines the NUMBER (singular or plural) and the GENDER (masculine, feminine, or neutral) of the Noun Phrase as a whole. This can be seen by considering what pronoun could be used to replace the NP in a sentence:

[3] their extremely subtle tactics – they, them
[4] their extremely subtle tactic – it
[5] an extremely subtle actress – she, her
[6] an extremely subtle actor – he, him.

Tactics, to take just the first example, is the plural head noun. So the NP as a whole is plural, as indicated by the fact that it could only be replaced by the plural pronouns *they* or *them*.

Before I make any further comments on the relation between NP and N, here is a phrase-marker of *their extremely subtle tactics*, in which I have filled in all the information about categories introduced so far:

[7]

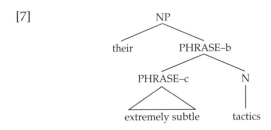

For the topmost node, all I have done is categorise PHRASE–a as a Noun Phrase (NP). In order to say that *tactics* is a noun, I have introduced an extra node, immediately dominating *tactics*, which I have labelled N.

Noun Phrases, of course, may contain more than one noun. But (with one exception to be discussed in a moment) **only one noun in a Noun Phrase can function as its head**. In each of the following sentences, first identify the subject NP, and then all the nouns contained in those subject NPs, indicating which is the head noun.

[8] The man devouring the plums is grinning broadly.
[9] The comedy actress John met in the foyer seemed happy.

In [8] the subject NP is *the man devouring the plums*. It contains two nouns, *man* and *plums*, and it is clear that *man* is the head noun. The appropriate pronoun to replace the whole Noun Phrase would be *he* – a singular masculine pronoun – which is consistent with the number and gender of *man* but not with the number and gender of *plums*. In [9] the subject NP is *the comedy actress John met in the foyer*. It contains the nouns *comedy*, *actress*, *John*, *foyer*. The appropriate pronoun is *she*, a feminine pronoun that is consistent only with the gender of *actress*. *Actress* is therefore the head noun.

As the discussion of these examples implies, **it is the HEAD NOUN that determines what sort of thing or person the whole NP refers to**. The subject NP of [8] refers to a man – it is a man (not plums!) that is doing the grinning. In [9] the NP refers to an actress – it is an actress who seemed happy (not John, or comedy – and certainly not the foyer!).

I have mentioned that, in an NP, constituents that modify the head noun are typically optional – they can be omitted without affecting the well-formedness of either the NP itself or the sentence in which it appears:

[10]   Their extremely subtle tactics confuse me.
[11]   Their tactics confuse me.
[12]   Tactics confuse me.

The question that I want to raise here concerns sentence [12]. On the one hand, I have said that *tactics* is a noun. On the other hand I have said that, wherever possible, sentences should be analysed into a two-part, NP + VP, structure. Clearly, the VP is *confuse me*. But this seems to suggest that *tactics* is therefore NP – i.e. a full Noun Phrase. In [12] then, is *tactics* just a noun, or is it a full Noun Phrase? There seems to be a conflict here. The same apparent conflict crops up with proper nouns, which generally don't appear with modifiers, as in [13]:

[13]   Max confuses me.

In [13], is *Max* just a noun or is it a full NP? Think about this question before reading further. Can you think of any way of resolving the conflict?

As suggested, the conflict is only apparent. We do not have to choose between these alternatives. *Max* in [13] (and *tactics* in [12]) is both a noun and a full NP. In saying this, I am allowing that **a Noun Phrase can consist simply of a head noun**. If you think about it, we must allow for this possibility: if we say that an NP consists of a (head) noun plus its modifiers, and if modifiers are typically optional, it follows automatically that NPs can consist just of a head noun.

In terms of a phrase-marker representation, then, we must allow for NP configurations like that shown in [14]:

[14]

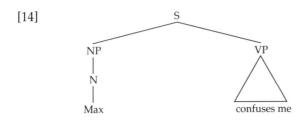

Some further remarks may help to clarify this point. Earlier I mentioned that pronouns stand in place of full NPs. Just as we can replace the subject NPs of [10] and [11] by *they*, so we can replace the subject NPs of [12] and [13] by pronouns (*they* and *he* respectively). On the other hand, if you try replacing a simple noun (as opposed to a full NP) with a pronoun, you will get very odd results. Consider again

[15] The ducks are paddling away.

The ducks is an NP and it contains the noun *ducks*. Only the whole NP can be replaced by a pronoun (as in [16]), not the simple noun *ducks* (see [17]):

[16] They are paddling away.
[17] *The they are paddling away.

This clearly shows that simple nouns as such cannot be replaced by a pronoun. Since *tactics* in [12] and *Max* in [13] can be replaced by pronouns, they must be analysed as being full NPs as well as simple nouns.

In [16] we see that the pronoun *they* has assumed the position and function of a full NP. So *they* is itself an example of a one-word NP. In terms of a phrase-marker it would be represented as in [18], with 'PRONOUN' abbreviated to PRO.

[18]

Now decide whether *tactics* in [10] (*Their extremely subtle tactics confuse me*) is a full NP or not.

By the pronoun test, it is not a full NP; cf. *Their extremely subtle they confused me. An NP consists of a simple noun and its modifiers.

Their and *extremely subtle* are the modifiers and *tactics* is the (simple) noun.

The discussion illustrates the close relation between the function of subject and the phrasal category of NP. In [12] and [13] *tactics* and *Max* are functioning as subjects. They therefore count as full NPs in those sentences. But in *their tactics confuse me*, it is the whole phrase, *their tactics*, that is functioning as the subject, not the simple noun *tactics* itself, which is just a constituent (albeit the central constituent) of the phrase that is functioning as subject.

So, more generally, when single words have the functions that full phrases have, it is standard practice to treat them as full phrases of the appropriate category. This means that we allow for **one-word phrases** in certain circumstances; not only one-word Noun Phrases, but one-word phrases of other categories as well. In fact, I opened Chapter 2 by discussing a sentence that consisted of two one-word phrases, namely *Ducks paddle*, where *ducks* is a simple noun that counts also as the subject NP, and *paddle* is a verb that counts as a VP. The latter counts as a full VP because it functions, by itself, as a complete predicate.

The idea of one-word phrases sometimes causes difficulty because WORDS are traditionally contrasted with PHRASES. After all, words are just words, but phrases are sequences, or strings, of words. However, in this context at least, it is necessary to understand 'word-sequence/string' as meaning 'a sequence/string of one of more words'.

Adjectives and adverbs

Dubious and *subtle* are adjectives. Any word that has the same distribution as those words is an adjective. Many adjectives have characteristic endings, such as *-able, -al, -ate, ful, -ic, -ing, -ish, -ive, -less, -ous, -y*. Examples are:

capable, economical, Italianate, beautiful, microscopic, surprising, priggish, inventive, hopeless, callous, fluffy.

There are other adjectival endings, and the endings given are only typical of adjectives, not an infallible guide. The more common adjectives tend not to have characteristic endings (e.g. *old, hot, short, tight, full, long*) and this goes for the colour adjectives (*blue, yellow*, etc.).

Many adjectives have the morphological possibility of taking a COMPARATIVE (*-er*) and a SUPERLATIVE (*-est*) inflection, as in *newer*, and *newest*, *subtler* and *subtlest*. Others do not (cf. **beautifuller/ *beautifullest, *dubiouser/*dubiousest*) but instead may be modified by the comparative and superlative DEGREE ADVERBS *more* and *most*, *less* and *least*. Yet others have irregular comparative and superlative forms (*good, better, best*).

I have mentioned the comparative and superlative degree adverbs *more* and *most*, *less* and *least*. Since the main function of degree adverbs is to modify adjectives (specifying the degree of the attribute expressed by the adjective), this seems the appropriate place to mention degree adverbs as a category. They are words having the same distribution as *rather* and *extremely*, for example:

very, quite, so, too, slightly, hardly, highly, moderately, completely, increasingly, incredibly, etc.

Adjectives that accept the *-er/-est* inflection or modification by degree adverbs are called GRADABLE ADJECTIVES. Unfortunately for the purposes of identifying adjectives, not all adjectives are gradable. NON-GRADABLE ADJECTIVES do not accept the *-er/-est* inflection, or modification by degree adverb. Here are some examples of non-gradable adjectives:

atomic, dead, potential, right, main, consummate, medical, fatal, final, second, third, supreme.

Note the oddity of the following: **supremer, *supremest, *more supreme, *very supreme, *rather supreme, *too supreme*.

As I introduce further categories in later chapters, we will encounter words which are adjectives but less obviously so. With these introductory remarks I have restricted myself to the clear cases.

Now, bearing in mind that adjectives have a variety of functions (not only the illustrated function of modifying nouns), identify the adjectives in the following passage. There are a few degree adverbs too. Make a note of them.

> The great architectural interest of the royal palace did not strike William at that precise moment, grotesque and flamboyant though it was. He had eyes only for Goneril's gorgeous purple hair. Could it be artificial? He found it difficult to believe she was so self-conscious as to have dyed it such a fantastic hue. She

seemed too modest for that. In silent admiration, he concluded that it had to be completely natural.

The adjectives are: *great, architectural, royal, precise, grotesque, flamboyant, gorgeous, purple, artificial, difficult, self-conscious, fantastic, modest, silent, natural*. The degree adverbs are: *so, too, completely*.

Adjective Phrases and Adverb Phrases

Rather dubious, extremely subtle, and *too modest* are Adjective Phrases. As with the NP, the phrase is of the same category as its head word, i.e. Adjective Phrase (AP) is centred on adjective (A). And, again like NPs, an AP can consist of an unmodified head, a simple adjective.

For example, in *Aldo's very colourful pizzas* the AP, *very colourful*, functions as the modifier of *pizzas* and *colourful* is a simple adjective functioning as the head of the AP. On the other hand, in *Luigi's colourless pizzas*, the simple adjective functions both as the head and, in itself, as the complete modifier of *pizzas*, so it counts as a full AP as well.

By contrast with adjectives and nouns, **degree adverbs cannot themselves be modified**. So there is no distinction between a degree adverb and a degree Adverb Phrase. In phrase-markers, then, I shall simply employ the label 'DEGREE' (shortened to 'DEG').

You should now be able to draw the phrase-marker for *very energetic*, using all the appropriate category labels. It is given as phrase-marker (a) at the end of this chapter.

Other constituents can appear in adjective phrases. I shall mention here only the GENERAL ADVERBS. Examples are:

frankly, potentially, oddly, enthusiastically, immediately, suspiciously, awkwardly.

As these examples illustrate, the vast majority of general adverbs (and, you will have noted, some of the degree adverbs) are formed from adjectives by the addition of *-ly*, and so are easily identified.

Like degree adverbs, general adverbs can modify adjectives within Adjective Phrases (though general adverbs typically have other functions as well): cf. *theoretically untenable, oddly inconclusive, diabolically tinted, immediately recognisable.*

General adverbs differ from degree adverbs in specifying a wider range of concepts than just degree. But this, in itself, is not the reason for distinguishing between general adverbs and degree adverbs in terms of syntactic category. The reason for the categorial distinction is that general adverbs can themselves be modified by degree adverbs, to form ADVERB PHRASES (AdvPs) – for example, *very oddly, quite frankly.* Since modification of a general adverb by a degree adverb is optional, an AdvP (like an NP and an AP) can consist of just a simple (general) adverb.

By way of a summary, I will give an analysis of *more obviously artificial.* As you read this paragraph, construct a labelled phrase-marker of the phrase. It is an ADJECTIVE PHRASE (AP), whose immediate constituents are the (head) ADJECTIVE (A) *artificial* and the (modifying) ADVERB PHRASE (AdvP) *more obviously.* This in turn consists of the (head) ADVERB (Adv) *obviously* and the (modifying) DEGREE ADVERB (DEG) *more.* The phrase-marker is given as (b) at the end of the chapter.

Prepositions and Prepositional Phrases

Recall the discussion of *beside a stream. Beside* is a preposition (P), and it is the head of the whole phrase. So the whole phrase is a PREPOSITIONAL PHRASE (PP). *A stream*, we decided, is functioning as complement to that head.

Prepositions are generally short words that express relations, often locational relations in space or time. Other examples are: *to, from, with, towards, within, off, by, up, down, since, before, after, during, until.* Prepositions don't always express locational concepts, though (IN *an accident*, IN *a blue coat*, OFF *work*, UNDER *pressure*, AT *great speed*, ON *the make*). The most commonly used preposition *of*, does not.

In this book, I shall only consider basic Prepositional Phrases (PPs) like *beside a stream* and *to Max*, making the traditional assumption that all Prepositions take complements and that their complements are always Noun Phrases. In fact Ps and PPs are more interesting than this. However, this simplification is convenient for you, since it allows you to assume that, whenever you encounter a preposition (P), it will always be dominated by

PP and always have a (complement) NP as a following sister, as in [19]:

[19]

Now draw the phrase-marker of *to Max*, including all the categorical information. (Phrase-marker (c) at the end of the chapter.)

PPs, if they contain very long and complex NPs can appear to be long and complex themselves (e.g. *through the trampoline he'd just bought off Jim*). Nevertheless, with one exception to be discussed immediately, such PPs can always be analysed as consisting simply of a P and an NP.

Co-ordinate Phrases

I have now introduced four main lexical categories, NOUNS, ADJECTIVES, ADVERBS (general and degree), and PREPOSITIONS, and taken a brief look at the phrasal categories associated with them. I will conclude this chapter with a very general point about categories and constituency.

Discussing nouns and Noun Phrases, I mentioned that, in an NP, only one noun can be head of the phrase. I pointed out that there was an important exception to this. The exception is illustrated in the following examples.

[20a] Max and Adrian are being melodramatic.
[20b] The clowns and the acrobats declined to co-operate.

Identify the subject NP of each of these sentences.

Now identify the nouns in those NPs.

Of the nouns in each NP, can you, in fact, decide which is the head noun?

The subject NPs are [20a] *Max and Adrian* and [20b] *the clowns and the acrobats*. The first contains the two nouns *Max* and *Adrian* and the second *clowns* and *acrobats*. In each subject NP it is in fact impossible to identify any single noun as being the head. Of *Max* and *Adrian* neither seems more central than the other. It is not just Max, nor just Adrian, who is being melodramatic, both are. The same goes for the clowns and the acrobats.

In such cases, if any noun is head of the NP, then both nouns must be. In phrases such as these, we must allow that NPs can have more than one head. Both *Max* and *Adrian* are the noun heads of the NP *Max and Adrian*. Such phrases are called CO-ORDIN-ATE PHRASES. *Max and Adrian* is a CO-ORDINATE NOUN PHRASE, with *Max* and *Adrian* co-ordinated by *and*. **Co-ordinate NPs have as many heads as there are nouns co-ordinated in them**. Other CO-ORDINATORS are *but* and *or*.

In view of all that has been said so far, you might feel inclined to say that *Max and Adrian* does not constitute a single phrasal constituent but is a sequence of two separate subjects. The weight of evidence is against this view. Can you think of any arguments against it?

In the first place, you have already identified *Max and Adrian* as a single constituent in saying that the sequence functions as the subject of its sentence. You can check for yourself that it is that complete phrase (rather than any sub-part of it) that changes position in the question. Also, we can use an interrogative pro-noun to replace the complete phrase, and answer the resulting question with it:

[21] Who is being melodramatic? – Max and Adrian.
[22] Who declined to co-operate? – The clowns and the acro-
     bats.

Likewise, the co-ordinate NP can be replaced by *they*:

[23] They are being melodramatic.
[24] They declined to co-operate.

As you may have noted, with co-ordinate NPs it is usual to find that the NP as a whole is PLURAL regardless of whether the heads are singular or plural. Hence, although *Max* and *Adrian* are individually singular, the NP as a whole needs to be replaced by the plural pronoun *they*.

What, then, is the structure of these phrases? Ask yourself first whether the subject NP of [20b] consists directly of the nouns it contains (plus *and*), or whether you can identify any intermediate constituents. If you can, what are their categories?

It should have been a simple matter to identify both *the clowns* and *the acrobats* as constituent phrases. They are NPs themselves. This can be demonstrated by showing that, even within the co-ordinate NP, they can themselves be replaced by pronouns, as in [25] and [26]:

[25] They and the acrobats declined to co-operate.
[26] The clowns and they declined to co-operate.

What about *Max* and *Adrian* in [*Max and Adrian*]? Are they just nouns or full NPs as well?

---

[27] and [28] are both well-formed:

[27] He and Adrian are being melodramatic.
[28] Max and he are being melodramatic.

This indicates that both *Max* and *Adrian*, in addition to being simple nouns, are full NPs in their own right.

In short, the subject NPs of [20a] and [20b] are co-ordinations of NPs. The whole co-ordinate phrase and the elements that are co-ordinated in them have the same distribution and so are of the same category. They can be represented as in [29] and [30]:

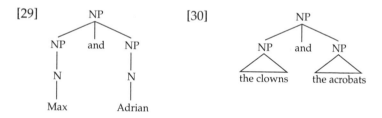

There is a general point here which I will approach by first asking you to judge which of the following strings are well-formed phrases and which not.

[31] Max and quickly
[32] the acrobats and wellnigh incomprehensible
[33] the actress that John met in the foyer and the acrobats
[34] in the foundations and under the rafters
[35] obviously intelligent and to Porlock
[36] moderately cheap and extremely nasty
[37] rather and inconsistent

For the purposes of this exercise, let's assume that we agree in our judgements: [33], [34], and [36] are well-formed phrases; [31], [32], [35], and [37] are ill-formed. Can you suggest a general explanation for the ungrammaticality of the latter set of examples?

Let us approach this by considering first the well-formed phrases. Consider [33]. What category of phrase is it, and how do you know?

---

[33] passes all the tests for NP. In the light of the above discussion, one could reliably guess that it is an NP since it is a co-ordination of phrases that have already been identified as NPs. Now identify the category of phrases that are co-ordinated in [34] and [36] and make a (reliable!) guess as to the category of the phrases as a whole.

In the foundations and *under the rafters* are both PPs. You will probably not be surprised to hear that [34] is itself a PP. *In the foundations* has the same distribution as *in the foundations and under the rafters* (wherever the one could appear so could the other) – so they must belong to the same category. In [36] *moderately cheap* and *extremely nasty* are both APs. Not surprisingly, [36] is an AP.

Now identify the phrases that have been co-ordinated in the ill-formed examples. On the basis of that, try to decide the category of the whole string. The difficulty you will experience in attempting to do this provides the explanation for their oddity. Try to formulate in your mind what the problem is.

---

[31] is a co-ordination of a Noun Phrase and an Adverb Phrase. How do we decide what category the whole co-ordination should belong to? We cannot decide. Both phrases are heads of the co-ordinate phrase, but their categories conflict. In [32] a Noun Phrase and an Adjective Phrase have been co-ordinated and we have the same problem. In [35] it is a Prepositional Phrase and an Adjective Phrase, in [37] a Degree Adverb and an Adjective Phrase. And again, there is no way of deciding what the category of the whole string is.

To sum up, **any constituent, of any category, can consist of a co-ordination of constituents of the same category.** It follows from this that only constituents of the same category can be co-ordinated.

This very general principle has provided an often-used test in language study. It has been used as a test of two things, (a) constituency and (b) category. As regards (a), notice that the general principle allows only *constituents* to be co-ordinated. So if you can co-ordinate a string of words with another string of words, this indicates that each of those strings can be a constituent. As regards (b), if you know the category of one of those strings of words, you know that the other string of words must be of the same category, since only identical categories can be co-ordinated.

I have illustrated this general principle with co-ordinations of phrasal categories only. But the principle holds for all categories, including lexical categories and sentences themselves. Compare [38] and [39]:

[38] Stuffy and too hot.
[39] Too hot and stuffy.

Both are APs. [38] is a co-ordination of APs (the first consisting of a simple A). The most likely interpretation of [39], on the other hand, is that it means the same as *too hot and too stuffy*. In this case, the modifier of *hot* is shared by *stuffy*, so that *too* modifies not just *hot* but the whole phrase *hot and stuffy*. *Hot* and *stuffy*, therefore, are each simple adjectives, and *too* must be analysed as modifying a CO-ORDINATE ADJECTIVE. So, as with many other APs discussed, this AP consists of a degree adverb and a (co-ordinate) adjective, as shown in [40b]:

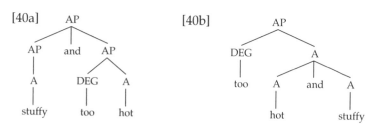

Up and down the staircase is a Prepositional Phrase (PP). It contains a co-ordination of prepositions (Ps). Draw the phrase-marker for the whole PP (using the triangle notation for the NP).

Now draw the phrase-marker for the PP *in the foundations and under the rafters.*

As noted, those phrases are both PPs, but the first contains a lexical co-ordination (with *the staircase* complementing a co-ordination of Ps) while the second is a phrasal co-ordination (of PPs):

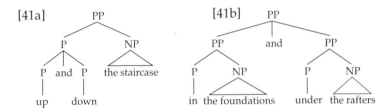

[41a] [41b]

The important point to notice about all these co-ordinations is that **the mother and the sisters of the co-ordinator (*and* in this case) all have the same category label**.

In these first three chapters, I have discussed constituency, function, and category, and how these concepts relate to each other. I conclude the chapter by showing how the points made about constituency and category in connection with co-ordination can be looked at in terms of function.

Co-ordinations of different categories are ill-formed because they could have no coherent function. Consider again [31] – *Max and quickly* – the co-ordination of an NP and an AdvP. Both the NP and the AdvP, remember, are heads. Attempting to make the whole co-ordinate phrase function in the way that an NP does, while all right as far as *Max* is concerned, involves making the AdvP function like an NP. But if it could function like an NP, it would be an NP, not an AdvP. And if we attempt to make the whole phrase function like an AdvP, the same problem arises in respect of the NP. So the phrase as a whole is without any possible function. In fact, it may well be that this lack of any possible function will turn out to be more important than the mixing of categories: for when the different categories can function in the same way it is sometimes possible to co-ordinate them. An example of this is *in a pickle and very worried*, which is a co-ordination of PP and AP. Such examples are awkward for linguistic analysis and are the subject of hot debate: it is not immediately clear how we should label the phrase a whole. For that reason, in this book I will not be troubling you further with examples like it.

Diagrams for in-text exercises

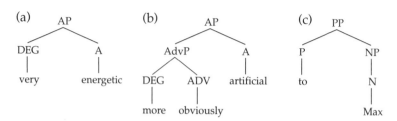

Exercises

1. Identify the following lexical categories in the passage below: (a) nouns, (b) adjectives, (c) degree adverbs, (d) general adverbs, and (e) prepositions.

   On the court, she openly displayed a perfectly outrageous cheek towards the officials who had recently been appointed by the club. At home, she was an incredibly warm and loving human being, full of sensitivity for people's feelings.

2. We have now identified two functions of NPs: subject, and complement to a preposition. There are other functions. Bearing this in mind, identify the NPs in the first sentence of the above passage. Remember to identify first the largest NPs and only then any NPs that may be contained within them. Then identify the head noun of each NP. Which NPs are functioning as subject? Which NPs are functioning as the complement to a preposition? Is there an NP functioning in some other way?

3. Draw the phrase-markers for the following expressions. In some cases, you will find that you do not have all the information necessary to give a complete analysis. Where this is so (and only where this is so!), follow the example of the preceding chapters – use the triangle notation, as appropriate.

   (a) for you and Pete
   (b) rather nervous but very excited
   (c) slowly and very carefully

(d) Ramon drank brandy and smoked cheroots.

(e) Herbert struck the board and I had to mend it.

4. In this chapter, we have seen that adjectives can be modified by degree adverbs (forming an AP) and on page 64 I said that degree adverbs cannot themselves be modified. It is possible, though, for an AP to contain sequences of degree adverbs.

(a) so very touchy

(b) so completely stupid

(c) very very odd

Suggest an analysis for these APs. You will need a hint here and it comes in two parts: (i) remember that (a), (b) and (c) are APs; (ii) remember that *very touchy*, *completely stupid* and *very odd* are also APs.

Discussion of exercises

1. NOUNS: *court, cheek, officials, club, home, being, sensitivity, people, feelings*
   ADJECTIVES: *outrageous, warm, loving, human, full*
   DEGREE ADVERBS: *perfectly, incredibly*
   GENERAL ADVERBS: *openly, recently*
   PREPOSITIONS: *on, towards, by, at, of, for*

2. NPs: (a) *the court*   (b) *she*   (c) *a perfectly outrageous cheek*   (d) *the officials who had recently been appointed by the club*   (e) *the club.* You may have missed *she*: it is a pronoun having one of the functions of full NPs. *The officials* has not been analysed as an NP for reasons to be outlined in Chapter 7, alluded to in Chapter 1, pages 20–22 (cf. the discussion of *a stream that had dried up*).
   HEADS: (a) *court*   (b) *she*   (c) *cheek*   (d) *officials*   (e) *club.*
   FUNCTIONS: *the court* is functioning as the complement of the preposition *on*. *She* is functioning as subject. *A perfectly outrageous cheek* has a function other than subject or complement to a preposition. *The officials appointed by the club* is complement to the preposition *towards*. *The club* is complement to the preposition *by*.

3. (a)

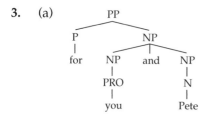

(b)

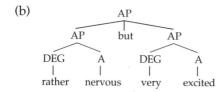

(c)

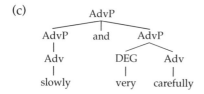

(d)

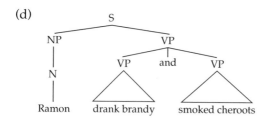

(e)

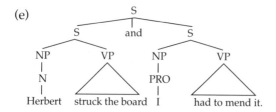

4. Those APs must be analysed as containing a further AP modified by DEG:

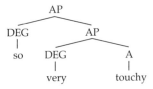

An alternative analysis would allow that degree adverbs *can* be modified and would analyse *so very touchy* as: [*so very*] + [*touchy*]. You might like to think about the possible analyses, then, of APs such as *very much more beautiful* and *so very much taller*.

Further exercises

1. *Between the black pages of the album, ancient photographs dimly revealed the grim faces of ancestors nervelessly paralysed in different attitudes of thought and apparent concentration.*

(a) Identify all the (i) nouns, (ii) adjectives, (iii) adverbs, (iv) prepositions in the above sentence.
(b) Identify its subject.

As mentioned in the chapter, we are assuming that PPs always take the form [P + NP]. If the NP is long and complicated the PP will appear complicated, though the overall structure is in fact simply [P + NP]. In fact there is no limit to how long a PP can be. One reason for this is that the NP within it can itself contain a PP (which will contain another NP (which can contain another PP (and so on (and so on)))). Bearing this in mind,

(c) for each preposition in the above sentence, identify the PP of which it is head, and
(d) for each N, identify the NP of which it is the head.

Example: The first P is *between*, which is complemented by the NP *the black pages of the album*. So *between* is the head of the PP *between the black pages of the album*. The next P is *of* ....

2. In the following sentences, a co-ordinator has been italicised. In each case, identify the constituents it co-ordinates and their category, attending carefully to the meaning. For example, in (i) *and* clearly does not co-ordinate just the single words on either side of it (*icy* and *her*). So how much of the preceding and following material must be included in the co-ordination? One of them is ambiguous.

    (i) It was icy *and* her wimpish friends simply refused to go swimming.
    (ii) He kept a towel *and* razor hidden in one of the lifeboats.
    (iii) The driver stopped the car *and* offered them a lift to the castle.
    (iv) She wouldn't take John's dog *or* any of the pets from the cage.
    (v) They were slowly *but* surely getting to grips with syntax.
    (vi) All the applause during the performance *and* at the following party made him feel quite elated.

3. Draw phrase-markers for the co-ordinate elements in the above sentences. Use triangles for the co-ordinated constituents. This means that for each, you will only need *one* category label (used three times in each case). See phrase marker [30] in the chapter, for an example.

4. I have claimed that every sentence in English has a subject (NP) and a predicate (VP). But consider now the following IMPERATIVE sentences:

    (i) Jump now!
    (ii) Release the clutch gently!
    (iii) Hold your breath for a minute!
    (iv) Leave some money to charity in your will!
    (v) Give yourself a rest!
    (vi) Help yourselves to champagne!

    These imperative sentences seem to consist of just a VP. Are they then counter-examples to the claim that every English sentence must have a subject NP? It is relevant, in connection with (v)–(vi), to consider the circumstances under which reflexive pronouns (e.g. *yourself, himself, themselves*) can be used and to note the oddity of *Give herself a rest! Help themselves to champagne*! In connection with (iii), note the oddity of *Hold my/his breath for a minute*! and, in connection with (iv), the oddity of *Leave some money to charity in his/John's will*!

Chapter 4

The Verb Phrase

You know that the basic sentence consists of a Noun Phrase (as subject) and a Verb Phrase (as predicate), and you have encountered several examples of VPs, though very little has been said about them. This chapter is concerned with the general structure (the immediate constituents) of the VP half of the basic sentence. *Paddle, sunbathed beside a stream, love fish, hate chips, dreads affectionate cats,* and *seemed happy* are all VPs. As these VPs illustrate, categories introduced in previous chapters may appear in the VP, including Noun Phrases themselves. In the VP, however, NPs have different functions. It is with these different functions that I am primarily concerned here.

A first look at verbs and the Verb Group

The one constituent that a Verb Phrase (VP) must contain is the VERB GROUP (Vgrp). The Verb Group consists of a (LEXICAL) VERB which is optionally preceded by other (AUXILIARY) verbs.

Lexical verbs are very easily identified by their morphological possibilities. They are those words that can take some if not all of the following INFLECTIONS: *-s, -ing, -ed, -en.* For example:

play: *plays, playing, played*
write: *writes, writing, written.*

Examples of COMPLEX Verb Groups (that is, Vgrps in which the head verb has auxiliary modification) are:

[1]   is writing
[2]   may have written
[3]   could have been writing.

A general point to note in identifying categories, one that applies particularly to verbs, is that **words can belong to more than one category**. For example, *interest* is certainly a verb: cf. *interests, interesting, interested*. It is functioning as a verb in [4].

[4]   Her hair interested him.

But both *interest* and *interests* can also be nouns (singular and plural respectively) as in [5].

[5]   Its great architectural interest did not strike him.

And *interesting* and *interested* can be adjectives, as in [6] and [7].

[6]   A very interesting manoeuvre was executed.
[7]   He wasn't very interested in the bean production.

When you find such words functioning in the context of a sentence, no confusion should arise. Notice in passing that the adjectives *interesting* and *interested* are gradable and so can be modified by *very*. By contrast, no verb can be modified by *very*:

[8]   *Her hair very interested him.

Decide on the category (or categories) of the following words. Most of them belong to more than one category. You may find it helpful to construct sentences in which they can function.

open, impossible, appeal up, content, between, export, edit. The exercise is discussed at the end of the chapter (**Discussion 1**, page 92).

The Verb Group itself, together with the morphology of the verb and the lexical/auxiliary distinction, is treated in Chapter 6. For the moment, all that is required is that you be able to identify verbs, and the above should suffice for that purpose. Since I am not concerned with the structure of the Vgrp here, I shall use the triangle notation to represent it in phrase-markers and say no more about it in this chapter.

The complements of the Verb Group

This chapter is concerned with the functional relations between the Verb Group (Vgrp) and the other constituents that appear in the basic Verb Phrase (VP). In Chapter 2 I discussed the function of *affectionate cats* in the sentence

[9]   Phil dreads affectionate cats.

The VP is *dreads affectionate cats*, and *dreads* is the single-word verb of the Vgrp. We concluded that the relation between the Vgrp (*dreads*) and the NP (*affectionate cats*) is one of complementation: there is a two-way dependency between the Vgrp (as head) and the NP (as complement). The use of *dreads* without a following NP is ungrammatical, and so is the use of the NP without *dreads*:

[10]   *Phil dreads.
[11]   *Phil affectionate cats.

Not all Vgrps do require a following NP. In fact, if we change the verb from *dread* to *sunbathe*, for example, we get a pattern of grammaticality exactly the opposite of the pattern in [9] and [10]:

[12]   *Phil sunbathed affectionate cats.
[13]   Phil sunbathed.

Dread, it seems, must take an NP, while *sunbathe* cannot take an NP. So the NP depends not just on there being Vgrp present but also on what kind of verb is the head of the Vgrp. *Dread* and *sunbathe* are examples of two very general SUB-CATEGORIES of the verb category (and of the Vgrps of which the verbs are head). **Verbs are SUB-CATEGORISED according to what other elements must appear with them in the VP. In other words, they are sub-categorised in terms of their COMPLEMENTATION types (in terms of what complements they must take).**

Just because an NP cannot follow the Vgrp *sunbathed* does not mean that nothing can follow the Vgrp. We have seen, for example, that the PP *beside a stream* can. But this PP is not part of the complementation of *sunbathe*, in the sense that it is not required to complete the meaning of the VP. It just gives extra information. If we omit it, we are not left with an incomplete predicate. So, in the VP *sunbathed beside a stream*, the PP is not functioning as a complement but as an optional modifier. The fact that a PP can follow *sunbathe* cannot therefore be used to sub-categorise the verb; **all VPs optionally include modification by a PP.** Notice, for example, that a PP can be added after *dreads affectionate cats*:

[14] Phil dreads affectionate cats *in the hay-fever season.*

In short, *dread* and *sunbathe* can be distinguished by the obligatory presence or absence of a following NP, but not by the (optional) presence or absence of a following PP.

For the moment I shall concentrate on the complementation of the verb. More is said about the distinction between complementation and modification in the VP in Chapter 5.

To see how general these sub-categories are, decide which of the following verbs belong to the same sub-category as *dread* (requiring an NP) and which to the same sub-category as *sunbathe* (requiring no NP). One of them belongs to both sub-categories.

disappear, make, inspect, die, vegetate, play, decamp, spot, throw.

Taking just the first two examples, note the following patterns of grammaticality:

[15a] Max disappeared.   [16a] *Max made.
[15b] *Max disappeared Bill.   [16b] Max made a noise.

Disappear clearly belongs to the same sub-category as *sunbathe*, as do *die, vegetate,* and *decamp*: none of these verbs allows a following NP. But *make* clearly belongs with *dread*, as do *inspect, spot* and *throw*: these demand a following NP. *Play*, on the other hand, belongs to both sub-categories, since both [17] and [18] are well-formed:

[17] The children played (beside a stream).
[18] Max plays the tuba (beside a stream).

Paddle, reflect, and *break* are further examples of verbs that belong to both sub-categories. Check this for yourself. Sentences containing them in their different uses are given at the end of the chapter (**Discussion 2**, page 92).

The two sub-categories discussed above are not the only ones. I shall deal here with **six main sub-categories of Vgrp**:

(1) TRANSITIVE **(sometimes called** MONOTRANSITIVE**),**
(2) INTRANSITIVE,
(3) DITRANSITIVE,
(4) INTENSIVE,
(5) COMPLEX TRANSITIVE,
(6) PREPOSITIONAL.

Monotransitive Vgrps

A monotransitive Vgrp is one which requires a single Noun Phrase to complement it. Of the verbs considered above, then, *dread, make, spot, throw,* and *inspect* are monotransitive verbs.

The NP that complements a transitive verb is said to function as its DIRECT OBJECT. So, in *Phil dreads affectionate cats,* the NP within the VP (*affectionate cats*) is complementing the transitive verb *dread* as its direct object.

Notice that, where an NP functioning as the direct object of a verb is a pronoun, it has a special form. This form is called the OBJECTIVE CASE (or, more traditionally, the accusative case). Thus the direct object pronouns in the objective case are grammatical in [19], but the corresponding pronouns in the SUBJECTIVE (traditionally, the nominative) CASE are ungrammatical, [20]:

[19] Phil dreads ⎰ me / her / him / us / them

[20] *Phil dreads ⎰ I / she / he / we / they

When the form of an NP is determined by its complement relation with another constituent, it is said to be GOVERNED by that other constituent (in this case, the verb). Notice that this goes for NPs complementing prepositions in PPs. The preposition governs the NP, demanding that it appear in the objective case: *for him* vs. **for he, against them* vs. **against they. You* and *it* are the only pronouns that do not have a special distinct form in the objective case.

Since the Vgrp and the NP are in a functional relationship, the NP needs to be represented as a sister of the Vgrp (and therefore as a daughter of the VP) as in [21]:

[21]

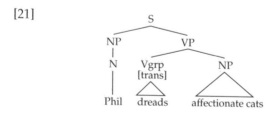

In [21] I have added to the Vgrp node the extra label '[trans]', short for '(mono)transitive'. This extra label is called a FEATURE, and it simply sub-categorises the Verb Group as being monotransitive. This sub-categorisation feature is needed in order to specify the function of the following NP in terms of the phrase-marker itself. Thus, **when an NP is the sister of a Vgrp bearing a [trans] feature, we know that the function of the NP is that of direct object**. The point of having this feature within the phrase-marker will become more apparent when I deal with other sub-categories of verb.

Intransitive Vgrps

An intransitive Vgrp is one that does not require any further constituent as a sister in the VP. So, *disappear, die, vegetate* (and *play* on one interpretation) are intransitive verbs.

Since an intransitive Vgrp does not require any further element to form a complete predicate, a single-word verb can count not only as a complete Vgrp but also as a complete VP. (Remember the discussion of *Ducks paddle* in Chapter 3.) So, a very simple sentence like *Omar sighed* is represented as in [22] – with an [intrans] feature on the Vgrp.

[22]

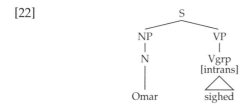

Ditransitive Vgrps

A ditransitive Vgrp is one which requires TWO NPs as its complementation. Examples are *give, send*, and *buy*:

[23a] William is giving **Goneril** *the bleach.*
[24a] The staff have sent **the general** *a message.*
[25a] Max will buy **his butler** *a salami-slicer.*

In [23a]–[25a] **the first complement NP (in bold) functions as the INDIRECT OBJECT of the ditransitive verb. The second complement NP (in italics) functions as the DIRECT OBJECT** (i.e. it has the same function as the NP that complements a monotransitive Vgrp). Here is a phrase-marker of [23a] – with a [ditrans] feature on the Vgrp:

[26]

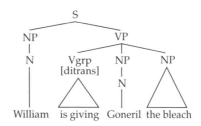

Both NPs are governed by the Vgrp *is giving* and would appear in the objective case if they were pronouns.

Now decide which of the following verbs are ditransitive.

(a) *show*   (b) *offer*   (c) *see*   (d) *tell*   (e) *announce*

Consider the following sentences:

[27] Max has already shown **Mathilda** *his collection of razors*.
[28] Tarzan offered **Jane** *his hairy arm*.
[29] Hazeltine told **his boss** *the news*.

(a), (b), and (d), since they accept two consecutive NPs, are ditransitive verbs. (c) and (e) do not:

[30] *Max saw Mathilda his collection of razors.
[31] *Hazeltine announced his boss the news.

An important characteristic of VPs consisting of a ditransitive verb complemented by two NPs is that they are systematically related to VPs in which **the indirect object NP (bold in [23a]–[25a]) corresponds to a Prepositional Phrase (PP) in a position following the direct object**. Thus [23a] corresponds with [23b]:

[23b] William is giving *the bleach* **to Goneril**.

The PPs that correspond in this way with indirect objects are always introduced by *to* or *for*.

What are the appropriate [b] forms for [24a] and [25a]?

[24b] The staff have sent *a message* **to the general**.
[25b] Max will buy *a salami-slicer* **for his butler**.

These [b] sentences can be represented as in [32]:

[32]

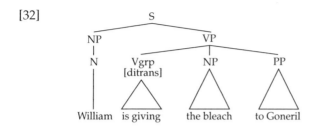

The PP corresponding to an indirect object NP has a rather special status. With monotransitives, when a PP follows the direct object NP, it is not part of the complementation of the verb but is an optional modifier. However, in using a ditransitive verb such as *send*, we need to specify not only (a) a sender (usually subject), and (b) what is sent (usually the direct object), but also (c) to whom it is sent (usually indirect object). **The indirect object can be specified either by an NP or by a PP containing *to* or *for*.** So PPs that correspond to indirect objects *are* part of the complementation of ditransitive verbs. Whether they appear within PPs or not, I shall always refer to NPs like those in bold in [23a]–[25a] and [23b]–[25b] as indirect objects.

INDIRECT OBJECT, then, is either the first of two NP sisters of a Vgrp bearing a [ditrans] feature (as in [26]) or the NP daughter of a PP which is a sister of a Vgrp bearing a [ditrans] feature (as in [32]). As for DIRECT OBJECT, as well as being the NP sister of a Vgrp bearing a [monotrans] feature, it can in addition be either the second of two NP sisters of a [ditrans] Vgrp, or the NP sister of a [ditrans] Vgrp which also has a PP sister.

Intensive Vgrps

Intensive Vgrps require a single complement, which can take the form of an Adjective Phrase, or a Noun Phrase, or a Prepositional Phrase. The most obvious intensive verb is *be*. As the most central example of the intensive sub-category of verb, *be* **is called 'the copula'.**

[33] Ed is *rather extravagant.* (AP)
[34] Sigmund was *an auctioneer.* (NP)
[35] Oscar should be *in the engine room.* (PP)

The complement of an intensive Vgrp functions (more specifically) as a PREDICATIVE. Other intensive verbs (other verbs taking a predicative as complement) are: *become, seem, appear, turn, remain, look, taste, feel, smell, sound.*

When a verb is complemented just by an AP (Vgrp + AP), you can be sure you are dealing with an intensive Vgrp + predicative, because [intensive] is the *only* sub-category of verb that can take just an AP complement. This point is worth noting because, as mentioned, intensives can be complemented by an NP or a PP. When a verb is complemented by an NP, then, you will have to decide whether [Vgrp + NP] is an example of [monotransitive Vgrp + direct object] or an example of [intensive Vgrp + predicative]. Understanding the concept of 'predicative' involves understanding **the difference between predicative and direct object**. I explain this now.

Compare [34] above (repeated here as [36]) with [37]:

[36] Sigmund was an auctioneer.
[37] Sigmund spotted an auctioneer.

In both, we have a verb complemented by an NP. In [37] the verb is monotransitive; so the NP complement functions more specifically as direct object. As a direct object, the NP identifies an individual distinct from Sigmund (referred to by the subject NP *Sigmund*). In saying that Sigmund *spotted* an auctioneer, we mention *two* distinct individuals (Sigmund and the auctioneer) and state that the former spotted the latter. It is in the nature of spotting that it is a relation between two individuals (or, participants), a spott*er* (subject) and a spott*ee* (direct object). That is what makes *spot* a (mono)transitive verb.

A moment's thought will show something quite different going on in [36]. [36] does *not* express a relation between two individuals. In [36] only *one* individual is mentioned (by means of the subject *Sigmund*). The rest of the sentence (the VP) is used to characterise the subject. If [36] expresses a relation, it is a relation between an individual and a *property*: the sentence expresses the idea that Sigmund has the property of being an auctioneer. **Predicatives are used to attribute** PROPERTIES **to the things picked out by (or, referred to) other expressions**; predicatives (unlike direct or indirect objects) do not themselves refer to things in the world. It is because intensive verbs only take predicatives that they can be complemented by Adjective Phrases: APs only ever identify properties. Thus, [33] mentions Ed and simply attributes the property of extravagance to him. NPs, by contrast, can be used both to identify properties and to refer to individuals. This is why an NP can function both as predicative (complementing an intensive verb) and as direct object (complementing a monotransitive verb).

Most of the intensive verbs listed above also belong (though with a different meaning) to the monotransitive verb subcategory. This difference between monotransitive (+ direct object) and intensive (+ predicative) can be made quite vivid by comparing the two senses of such verbs. For each of the following decide whether the (italicised) complement NP is complementing a monotransitive verb as direct object or complementing an intensive verb as predicative:

[38] Max turned *a subtle shade of green*.
[39] Max turned *another card*.
[40] Tarzan felt *a tap on his shoulder*.
[41] Tarzen felt *a real idiot*.
[42] The leopard-skin pillbox hat didn't become *her*.
[43] The hat became *a very useful wastepaper basket*.
[44] The captain sounds *an absolute tyrant*.
[45] The captain sounded *the ship's horn*.

The NPs are functioning as direct objects (complementing those verbs in their monotransitive senses) in [39], [40], [42], and [45]. They are functioning as predicatives (complementing those verbs in their intensive senses) in [38], [41], [43], and [44]. In the latter cases, those NPs could be replaced by APs without changing the sense of the verb (*green* in [38], *idiotic* in [41], *ever more useful* in [43], and *absolutely tyrannical* in [44]).

I have said that predicatives are used to attribute properties to the things referred to by *other* expressions. We have seen that, in the case of intensive verbs, that other expression is always the subject. So, **to be more specific about the function of the italicised complement expressions in [33]–[35]: they are predicatives; and more specifically yet, they are** SUBJECT-PREDICATIVES. In the next section, I will need to refer to object-predicatives.

I can now show more clearly what the point is of attaching a sub-categorisation feature to the Vgrp in phrase-markers. Without such a feature, [36] and [37] – and all the examples [38]–[45] – would receive exactly the same analysis. It is the distinction between the features, [intens] and [monotrans] that distinguishes them, as in [46a–b], for example.

[46a]

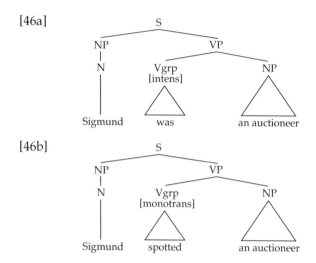

[46b]

An [intensive] verb, by definition, takes a subject-predicative; and a [monotrans] verb, by definition, takes a direct object. So, by using those features, you are effectively assigning a (more specific) function to the complement of the verb.

A word now about PPs functioning as subject-predicatives. I have already mentioned that all VPs can include optional modification by PPs. PPs should only be treated as part of the necessary complementation of an intensive verb (i.e. as subject-predicatives) if they cannot be omitted. So, *in the engine room* in [35] IS a predicative since [47] is not a complete sentence (even though the missing element might be understood in context – see Chapter 5):

[47]   *Oscar should be.

I look again at PP complements below.

Complex transitive Vgrps

Complex transitive Vgrps take two complements: a direct object (NP) and an object-predicative. Again, the predicative can take the form of an AP, or an NP, or a PP. Here are some examples, with the direct object in italics and the predicative in bold.

[48]   Melvin found *his own jokes* **extremely funny**. (AP)
[49]   They are making *Stella* **their spokesperson**. (NP)
[50]   Liza has been putting *the liquor* **under the bed**. (PP)

Everything I said about predicatives above goes for the predicative in a complex VP, with one big difference. The difference is that **the predicative in a complex transitive VP characterises (attributes a property to) the direct object, not the subject, hence the name 'object-predicative'.** The semantic relation between direct object and object-predicative in a complex transitive VP, then, parallels that between subject and subject-predicative in an intensive sentence. For example, if [48] is true, then, at least as far as Melvin is concerned, his own jokes **are** extremely funny; if [49] is true, then Stella is going to **become** their spokesperson; and if [50] is true, then the liquor **is** under Liza's bed.

Here is a phrase-marker representation of [48]:

[51]

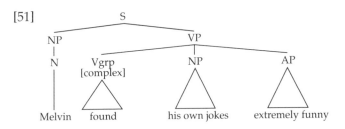

In assigning the feature [complex] to the Vgrp, we are making the whole phrase-marker represent the function of *his own jokes* (direct object) and of *extremely funny* (object-predicative). This is particularly needed in a case like [52a].

[52a] Max found Bill an amusing companion.

This example is ambiguous. Satisfy yourself as to the two interpretations and then explain the ambiguity by assigning different functions to the complements of the verb. On the basis of that, you should be able to assign two different sub-categorisation features to the Vgrp *found*.

On one interpretation, [52a] corresponds in meaning with (a) *Max found an amusing companion* FOR *Bill*. On this interpretation, the verb *find* is ditransitive, *Bill* (the recipient) is the indirect object, and *an amusing companion* is the direct object. Notice that *three* participants are involved on this (ditransitive) interpretation. On the other interpretation, it corresponds with (b) *Max found Bill* TO BE *an amusing companion*; *Bill* and *an amusing companion* have the functions associated with the complementation of complex transitive verbs, direct object (*Bill*) and object-predicative (*an amusing companion*). On this (complex transitive) interpretation, there are only *two* participants, Max and Bill; *an amusing companion* merely attributes a property to Bill. The distinction in meaning between (a) and (b) (and hence the ambiguity), and the different functions of *Bill* and *an amusing companion,* is all accounted for simply by the difference in sub-categorisation feature attached to the Vgrp.

[52b]

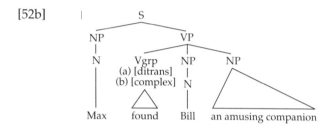

Prepositional Vgrps

Glance, reply, refer, and *look* are examples of prepositional verbs – they must be complemented by a Prepositional Phrase. Take *glance*, for example:

[53] *Max glanced
[54] *Max glanced the falling acrobat
[55] Max glanced at the falling acrobat.

[56]

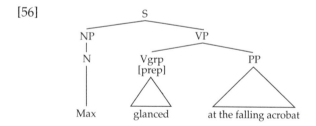

As we shall see in the next chapter, these need to be distinguished from [intransitive] verbs with optional modification by PP (e.g. *Sam sunbathed beside a stream*). I shall call the PP that complements a [prepositional] Vgrp, a PREPOSITIONAL COMPLEMENT. In the sub-categorisation offered in this chapter such Vgrps also need to be distinguished from [intensive] Vgrps when these are complemented by a PP, as in *Oscar should be in the engine room* – [35]

above. The Vgrp in [35] has been sub-categorised as [intensive] rather than [prepositional] because it can alternatively be complemented by an AP or an NP functioning as subject-predicative. Prepositional verbs can only be complemented by PPs.

We have now looked at a six-way distinction among Verb Groups and their associated sentence patterns. Not all verbs (and not all uses of all verbs) fit neatly into this classification or do so only with a certain amount of ingenuity on the part of the analyst. The distinctions given nevertheless provide an introduction to the topic of sub-categorisation and in discussing them, I have mentioned all the major constituent functions.

As mentioned, other elements may optionally appear. These, though, are not part of the necessary complementation of the verb, but are modifiers. Chapter 5 is concerned with these and with some of the factors that need to be taken into account in distinguishing between complements and modifiers in the VP.

The sub-categorisation can be summarised as follows:

MONOTRANSITIVE – '[trans]':
   subject – Vgrp – direct object
   (S)   (dO)

INTRANSITIVE – '[intrans]':
   subject – Vgrp
   (S)

DITRANSITIVE – '[ditrans]':
   subject – Vgrp – indirect object –   direct object
   (S)   (iO)   (dO)
or:
   subject – Vgrp – direct object – *to/for* indirect object
   (S)   (dO)   (iO)

INTENSIVE – '[intens]':
   subject – Vgrp – subject-predicative
   (S)   (sP)

COMPLEX TRANSITIVE – '[complex]':
   subject – Vgrp – direct object –   object-predicative
   (S)   (dO)   (oP)

PREPOSITIONAL – '[prep]':
   subject – Vgrp – prepositional complement
   (S)   (PC)

Discussion of in-text exercises

1. The following sentences illustrate the different uses of the words given. The category of the word in each sentence is given below. You may find it useful to treat the sentences as an exercise: identify the category of the italicised word in each sentence.

> 1. Morgan *opened* his mouth.
> 2. Morgan's *open* mouth admitted the fly.
> 3. That was clearly *impossible*.
> 4. Mary *appealed* to John to take the rubbish out.
> 5. Her repeated *appeals* were unsuccessful.
> 6. He booted his drunken colleague *up* the gangway.
> 7. They *up* the rent every other month.
> 8. Georgette is perfectly *content*.
> 9. Jenny criticised the *content* of the paragraph.
> 10. Watching you work so hard *contents* me.
> 11. The recalcitrant mango slipped *between* Grace's fingers.
> 12. Toffee-wrappers are the main *export*.
> 13. Boggis and Stone *export* toffee-wrappers to Mesopotamia.
> 14. Max has *edited* a grand total of 253 books.

open: 1. Verb. 2. Adjective. *impossible*: 3. Adjective. *appeal*: 4. Verb. 5. Noun. *up*: 6. Preposition. 7. Verb. *content*: 8. Adjective. 9. Noun. 10. Verb. *between*: 11. Preposition. *export*: 12. Noun. 13. Verb. *edit*: 14. Verb.

2. 1. The ducks are paddling (across the lake). – [intransitive]
    2. He paddled the raft (across the lake). – [monotransitive]
    3. Morgan is reflecting (quietly). – [intransitive]
    4. The glass reflected Max's ugly mug. – [monotransitive]
    5. The samovar broke. – [intransitive]
    6. Anna broke the samovar. – [monotransitive].

Exercises

1. Identify the major functions in the following sentences (subject, direct object, indirect object, subject-predicative, object-predicative and prepositional complement). Identify the Vgrps and sub-categorise them. Example:

Otto	is devouring	the cous-cous
(subject)	(Vgrp)	(direct object)
	[trans]	

(1) The girl in the palace had dyed her hair deep purple.
(2) The balloons are ascending.
(3) Richard has promised me his spaghetti machine.
(4) This sedan-chair should prove useful.
(5) Someone has stolen my contact-lenses.
(6) It doesn't sound much fun.
(7) The candidate's antics did not amuse the board of examiners.
(8) The committee nominated her Acrobat of the Year.
(9) Egbert has been feeding the cat smoked salmon.
(10) I would like my curry as hot as you can make it.
(11) We don't allude to his third ear.
(12) The main witness for the prosecution has disappeared.
(13) He has applied for a gun licence.

2. Decide whether the PP in the following sentences is part of the complementation of a DITRANSITIVE Vgrp or not.

(1) Holden is writing letters to Africa.
(2) Holden is writing letters to The White House.
(3) Max took the hyena to the station.
(4) Max lent his hyena to the Dramatics Society.
(5) William baked a cake for Goneril.
(6) William baked a cake for Christmas.
(7) She is saving the money for a Bechstein Grande.
(8) She is saving a place for Sophie.

3. Using any of the following phrases, construct (a) a sentence in which *smelt* is used as an intransitive Verb Group; (b) a sentence in which it is used as a monotransitive Verb Group; (c) a sentence in which it is used as an intensive Verb Group.

   (i) *smelt* (ii) *the apprehensive butler* (iii) *Jim's attempt at a stew* (iv) *loathsome*.

4. The functions of the major constituents in

(a) Widmerpool will make Pamela a disastrous husband.

are difficult to accommodate within the six-way subcategor-
isation introduced in this chapter. Explain why. You may
find this easier if you compare it with (b) and (c)

(b)   Widmerpool will make Pamela a good wife.
(c)   Widmerpool will make Pamela lots of money.

which are much more easily handled (though in different
ways).

5.   Using the triangle notation for all major constituents (as
used in this chapter) draw phrase-markers for the following
sentences.

(a)   Nicholas was feeling strangely euphoric.
(b)   The gallery wouldn't lend them the triptych.
(c)   The condition of the cakes left out overnight had deteriorated.
(d)   They voted the Grand Master out of office.
(e)   A bucket of cold water will revive this particular patient.
(f)   The Venetians have submitted to Napoleon's demands.

Discussion of exercises

1.(1) [The girl in the palace] [had dyed] [her hair] [deep purple].
       S   Vgrp   dO   oP
                               [complex]

(2)   [The balloons] [are ascending].
         S   Vgrp
                        [intrans]

(3)   [Richard]   [has promised] [me] [his spaghetti machine].
         S   Vgrp   iO   dO
                     [ditrans]

(4)   [This sedan-chair] [should prove] [useful].
           S   Vgrp   sP
                            [intens]

(5)   [Someone]   [has stolen]   [my contact lenses].
         S   Vgrp   dO
                    [trans]

(6)   [It] [doesn't sound] [much fun].
        S   Vgrp   sP
               [intens]

(7) [The candidate's   [did not amuse]   [the board of
     antics]   examiners].
        S   Vgrp   dO
                        [trans]

(8) [The committee] [nominated] [her] [Acrobat of the Year].
         S   Vgrp   dO   oP
                [complex]

(9) [Egbert] [has been feeding] [the cat] [smoked salmon].
     S   Vgrp   iO   dO
            [ditrans]

(10) [I] [would like] [my curry] [as hot as you can make it].
     S   Vgrp   dO   oP
       [complex]

(11) [We] [don't allude] [to his third ear].
     S   Vgrp   PC
         [prep]

(12) [The main witness for the prosecution] [has disappeared].
                  S   Vgrp
                                        [intrans]

(13) [He] [has applied] [for a gun licence].
     S   Vgrp   PC
       [prep]

2. As mentioned in this chapter, a PP is counted as part of the complementation of a ditransitive verb only if it corresponds to an NP functioning as an indirect object. Take examples (1) and (2). (1a) (below) is not a reasonable paraphrase of (1), but (2a) (below) is a reasonable paraphrase of (2):

(1a) Holden is writing Africa letters.
(2a) Holden is writing The White House letters.

So the PP in (2) is part of the complementation of the verb, and *write* in that sentence must be sub-categorised as [ditrans]. In (1), on the other hand, *write* is a monotransitive verb, complemented by the direct object *letters* or perhaps *letters to Africa*. Note that, if *to Africa* is not part of the direct object NP in (1), then it must be analysed as an optional modifier within the VP. I discuss why there should be this difference between (1) and (2) after dealing with the remaining examples.

(3) No. cf. *Max took the station his hyena*. The PP is a modifier.
(4) Yes. cf. *Max lent the Dramatics Society his hyena. Lend* is a [ditrans] verb.
(5) Yes. cf. *William baked Goneril a cake.*
(6) No. cf. * *William baked Christmas a cake.*
(7) No. cf. **She is saving a Bechstein Grande the money.*
(8) Yes. cf. *She is saving Sophie a place.*

Notice that it is only NPs denoting ANIMATE things (or things that could be interpreted as being animate) that can be indirect objects. For example, the moment you interpret *Christmas* as a person rather than a festival, *William baked Christmas a cake* sounds perfectly grammatical. Even in (2a) *The White House* can be an indirect object because, as well as being a building, it is an organisation of human beings, as is the Dramatics Society. On the other hand, since there is no single human institution that represents Africa as a whole, *Africa* remains an inanimate location, and cannot function as indirect object.

3.   INTRANSITIVE: 1. The apprehensive butler smelt.
                              2. Jim's attempt at a stew smelt.

      MONOTRANSITIVE: 1. The apprehensive butler smelt
                                    Jim's attempt at a stew.

      INTENSIVE: 1. The apprehensive butler smelt loathsome.
                        2. Jim's attempt at a stew smelt loathsome.

5.   The sub-categorisation problem posed by the (a) sentence can be made clear by showing that it corresponds with

      (d) Widmerpool will make a disastrous husband FOR Pamela.

Here the NP *Pamela* in (a) has moved and become a PP. This suggests that *make* in (a) is a [ditrans] verb, since *Pamela* seems to be functioning as INDIRECT OBJECT. But if *make* in (a) is [ditrans], we should expect *a disastrous husband* to be functioning as DIRECT OBJECT (since ditransitive complementation consists of indirect object + direct object). But it isn't. It does not mention an individual distinct from the subject *Widmerpool*. This suggests that it is a subject-predicative. So, it seems that in (a) we have:

subject – verb – indirect object – subject-predicative.

If you look at the summary of the sub-categories given in this chapter, you will see that this particular combination of complements (indirect object + subject-predicative) is not allowed for. Indirect object only combines with direct object (in ditransitive sentences) and subject-predicative only occurs by itself (in intensive sentences). We appear to have a combination of intensive complementation and one half of the ditransitive complementation.

This is a very unusual example. In fact, I cannot think of another example like it, so I shall not go to the bother of establishing a further (rather exotic) sub-category to handle it.

The (b) and (c) examples which were offered for comparison present no problem. (b) is straightforwardly handled as complex transitive – direct object + object-predicative (under Widmerpool's guidance, Pamela will become a good wife). (c) is a straightforward ditransitive structure – indirect object + direct object (Widmerpool will make a lot of money *for* Pamela).

5.

(a)

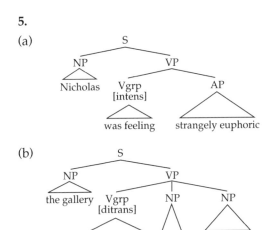

(b)

(c)

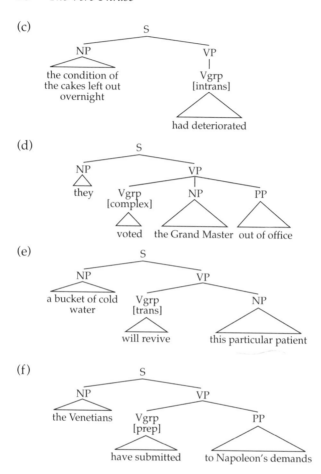

(d)

(e)

(f)

As you may have noticed, in these six phrase-markers, all six complementation types are represented, and hence all six types of basic sentence considered in this chapter.

Further exercises

1. For each of the following sentences
(a) identify the Verb Group;
(b) Identify all the major functions: subject (S), direct object (dO), indirect object (iO), subject-predicative (sP), object-predicative (oP), prepositional complement (PC);

(c) Give the sub-category of the Vgrp. Make sure the sub-category is consistent with the functions you have assigned (in (b) above) to the other constituents.

(d) Give the category of each of the constituents you have identified under (c) above.

Example:

	[*Phil*]	[*dreads*]	[*affectionate cats*]
Function:	S	Vgrp [trans]	dO
Category:	NP		NP

(1) Petrol is getting more expensive.
(2) Alexander's father left him.
(3) Alexander's father left him the theatre.
(4) Alexander's father left him in the care of the bishop.
(5) Several of the men he had hired were complaining.
(6) He may have been referring to the fact that you had no clothes on.
(7) Customers must not sit their children on the counter.
(8) Her mother and father didn't approve of Matilda's behaviour.
(9) Most of the students will have done the work you set.
(10) Col. Mustard has locked Miss Scarlet in the library.
(11) Children in ragged clothes were shinning up the drainpipes.
(12) Your Kentucky Fried Chicken and chips have gone cold and greasy.
(13) The obliging manager poured everyone a gigantic glass of wine.
(14) Joan placed it in the gaping hole.
(15) Karen peered into the gaping hole.
(16) The new chef is liquidising last week's uneaten fritters.
(17) This would make a perfect picnic place.
(18) Bill has made a brilliant picnic table.
(19) This so-called music makes me mad.
(20) He should have made the men a decent meal.
(21) The exhausted team members made for the nearest pub.

2. Draw phrase-markers for (at least some of) the above sentences, using the triangle notation for all the constituents you identified under 1(a)–(b) above. (For examples, see the Discussion of Exercise 5 above.)

3. Prepositional Phrases have a variety of functions. We have looked at four so far. As (obligatory) **complements of verbs**, they may function as

[A] subject-predicative in [intensive] VPs,
[B] object-predicative in [complex] VPs,
[C] indirect-object in [ditransitive] VPs (but only with *to* or *for*),
[D] prepositional complement in [prep] VPs.

And, we shall see, they can also function as (optional) **modifiers**:

[E] modifiers within the structure of NP (e.g. *the book in your pocket*),
[F] modifiers within the structure of VP (e.g. *sunbathed beside a stream*).

Decide which one of these functions the bracketed PPs have in the following sentences (this can be done by giving one of the above letters). NB. Some may admit of discussion, allowing of more than one reasonable answer. This is particularly true of (15). (3) and (13) are ambiguous. In (13) the bracketing given is wrong on one of the interpretations. Explain this.

(1) Berthold is the man [for the job].
(2) She was very happy [in the Spring].
(3) I touched the man [with the umbrella].
(4) This award is [for outstanding culinary achievement].
(5) I'm doing this course [for my own satisfaction].
(6) Eliot left most of his manuscripts [to the museum].
(7) Eliot left most of his manuscripts [at the museum].
(8) He passed the wine [to Tessa].
(9) He passed the house [on the way].
(10) We are staying [for the moment].
(11) We are staying [at the Hotel Mortification].
(12) He knocked a glass [of wine] [onto the floor].
(13) He always talks [about reconciliation] [with John].
(14) He remained [in a state of shock] [for ten days].
(15) Dionysus remained [in the bar].

Chapter 5

Adverbials and Other Matters

Adjunct adverbials in the Verb Phrase

In this chapter I look more closely at the distinction between verb complements and modifiers in the Verb Phrase.

You have already encountered PPs functioning as modifiers in the VP. Examples are:

[1]   Old Sam sunbathed *beside a stream.*
                       like a maniac.

[2]   Max spotted those wildcats *in the Spring.*
                                 with his binoculars.

As mentioned, since the (italicised) PPs are optional and can occur with almost any verb, they cannot be used to sub-categorise the verb. They are not functioning as complements. They give additional, though not essential, information. When a constituent functions as the PPs in [1] and [2] are functioning, it is said to function as an ADJUNCT ADVERBIAL.

[1] and [2] are examples of intransitive and monotransitive sentences with adjunct adverbials. Here are further examples of PPs functioning as adjuncts in intensive [3], [4], and [5], ditransitive [6], and complex transitive [7] structures:

[3]   Ed was rather extravagant *in the bazaar.*
[4]   Sigmund was an auctioneer *for three years.*
[5]   Oscar was in the engine-room *in a flash.*
[6]   William gave Goneril the bleach *on her birthday.*
[7]   Liza put the liquor under the bed *for safekeeping.*

As the adjunct PPs in these examples illustrate, adjuncts express a wide range of ideas, including manner, means, purpose, reason, place, and time (including duration and frequency).

They tend to answer questions like *Where? Why? When? How? What for? How long? How often? How many times?*

Since adjunct is one type of ADVERBIAL function, you should not be surprised to learn that, **in addition to PPs, ADVERB PHRASES (AdvP) can also function as adjunct adverbials**. Nevertheless, take care not to confuse the term ADVERBIAL (which denotes a function, not included in phrase-markers) and the labels ADVERB/ADVERB PHRASE (which are category labels and do figure in phrase-markers). We have seen that AdvPs can have functions other than that of adverbial. (They can modify adjectives, within APs.) Conversely, you know that not all constituents functioning as adverbials are AdvPs: we have just seen that PPs can function as adverbials. Here are examples of AdvPs functioning, like the PPs above, as adverbials:

[8]   Sam sunbathed *frequently*.
[9]   He spotted the wildcats *quite accidentally*.
[10] She put it under the bed *surreptitiously*.

Many adverbs are not as easily identified as such by their *-ly* morphology, in particular the interrogative adverbs, *how, where, why, when*, and adverbs relating to time: *here, there, now, then, again, yet, still, already, seldom, often, ever, never.*

In addition to AdvPs and PPs, **certain NPs can function as adverbials**: *home, last year, yesterday, tonight, tomorrow, the day before yesterday, the day after tomorrow, this afternoon* ....

Levels of Verb Phrase

How do adjunct adverbials fit into the structure of sentences? I have described adjuncts as modifiers within the VP but so far I have avoided saying exactly what they modify. Two possibilities seem to offer themselves. In [2], for example, does *in the Spring* modify just the Vgrp *spotted*, or does it modify *spotted those wildcats* – that is, the Vgrp plus its direct object? What do you think?

Answering this question involves making a decision about the constituent analysis of *spotted those wildcats in the Spring*. If the PP modifies just the Vgrp *spotted*, then it should be a sister of the Vgrp, along with *those wildcats*, as in [11]:

[11]

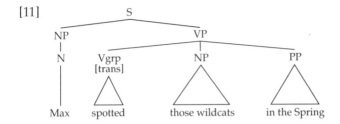

If, on the other hand, we want to say that *in the Spring* modifies *spotted those wildcats*, then it must be a **sister of a constituent consisting of the Vgrp + direct object NP**. In other words, Vgrp + NP must form a constituent. They don't form a constituent in [11], do they? So, if we choose this second option, [11] cannot be the right analysis.

I shall choose this second alternative. Intuitively the adjunct PP does seem to modify a constituent consisting of Vgrp + NP rather than just the Vgrp by itself. I have already noted that *those wildcats,* as a complement, completes the sense of the verb and, together with that verb, forms a unit of sense. It does this independently of the adjunct *in the Spring.*

We have seen that *Max spotted those wildcats in the Spring* is a good subject-predicate sentence. *Max* is the subject NP. So *spotted those wildcats in the Spring* is clearly a VP. Now, on the analysis we are adopting, we are saying that *in the Spring* modifies a constituent of the Vgrp + NP (*spotted those wildcats*). Bearing in mind that *Max spotted those wildcats* is itself a good subject-predicate sentence, what category label should we attach to *spotted those wildcats*? In other words, what kind of constituent is it?

Having decided that, draw a phrase-marker for the whole sentence (*Max spotted those wildcats in the Spring*). Use the triangle notation for *spotted, those wildcats,* and *in the Spring.*

Spotted those wildcats must be a VP in its own right (consisting of a monotransitive Vgrp plus its direct object NP). That VP is a constituent of another, larger, VP – namely *spotted those wildcats in the Spring*. So the whole phrase-marker must look like [12], in which, for ease of reference, I have numbered the two VPs.

[12]

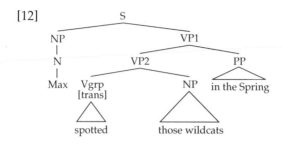

This analysis has the effect of creating two levels of VP and thus allowing us to represent, within the phrase-marker configuration, the difference in function between the NP *those wildcats* (functioning as a COMPLEMENT, more specifically as direct object) and the PP *in the Spring* (a MODIFIER, more specifically, an (adjunct) adverbial). Thus, **adjunct adverbials are modifiers of VPs**. As such, they must be represented, in phrase-markers, as sisters of VPs.

If there is just one big idea in this chapter, it is this: this difference in function between (obligatory) complements of the verb and (optional, modifying) adjunct adverbials is to be represented in phrase-markers as follows:

- COMPLEMENTS **of the verb are sisters of Verb Group (Vgrp)**
- ADJUNCT ADVERBIALS **are sisters of Verb Phrase (VP).**

A piece of evidence that supports this analysis was alluded to in the introduction. But first, draw the phrase-markers for [13] and [14] in the light of the discussion so far, bearing in mind that *mend* is a [monotransitive] verb and *put* is a [complex transitive] verb.

[13] Bevis mended his car in the garage.
[14] Bevis put his car in the garage.

Since *put* is [complex transitive], the PP in [14] is part of the complementation of the verb. By contrast, the PP in [13] is an (optional) adjunct adverbial. Thus, on the analysis adopted here,

[15] and [16] are the appropriate phrase-markers (in which I have numbered the VPs for ease of reference).

[15]

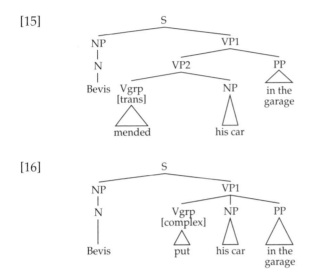

[16]

In the Introduction, I noted that [17] was grammatical, but [18] ungrammatical.

[17] Bevis mended his car in the garage and Max did so in the lay-by.
[18] *Bevis put his car in the garage and Max did so in the lay-by.

What is the explanation for this? The expression *do so* is used to avoid repeating material that has already appeared in the sentence. It stands for, or replaces, that material. Expressions that perform this function are called PRO-FORMS. Pronouns are pro-forms. They replace NPs (and so should really be called 'pro-NP's). *Do so* (*did so*, etc.) always and only replaces a VP. So if a constituent is a VP, it can be replaced by a form of the expression *do so*, otherwise it can't.

In [17] we understand that *did so* is replacing *mended his car*. This is fine because, as [15] shows, *mended his car* is a VP (namely, VP2). If, as is natural, we take [18] to mean that Max put his car in the lay-by, we must conclude that *did so* is replacing *put his car*. But, as a glance at [16] shows, *put his car* is NOT a VP (in fact, it is not even a constituent). Since *did so* only ever replaces VPs, it is thus predictable that [18] is ungrammatical.

We have seen that *did so* in [17] replaces VP2 (*mended his car*) in [15]. Let's now check whether it can replace VP1 (*mended his car in the garage*) in [15]:

[19] Bevis mended his car in the garage and Max did so (too).

We understand this to mean that Max 'mended his car in the garage'. Since it is replacing a VP, it is grammatical (though perhaps more natural as ... *and so did Max*). You can check for yourself that *did so* can replace the single VP of [14]/[16].

The fact that *did so*, which replaces only VPs, can grammatically replace two strings of words (one contained within the other) in [13] provides vivid evidence that [13] does contain two VPs, as represented in [15].

It is also good evidence for the distinction between complements and (modifying) adjuncts in the VP, and for representing the difference in terms of the distinction between **sister-of-Vgrp (complement)** and **sister-of-VP (adjunct)**. Remember, complements are required by certain Vgrps to complete their meaning and to make up a full and grammatical VP. A Vgrp that requires a complement (that is, all Vgrps except [intransitive] ones) does not form a full VP on its own – that, after all, is *why* the complement is obligatory. For example, *mend* is a monotransitive verb: it does not form a VP without a direct object NP. So, were we to replace just *mended* in [13] by *did so*, we would replacing, not a Verb Phrase (VP), but a Verb Group (Vgrp) – and the result is ungrammatical:

[20] *Bevis mended his car in the garage and Max did so his bike in the lay-by.

In the light of this discussion, what do you suggest should be the phrase-marker for *Sam sunbathed beside a stream*? It is important to bear in mind that *sunbathe* is an intransitive verb and therefore does form a full VP in its own right. The phrase-marker is given as **Discussion 1**, page 116.

Notice that, since the occurrence of adjuncts is not determined by the verb and its sub-category, there is no reason why we should not reiterate adjunct adverbials (aA) to our hearts' delight, as in [21]:

[21] He   guzzled   cream cakes   noisily   under the blankets
       S   Vgrp   dO   aA   aA

in the outhouse   every night
aA   aA

Now draw a phrase-marker of [22]:

[22] Humphrey drove his car on the left in France.

bearing in mind that [23], [24], and [25] are all grammatical:

[23] He drove his car on the left in France and Claude did so too.
[24] He drove his car on the left in France and he did so in Germany too.
[25] He drove his car on the left in France but did so on the right in the States.

(The phrase-marker is given at the end of the chapter – **Discussion 2**, page 117.)

The mobility of adverbials

Well, this division of complements into a lower VP and adjunct adverbials into a higher VP looks very neat. Unfortunately, a very prominent characteristic of adverbials is that they can appear in all sorts of positions in the sentence, not just following the Vgrp and its complements. Indeed, the very fact that you can move a PP around a sentence is a sure sign that it is functioning as an adverbial and not as the complement of the Vgrp, see [26].

[26] Beside a stream, old Sam sunbathed.

Which positions can *surreptitiously* occupy in [27]?

[27] She put it under the bed.

[28] Surreptitiously, she put it under the bed.
[29] She surreptitiously put it under the bed.
[30] She put it surreptitiously under the bed.
[31] She put it under the bed surreptitiously.

Notice in passing that it cannot come between the Vgrp and its direct object.

The position of the adjunct in [31], of course, poses no problem for the analysis of adjuncts as modifiers of VP within a higher VP. And neither does its position in [29]. What would you suggest as the most appropriate phrase-marker for [29]?

We can simply analyse *surreptitiously* as a PRECEDING sister of the VP within another VP as in [32]:

[32]

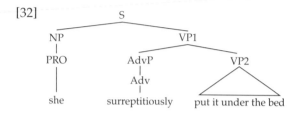

In [30], however, *surreptitiously* is going to have to appear within VP2 since it appears between the complements of the Vgrp, between the direct object and the object-predicative. This is awkward for our analysis. If we want to say that the adjunct modifies the VP, it is odd to find it actually inside that VP.

And [28], of course, poses a problem because in it the adjunct is completely removed from the VP.

It is beyond the scope of this book to discuss this aspect of adverbials and its implications, important though it is. I shall not attempt to represent these 'displaced' adverbials in phrase-markers. Instead, I shall adopt a standard representation in which adjunct adverbials are always sisters of a VP within a higher VP. You should bear in mind, however, that this is a simplification of the facts. Of course, if we are simply enumerating the major functions in a sentence, ignoring constituency, no problems arise: [28] can be enumerated as aA–S–Vgrp–dO–oP, [29] as S–aA–Vgrp–dO–oP and [30] as S–Vgrp–dO–aA–oP.

Phrasal verbs

PPs functioning as adjuncts or complements within VP must be distinguished from another apparently similar structure. Consider the difference between [33] and [34]:

[33] He called up the street.
[34] He called up the boss.

In [33] *up the street* is a PP functioning as an adjunct modifying a VP that consists of the intransitive Vgrp *called*. By contrast, you will have noticed that the string *up the boss* does not form a unit of sense in [34] – and in fact is not a constituent, and hence not a PP. Instead, *up* belongs more with *call*, to form the PHRASAL VERB *call up*. Now, if *called up* is the Vgrp of [34], what do you suggest is the function of the NP *the boss*?

It is the single NP complement of the Verb Group, so it must be either subject-predicative or direct object. In fact, it is the direct object (if this is not clear, check in Chapter 4 on the difference between dO and sP). *Call up*, then, is a transitive phrasal verb. [34] can be represented as in [35]:

[35]

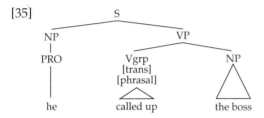

There are many such phrasal verbs in English – some more idiomatic than others, some transitive, some intransitive, e.g.

TRANS: *call off, look up, put down, hand down, hand over*
TRANS and INTRANS: *give up, give in, drink up.*

Although *up, off, down, over* look suspiciously like prepositions, they are traditionally distinguished from prepositions in this position and categorised as PARTICLES. So **a phrasal verb consists of a verb + a particle**.

Notice that [36] is ambiguous.

[36] He looked up the street.

On one interpretation, the VP is analysed as Vgrp + PP. This is the interpretation on which he would be looking up the street to see who was coming, for example. On the other interpretation, it is to be analysed as a phrasal verb with the NP functioning as direct object (as in [34]). On this interpretation he would be trying to locate the street in a street atlas.

A characteristic of particles is that they can appear in a position after the direct object. Thus, [34] is acceptably paraphrased by [37].

[37] He called the boss up.

But [33] is not paraphrased by [38].

[38]   *He called the street up.

The VP of [37] can be represented as in [39], with 'particle' abbreviated to 'Prt'.

[39]

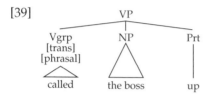

Indeed, when the direct object is a pronoun, the particle must appear after it:

[40a] He called him up.
[40b] *He called up him.

Only the particle of a phrasal verb can move over the NP in this way. The preposition in a PP can never move to a position following its NP complement. So, **particle movement provides a very reliable test for distinguishing between [phrasal verb + (direct object) NP] and [verb + PP]**. Notice that, while [36] is ambiguous, *He looked the street up* is not. Since *up* has moved, it cannot be the P of the PP *up the street*; it must be the particle of the phrasal verb *look up*.

Decide, for each of the following, whether it is a phrasal verb + (direct object) NP or a verb + PP. **Discussion 3**, page 117.

(i) shouted out the answers	(ii) looked out the window
(iii) hangs about the office	(iv) handed over the money
(v) viciously turned on John	(vi) saw through the term
(vii) gave in my essay	(viii) saw through her disguise

Ellipsis

Now that I have introduced adjunct adverbials and distinguished them from the complements of the verb, we must look at a general issue that has a bearing not only on that distinction but on verb-sub-categorisation.

I have said that verb complements are a necessary part of sentence structure: they cannot be omitted without ungrammaticality. In this they contrast with adjunct adverbials. But look now at the following sentences:

[41] William gave the bleach *to Goneril.*
[42] William gave *Goneril* the bleach.
[43] William gave the bleach.

In Chapter 4 I sub-categorised *give* as a ditransitive verb. This is as good as saying that both the direct and the indirect object are necessary, non-omissible. But [43] does appear to be acceptable, even though it contains nothing that corresponds to an indirect object. Should we say, then, that the indirect object NP in [42] or the PP in [41] are optional? What effect would this have on the sub-category of the verb?

It would make *give* a monotransitive verb. If it is monotransitive, then the PP in [41] would be an adjunct rather than part of the complementation of the verb. Alternatively, we might want to assign *give* to both sub-categories, [ditrans] in [41] and [42], but [monotrans] in [43].

For various reasons, neither of these solutions is desirable. The most important reason is that neither solution does justice to the fact that, although [43] is acceptable, it nevertheless seems incomplete. Or, more to the point, it seems incomplete when considered OUT OF CONTEXT. Out of context, we would probably be prompted to ask who William gave the bleach to. However, in any context in which it could be understood who had been given the bleach, [43] is perfectly acceptable – for example, in the context of a conversation about Goneril's birthday presents. On the other hand, in the context of a discussion of what had happened to the bleach or of what William had done, its incompleteness would be unacceptable. Note the oddity of [44b] as an answer to [44a]:

[44a] Whatever happened to the bleach?
[44b] William gave it.

When a sentence is actually used by a speaker (i.e. when a speaker actually utters it), almost anything can be omitted, provided that the omitted elements can be understood from the context in which it is used. **The omission from sentences of required** elements capable of being understood in the context of their use is called ELLIPSIS. Ellipsis creates acceptable, but nonetheless grammatically incomplete sentences.

Even subjects can be ellipted, as in

[45] Visited Madame Sosostris this morning.

(Almost certainly the ellipted subject is *I*.) But we would not want to say, simply because the utterance of [45] is acceptable in certain contexts, that subject NPs are grammatically optional.

In saying that certain constituents are necessary (obligatory), I have been relying implicitly on a distinction that is important in language description:

The grammaticality of sentences vs. the acceptability of utterances (that is, the acceptability of uttering a particular sentence in a context).

The study of syntax, in its purest form, is more concerned with the concept of grammatical sentence than with the concept of acceptable utterance. In other words, **syntax is concerned with the form of sentences, without taking into account the effects of uttering sentences in a context**. Knowing what counts as a grammatical sentence plays an important part in a speaker's ability to interpret the utterances he actually hears (or reads), but it is only a part.

You may wish to apply the SENTENCE ANALYSIS offered here to UTTERANCES (that is, to actual uses of sentences by a speaker, whether in speech or in writing). If so, it will be useful to have a means of representing elliptical sentences. This is easily done. For example, we can capture the fact that, even though [43] has no indirect object, it still counts as a ditransitive sentence (albeit an elliptical one), as in [46]:

[46]

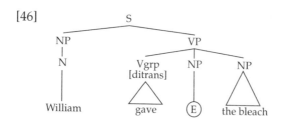

where (E) indicates an ellipted element, in this case an NP functioning as indirect object.

Before leaving ellipsis, it is worth spending a little time considering how ellipsis interacts with the analyst's decisions about sub-categorisation.

Compare [47] and [48]:

[47] Max played the tuba in the street.

[48] Max played in the street.

[47] is monotransitive with an adjunct PP (*in the street*). What about [48]? Well, in context, it could be an elliptical version of [47]. For example, if, as an utterance, it occurred in the context of a conversation about the players of the Chatanooga Stompers, and Max is known to be their tuba player, then [48] would reasonably be understood to mean exactly what [47] means. In such a context, it should be treated as an elliptical monotransitive sentence, with the dO ellipted.

Out of context, (that is, as a sentence rather than an actual utterance), or in another context, [48] is interpreted differently. Here, *play* means the same as 'play about' or 'amuse oneself'. This is an intransitive sense of *play*.

As sentences out of context, then, [47] and [48] indicate that *play* belongs to two sub-categories [monotrans] and [intrans]. It has a distinct sense in each.

Compare now [49] and [50].

[49] Jean-Pierre ate the cous-cous rapidly.

[50] Jean-Pierre ate rapidly.

Should we assign *eat* to two sub-categories, [monotrans] in [49] and [intrans] in [50]? Or should we treat [50] as an elliptical [monotrans] with the direct object omitted?

Eat is different from *play* in that one always has to eat something. As we saw, one doesn't always have to play something; it depends on the sense of *play*. This suggests that [50] should be treated as [monotransitive] with an ellipted direct object.

Sentence adverbials

All the adverbials looked at so far are adjunct adverbials. We have seen that they are modifiers of a VP within a higher VP. **Adjunct adverbials might then be called 'VP-adverbials'.** In this section I contrast them with other kinds of adverbial, which I shall group together as 'sentence adverbials' (S-adverbials).

Compare the [a] and [b] examples in the following pairs:

[51a] Buster admitted everything *frankly*.
[51b] Buster admitted everything, *frankly*.

[52a] Max can only do the tango *rather awkwardly*.
[52b] Max can only do the tango, *rather awkwardly*.

[53a] Mildred interfered *between you and me*.
[53b] Mildred interfered, *between you and me*.

In the [a] examples the italicised constituent functions as an adjunct adverbial, a VP modifier. In [51a], *frankly* tells us the manner of Buster's admission (Buster was frank). But this is not how you understand [51b], with the comma. Here, *frankly* describes how the speaker/writer of [51b] feels she herself is expressing what she has to say. Here it is the speaker/writer who is being frank in saying that Buster admitted everything. [52a], with the VP-adverbial, expresses the idea that the MANNER of Max's tango-dancing is awkward. It does not imply that the tango is Max's only dance. By contrast, in [52b], nothing is said about *how* Max dances the tango, but it does say that the tango is Max's only dance. [52b] expresses the idea that, however gracefully Max might dance the tango, the speaker/writer feels that its being Max's only dance is a rather awkward fact. The same sort of distinction goes for [53a/b]. In [53b] *between you and me* is being used to mean the same as *confidentially* (the speaker/writer of [53b] is being confidential is saying that Mildred interfered), but not in [53a].

All the [b] examples are sentence adverbials. Generally, S-adverbials provide some comment by the speaker/writer about the fact she is reporting or about how she feels she herself is expressing what she has to say. They are called 'S-adverbials' because, in contrast to the VP-adverbials of the last section and in the [a] examples above, the adverbial does not modify anything *within* the sentence. They are, in fact, only very loosely associated with the sentence. This feeling is borne out by the use of the comma in writing and by a distinct intonation in speech. Notice that the S-adverbial interpretation is the more natural (and in the case of [52b] the only possible one) when the adverbial occurs at the beginning of the sentence:

[51c] Frankly, Buster admitted everything.
[52c] Rather awkwardly, Max can only do the tango.
[53c] Between you and me, Mildred interfered.

Disparaging letters are often written to newspapers about the use of *hopefully* in [54b] as against its use in [54a]:

[54a] He will look up hopefully.
[54b] He will look up, hopefully. (Hopefully, he will look up.)

Why this should be is not clear. *Hopefully*, just like *frankly, between you and me, confidentially*, and *rather awkwardly* – and innumerable other adverbials – can (and does) function both as a VP-adverbial (as in [54a]) and as an S-adverbial (as in [54b]). *Stupidly* is another example: compare [a] *He answered the question stupidly* with [b] *Stupidly, he answered the question.*

As mentioned, instead of modifying some element within the rest of the sentence, the S-adverbial relates to the rest of the sentence as a whole, considered as a unit. Now, the rest of the sentence considered as unit is a perfectly good sentence itself. So, as suggested by the terms 'VP-adverbial' and 'S-adverbial', the distinction between [51a] and [51b] is the distinction between *frankly* functioning as a modifier of VP within a higher VP vs. functioning as a modifier of S within a higher S, as in [55].

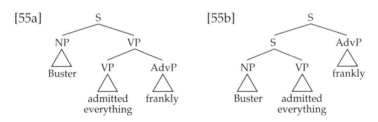

(If the S-adverbial appears at the beginning, it should be represented as a preceding sister of the S it modifies – just as, if the VP-adverbial appears between the NP and the VP, it should be represented as a preceding sister of the VP.)

We have only looked at adverbials that can function both as VP-(adjunct) adverbials and as S-adverbials. Some AdvPs and PPs can only be interpreted as VP-(adjunct) adverbials. Examples are: *sideways, daintily, noisily, with grace and speed.* Conversely, other AdvPs and PPs can only function as S-adverbials. Examples are: *unfortunately, admittedly, certainly, of course, perhaps, possibly.*

In particular, there is a group of AdvPs and PPs that have a quite specific interpretation and can only have an S-adverbial function. Examples are: (AdvPs) *nevertheless, therefore, furthermore, thus, how-*

ever, incidentally, and (PPs) *on the contrary, by contrast, in other words, for a start, in short, in conclusion, on the other hand.* Such S-adverbials are sometimes more specifically referred to as 'conjunct adverbials'. They indicate what kind of relation holds between the sentence they modify and the surrounding discourse. As S-adverbials, they have no function within the sentence they modify. They serve to link distinct and grammatically unconnected sentences into a coherent and structured discourse. As a result, notice that when a conjunct S-adverbial is present, the sentence sounds odd in isolation, as if it has been ripped out of a context:

[56] In short, you're fired.
[57] You've got no clothes on, for a start.
[58]

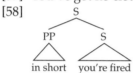

The representation of S-adverbials as sisters of S (within another S) is again a simplification, however. Like VP-(adjunct) adverbials, S-adverbials can appear in a variety of positions, not only at the beginning and the end of sentences, but actually inside the sentences they modify:

[59] Rashid, on the other hand, came dressed as a washing machine.

In these first five chapters, the general structure of simple sentences has been outlined. In the next two chapters, I go into more detail on the structure of simple sentences. Chapter 6 concerns the structure of the Verb Group itself and Chapter 7 discusses in more detail the structure of Noun Phrases.

Discussion of in-text exercises

1.

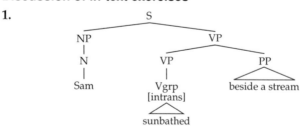

Beside a stream is a VP-adverbial. As an [intrans] Vgrp, *sunbathed* forms a VP in its own right. Notice that we could continue with *... and Ferdinand did so behind the gas-house* meaning 'Ferdinand sunbathed behind the gas-house'. Here *did so* replaces *sunbathed*.

2.

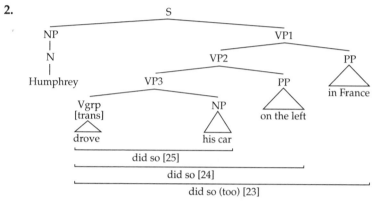

3. (i) Transitive phrasal verb + NP (cf. ☑ *shouted the answers/them out*).
 (ii) Prepositional verb + PP (cf. ☒ *looked the window/it out*).
 (iii) Prepositional verb + PP (cf. ☒ *hangs the office about*).
 (iv) Transitive phrasal verb + NP (cf. ☑ *handed the money/it over*).
 (v) Prepositional verb + PP (cf. ☒ *viciously turned John/him on*).

Viciously was included in order to rule out the interpretation in which John is excited/aroused. On this latter interpretation *turned on John* clearly is a phrasal verb + NP and in fact sounds much better with the particle moved (cf. ☑ *turned John/him on*).

 (vi) Transitive phrasal verb + NP (meaning 'completed the term') (cf. ☑ *saw the term/it through*).
 (vii) Transitive phrasal verb + NP (cf. ☑ *handed my essay/it in*).
 (viii) Prepositional verb + PP (cf. ☒ *saw the disguise through*).

What these examples show is that the distinction between phrasal verb (+ NP) and prepositional verb (+ PP) is not a distinction between an idiomatic construction and a non-idiomatic construction. As (iii), (v) and (viii) illustrate, the combination of prepositional verb and PP can be quite as idiomatic as a phrasal verb (+ NP). Idiomaticity is independent of, and cuts across, the phrasal/prepositional distinction.

Exercises

1. Identify the sub-category of the Vgrp and the functions of the major elements in the following sentences (i.e. S, V, dO, iO, sP, oP, PC, aA (for adjunct adverbial), and sA (for sentence adverbial).

    (i) This so-called music will drive me mad very quickly.
    (ii) I will be with you in two shakes.
    (iii) We can celebrate this with an Indian take-away tonight.
    (iv) The academy has turned out some inspired confidence trick-sters in its time.
    (v) Incidentally, I have sold your vests to the museum for a small fortune.
    (vi) Luckily enough, they gave in in seconds.
    (vii) Murdstone brought the child up too strictly, in my opinion.

2. Having checked the answers to exercise 1, draw phrase-markers for sentences (ii), (iii), (v), and (vi).

3. The following verbs are all monotransitive. Try and decide for each verb whether the absence of a direct object should be treated (a) as an instance of ellipsis or (b) as indicating that the verb also belongs to the intransitive sub-category (cf. the discussion of *play* in this chapter).
    read, launch, kick, jump, recall, pay.

4. Look carefully at the following sentences and decide on the sub-category of the Vgrp and the functions of the italicised constituents. Some questions to ask yourself: Does *appear* belong to one sub-category or to more than one? Is (v) elliptical? Does *appear* have the same sense in all cases? Are any of the sentences ambiguous?

    (i) Hieronimo appeared *rather jumpy.*
    (ii) Hieronimo appeared *a veritable tyrant.*
    (iii) Hieronimo appeared *in a flurry of snow.*
    (iv) Hieronimo appeared *in a dangerous mood.*
    (v) Hieronimo appeared.

5. Let us agree that the following sentence is ungrammatical:

    (i) *Tim went to the circus and Max did so to the zoo.

    And let us assume that it is supposed to mean (or is an ungrammatical way of saying) (ii)

(ii) Tim went to the circus and Max went to the zoo.

Now tackle the following questions in order:

(a) What string of words does *did so* replace in (i)?
(b) What does the UNgrammaticality of (i) tell you about the CATEGORY of the string it replaces?
(c) On the basis of your answers to (a) and (b), can you decide whether the PP *to the circus* is an adjunct or a complement of the verb?
(d) On the basis of your answer to (c), how should we sub-categorise *go* in (i)?
(e) Look at the following conversations:

   (iii) A: Where's Maria? B: She went.
   (iv) A: Huge party, wasn't it! B: Even Maria went!

   How do you suggest we handle the sub-categorisation of *go* in each of these uses?

Discussion of exercises

1. (i) This so-called music   will drive   me   mad   very quickly.
              S   Vgrp   dO   oP   aA
                             [complex]

  (ii) I   will be   with you   in two shakes.
      S   Vgrp   sP   aA
          [intens]

 (iii) We   can celebrate   this   with an Indian take-away
       S   Vgrp   dO   aA
             [trans]

    tonight.
      aA

 (iv) The academy   has turned out
         S   Vgrp
             [phrasal trans]

    some inspired confidence tricksters   in its time.
                dO   aA

  (v) Incidentally   I   have sold   your vests   to the museum
        sA   S   Vgrp   dO   iO
                    [ditrans]

    for a small fortune.
        aA

(vi) Luckily enough   they   gave in   in seconds.
     sA   S   Vgrp   aA
                       [phrasal
                       intrans]

(vii) Murdstone   brought   the child   up   too strictly
     S   Vgrp   dO   Prt   aA
              [phrasal
              trans]

in my opinion.
  sA

2. (ii)

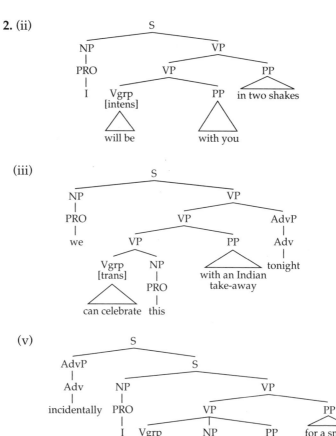

(vi)

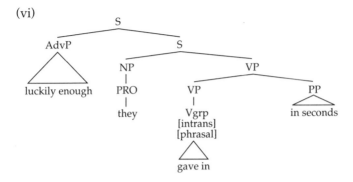

3. This exercise is a matter of judgement rather than getting the answer right or wrong. My judgements are as follows. The verbs seem to fall into three groups:

(i) *jump* and *kick*   (ii) *read* and *pay*   (iii) *recall* and *launch*

(i) *Jump* and *kick* are similar; you can jump a stack of books and kick an obstinate car but you can also jump without jumping something (as in jumping up and down) and you can just kick (babies do it all the time). So *jump* and *kick* clearly belong to both sub-categories [monotransitive] and [intransitive].

(ii) *Read* and *pay* are similar to *eat*. You do always have to read SOMETHING. And when after a meal you inform your partner that he/she is 'paying', they will understand that it is the bill that is to be paid. So both *read* and *pay* are [monotransitive] and the absence of a direct object is a matter of ellipsis.

(iii) I have grouped *launch* and *recall* separately from *pay* since, while they are clearly [monotransitive] and require a direct object, they require it so strongly that it is almost unacceptable to omit the object by ellipsis. These too are [monotransitive] only.

4. In (i) *appear* is complemented by an Adjective Phrase. This indicates that the verb is [intensive], with the AP functioning as subject-predicative. The complement NP in (ii) has the

same relation to the verb and the subject as the AP in (i), so again there is no reason not to take the verb in (ii) as [intensive], complemented by a subject-predicative. We usually find that [intensive] verbs can be complemented either by an AP, NP, or PP. So we might expect the verb in (iii) to be [intensive] again, with the PP functioning as subject-predicative. But notice that the sense of *appear* in (iii) is quite distinct from that in (i) and (ii). (i) and (ii) can be paraphrased by (vi) and (vii):

(vi) Hieronimo appeared *to be* $\left\{ \begin{array}{l} \text{rather jumpy.} \\ \text{a veritable tyrant.} \end{array} \right.$

(vii) *It appeared that Hieronimo was* $\left\{ \begin{array}{l} \text{rather jumpy.} \\ \text{a veritable tyrant.} \end{array} \right.$

where the verb has a sense similar to *seem*. (iii), on the other hand, cannot be paraphrased in these ways:

(viii) Hieronimo appeared to be in a flurry of snow.
 (ix) It appeared that Hieronimo was in a flurry of snow.

In (iii) the verb has the sense of 'come into view' or 'turn up'. It can be paraphrased by (x).

(x) Hieronimo appeared, and did so in a flurry of snow.

(Compare (i) and (ii).) In this sense the verb is to be treated as [intransitive] with the PP functioning as an (optional) adverbial.

Coming to (iv) now, notice that it is ambiguous: it can have either the sense it has in (i) and (ii) (*Hieronimo appeared to be in a dangerous mood*) or the sense it has in (iii) (*Hieronimo appeared and did so in a dangerous mood*). On the first interpretation, we have an [intensive] Vgrp complemented by a PP as subject-predicative; on the second, an [intransitive] Vgrp modified by an optional PP as adverbial.

As for (v) this must be taken as a non-elliptical [intransitive] sentence, not as an elliptical [intensive] sentence. Since *appear* also belongs to the [intransitive] sub-category, the subject-predicative cannot, in fact, be ellipted with the [intensive] sense of the verb. A speaker, in ellipting the subject-predicative, would risk having *appear* misunderstood and analysed by his hearers as [intransitive].

5.

(a) *Did so* replaces *went*.

(b) Since *do so* only replaces VPs and since (ii) is UNgrammatical, we may conclude that *went* does not constitute, in itself, a VP (though it is, of course, a Vgrp).

(c) Yes, we can decide this. If *to the circus* was an adjunct it would be the sister of a VP (within a higher VP). In that case, *went* would have to be analysed as a VP. But *went* isn't a VP (as we showed in (b)). So the PP cannot be an adjunct. If, on the other hand, the PP is a complement, then it must a sister of the Vgrp, and form a VP with that Vgrp. And notice that *do so* can indeed replace the string *went to the circus* as in:

Max went to the circus and Hogarth did so (too).

So, it appears that we must analyse the PP as a complement. It is only by doing this that we can avoid analysing *went* as a full VP in its own right.

(d) We must analyse *go* as a prepositional verb.

(e) Two quite different senses of *go* are involved. In (iii), the verb is used in the sense of 'leave' or 'depart' and is [intransitive]. *Go*, therefore, is both an [intransitive] and a [prepositional] verb. In (iv), on the other hand, the verb is interpreted, in the given context, as *went to the party*. The prepositional complement is understood. This is an elliptical use of the [prepositional] verb.

Further exercises

Here are three sets of sentences, illustrating all the points made in the last two chapters. Draw phrase-markers for them. Allow yourself plenty of room. Ambiguous examples will need two phrase-markers. The examples become more intricate, and may admit of more discussion, as the sets progress. Those in Set I do not include sentence-adverbials; this will allow you to concentrate more on the distinction between verb complements (sisters of Vgrp) and VP-(adjunct) adverbials (sisters of VP).

Example: *Their spokesman's pronouncements quickly landed him in gaol.*

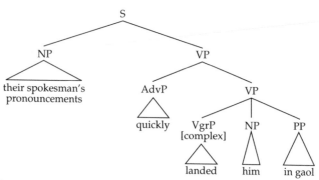

Set I

1. The trainees got much quicker during the Autumn months.
2. I shall make this the main point of my argument.
3. The plane will be landing in twenty minutes.
4. The unfortunate wizard looked up querilously.
5. The new arrival wished everyone present a very Merry Christmas.
6. Matilda had polished off the toast by eight thirty.
7. She never had believed in ghosts.
8. He opened his post very reluctantly on that particular day.
9. Martha left the bathroom in an awful hurry.
10. Martha left the bathroom in an awful mess. (ambiguous)
11. They decided on the train. (ambiguous; elliptical on one interpretation)

Set II

1. It was raining extremely hard on the Continent last night.
2. That would be a rather silly question to ask, obviously.
3. They often are nervous of the parachutes at first.
4. Incredibly, she allowed him total freedom without a thought for the consequences.
5. You've turned the high-wire into a death-trap, for your information!
6. The management of the circus and the ringmaster were hoping for an early meeting with the trapeze artists.
7. Floyd's supposedly surprise puddings always blew up in your face.

8. You can cook a most delicious meal with just semolina and ketchup for the price of a Coke.
9. The younger architects had positioned the ground-floor windows too close to each other in the earlier building.
10. The ferryboat is much too overloaded for a crossing in rough seas in my opinion.

Set III

1. He never looked back on his years at sea with much nostalgia, however.
2. The drunken new recruits to the unit were tripping over guy ropes repeatedly until the early hours.
3. Unfortunately, his newly invented rotting compound quickly leaked into the foundations.
4. Several figures gingerly edged towards the precipice in full view of the waiting police.
5. The dogs were barking at the gate. (ambiguous)
6. You should ignore all those people in the studio. (ambiguous)
7. You should keep all those people in the studio. (ambiguous)
8. The butler usually mopped up the crumbs after each course in the old days.

   (This last will need careful attention to the meaning in deciding what constituents each of the several adverbials is modifying.)

Chapter 6

The Verb Group

This chapter is concerned with the internal structure of the Verb Group itself. The structure of verbal elements in English is a matter of some controversy: several different analyses have been proposed in recent years. What I aim to do here, then, is to offer an analysis that will be useful whether or not you intend to concern yourself later with the issues involved in deciding between competing analyses of English verbs.

From the last two chapters you will have gained an idea of what Vgrps look like. **Every (non-elliptical) Vgrp contains a** LEXICAL **verb as its** HEAD. Lexical verbs are verbs that belong to the indefinitely large general vocabulary of the language (e.g. *run, eat, analyse, shatter, adjourn, depend* ...). The lexical head always appears last in the Vgrp.

The lexical head verb may or may not be modified by AUXIL-IARY **verbs.** Auxiliary verbs form a special and very restricted set of verbs. The clear ones are: *be, have, do, can, may, must, will, shall,* and *need.* (Less clearly, *dare, ought,* and *used* are (or resemble) auxiliaries, too, at least in some dialects.) Auxiliary verbs always have their function in respect of the lexical verb functioning as head of the Vgrp.

A Vgrp consisting of just a head verb (without auxiliaries) I shall call a SIMPLE Verb Group. A Vgrp with auxiliary verbs I shall call COMPLEX. A simple Vgrp will have just a lexical verb (V) as its daughter, as in [1], while a complex Vgrp will have two daughters, AUX and V, as in [2]. All the auxiliary verbs will fall under the AUX node.

[1]   SIMPLE   [2]   COMPLEX

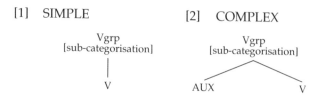

The simple finite Vgrp

A simple Vgrp contains just a single (necessarily lexical) verb. As the simple Vgrps in the following sentences illustrate, that verb can be further analysed:

[3a] Max mows the lawn.	[3b] Max mowed the lawn.
[4a] It soon cracks.	[4b] It soon cracked.
[5a] He slots it in.	[5b] He slotted it in.
[6a] He gives her ten.	[6b] He gave her ten.
[7a] She goes nowhere.	[7b] She went nowhere.
[8a] Max meets the guests.	[8b] Max met the guests.
[9a] He puts it in his ear.	[9b] He put it in his ear.

The [a] sentences are distinguished from the [b] sentences by a TENSE distinction in the verb. In the [a] examples, the verbs appear in a PRESENT TENSE FORM. In [b], they appear in their PAST TENSE FORM.

A Vgrp that contains a TENSED verb (as in [3]–[9] above) is traditionally called a FINITE Vgrp. Every sentence must contain one finite Vgrp (whether simple or complex). Sentences may or may not contain more than one Vgrp. In such cases the further Vgrps may or may not be tensed (contain a tensed verb). Vgrps without a tensed verb are NON-FINITE. Sentences with more than one Vgrp are not dealt with until Chapters 8–10. In this chapter, then, we will be concerned just with sentences with one Vgrp and – therefore – just with finite (tensed) Vgrps.

In examples [3]–[5] – which all contain regular verbs – the form the verb takes is readily separated into (i) the verb itself (called THE VERB STEM) and (ii) a PRESENT TENSE INFLECTION (e.g. *mow* + -*s*) or a PAST TENSE INFLECTION (e.g. *mow* + -*ed*). In the other examples, though, this separation is not so easily done. These all contain irregular verbs. In these, the verb form and the form of the marker of past tense are so bound up with each other that it is impossible to distinguish them. And sometimes there is no explicit marker of the tense at all – as in [9b].

You might ask: How do we know that *put* in [9b] IS the past tense form of the verb *put*? Well, consider [5a] and [5b]. The verbs in those sentences are very distinctly marked for present and past tense respectively. If I were to ask you to change just the verb in each of those sentences from *slot* to *put*, you would use *puts* instead of *slots*, and *put* instead of *slotted*. In short, you would use *put* as the past tense form of the verb *put*, just as you use *slotted* as the past tense form of the verb *slot*. (Other verbs that behave like *put* in not having a past tense form different from their stem form are *bet* and *hit*.)

Although it is irregular for a verb not to change its form in the past tense, in the present tense it is quite regular for verbs not to change their form. In fact, verbs only change their form in the present tense when (as in all the [a] examples above) the subject NP is *he, she, it,* or any full Noun Phrase that could be replaced by one of those pronouns. Such NPs and pronouns are described as THIRD PERSON SINGULAR NPs. Otherwise, the present tense form of the verb is identical to the stem form. The only exception to this general rule is the verb *be*:

[10]

NUMBER	PERSON	MOW PRES	BE PRES	BE PAST
singular	1st (I)	*mow*	*am*	*was*
	2nd (you)	*mow*	*are*	*were*
	3rd (he, she, it)	*mows*	*is*	*was*
plural	1st (we)	*mow*	*are*	*were*
	2nd (you)	*mow*	*are*	*were*
	3rd (they)	*mow*	*are*	*were*

This change of form in the finite verb according to the number and person of the subject NP is called SUBJECT-VERB AGREEMENT.

It is customary to recognise just present and past as the tenses of English. Future TIME is expressible in a variety of ways (for example, by means of the auxiliary verb *will*, as in *He will go*), but there is no future TENSE as such. It is important to recognise that **there is no simple correlation between the grammatical category tense and the notion of time.** For example, in the right circumstances, both present tense and past tense are compatible with the expression of future time, as shown by [11] and [12]:

[11] The boat *leaves* at ten this evening.
      (present tense – future time)
[12] If he *gave* me the bleach tomorrow, I'd use it.
      (past tense – future time)

Furthermore, *will* is capable of expressing ideas other than future time, as in [13]:

[13] He *will* keep burning the fritters!

How should we represent the tensed simple Vgrp? In this book I am primarily concerned with whether a verb is finite (i.e. whether it is tensed) and, if so, whether the tense is present or past. These are matters of syntax. I am less concerned with the actual FORM a verb may take when it is tensed for present or past. This is more a matter of morphology, phonology, and spelling. So I shall not attempt to segment a tensed verb into a verb stem on the one hand and a tense inflection on the other in phrase-marker diagrams. Instead, I shall add the tenses as a TENSE FEATURE to the V node. The simple present tense Vgrp *gives*, therefore, will have the representation in [14] and the simple past tense Vgrp *gave* that in [15].

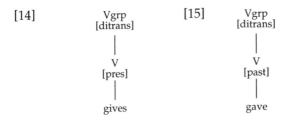

Auxiliary verbs in the complex Vgrp

There are two kinds of auxiliary verb:

PRIMARY AUXILIARIES: *be, have,* and *do.*
MODAL AUXILIARIES: *can, may, must, shall, will,* and *need.*

We shall see that, in addition to being auxiliary verbs, the primary auxiliaries can all function as lexical head verbs as well (and so can *need*).

Since some auxiliary verbs can also function as lexical verbs, I must mention some of the differences in behaviour between auxiliary verbs and lexical verbs. The two most important differences are:

1. In QUESTIONS an auxiliary verb can move in front of the subject NP. A lexical verb cannot.

2. The NEGATIVE PARTICLE (*not* or *n't*) can attach to an auxiliary verb but never to a lexical verb.

Compare the auxiliary verbs in [16] and [17] with the lexical verbs in [18] and [19]:

[16] [i] He can go.   [ii] Can he go?   [iii] He cannot go.
[17] [i] He is going.   [ii] Is he going?   [iii] He isn't going.

[18] [i] He spoke.   [ii] *Spoke he?   [iii] *He spoke not.
[19] [i] He drinks.   [ii] *Drinks he?   [iii] *He drinks not.

The correct forms for [18] and [19], of course, are

[20]   [ii] Did he speak?   [iii] He didn't speak.
[21]   [ii] Does he drink? [iii] He doesn't drink.

which involve the auxiliary verb *do*. This is explained further below.

Notice that there are two verbs *need*, one an auxiliary, the other lexical, with a subtle difference in meaning.

LEXICAL   AUXILIARY

[22a] He doesn't need $\left\{ \begin{array}{l} \text{to go.} \\ \text{a drink.} \end{array} \right.$ [22b] He needn't go.

[23a] Does he need $\left\{ \begin{array}{l} \text{to go?} \\ \text{a drink?} \end{array} \right.$ [23b] Need he go?

As indicated, the lexical verb can take a direct object NP (is monotransitive). The auxiliary verb cannot: *He needn't a drink*, *Needs he a drink?* Auxiliary verbs, remember, always have their function in respect of another *verb* (in a Vgrp). In the [b] examples, the relevant Vgrps are *needn't go* and *Need ... go*. In the [a] examples the relevant Vgrps are *doesn't need* and *Does ... need*. *To go* (like the NP *a drink*) is not part of that Vgrp; it is a distinct non-finite Vgrp. Here *to* ('the infinitive particle') is the marker of a distinct Vgrp (discussed in Chapter 10).

This then illustrates **a third distinction between auxiliary and lexical verbs: when a verb follows a lexical verb, it can be introduced by the infinitive particle *to*, but not when it follows an auxiliary verb** (within the same Vgrp).

The structure of AUX

AUX is highly structured and quite intricate. It can contain up to four immediate constituents, each with its own auxiliary verb:

1. **MODAL (M)**
2. **PERFECT ASPECT (PERF)**
3. **PROGRESSIVE ASPECT (PROG)**
4. **PASSIVE VOICE (PASS)**

The essential points to note are:

- All four are optional
- Any combination of them is possible, but
- They always appear in the order given
- Each may only appear once.

This allows for exactly sixteen different combinations, as you may check for yourself (see [42a] and [42b] below and Discussion 3 at the end of the chapter). Two further essential points are:

- Only the first verb is tensed (carries the tense feature)
- All four constituents of AUX determine the form of the NEXT verb in the Vgrp (the form of the verb that follows it in the Vgrp).

1. Modal (M)

M can be filled by any one modal verb. **Modal auxiliaries are distinguished from the primary auxiliaries and lexical verbs in *always* carrying tense.** They do not have untensed (non-finite) forms.

Some modals have both a present tense form and a past tense form:

PRESENT:	can	will	shall	may
PAST:	could	would	should	might

Compare [24] and [25]:

[24] (Present): He *says* he *will* come.
[25] (Past): He *said* he *would* come.

Must and *need* do not even have a past tense form but just the present tense form already given. Compare this situation with that which holds with a lexical verb like *give*. Besides its finite (present and past tense) forms, *give(s)* and *gave*, it has three non-finite forms: (i) *give* (the stem form, as in *to give*), (ii) *giving* and (iii) *given*.

I have just claimed that the auxiliary verb *need* has only a present tense form. But what about *needed*? Does the possibility of this form show that I was wrong?

---

*He needed go is not grammatical. By contrast, *He needed to go* and *He needed a drink* are fine. This shows that it is only the lexical

verb *need*, not the auxiliary verb (which is always followed by another verb) that can appear in a past tense form. So the claim about the auxiliary verb stands.

A defining peculiarity of modals is that they do not exhibit subject-verb agreement. That is, they do not change their form in the present tense even with a third person singular subject NP (so we have *He can go*, not **He cans go*).

I have mentioned that each constituent of AUX determines the form of the verb that follows it in the Vgrp. **The verb following the modal auxiliary in the Vgrp appears in its basic stem form.** This applies whether the following verb is another auxiliary or the lexical verb itself.

Here are phrase-marker representations of *can give* and *could die*:

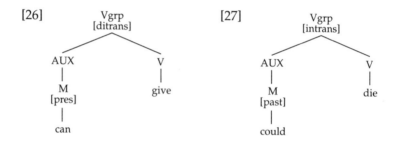

[26] can be described as a PRESENT MODAL Vgrp, [27] as a PAST MODAL Vgrp.

2.   *Perfect aspect (PERF)*

Here are some Vgrps with the PERF option chosen:

- [28] has forbidden (a present perfect Vgrp)
- [29] had gone (a past perfect Vgrp)
- [30] will have given (a present modal perfect Vgrp)
- [31] could have delayed (a past modal perfect Vgrp)

These all contain a form of THE PERFECT AUXILIARY verb *have*. In [28] and [29] perfect *have* is the first verb in the Vgrp, so it appears in a tensed form – present in [28], past in [29]. In [30] and [31], however, it follows a modal verb, so it must appear in its basic, untensed, stem form.

Remember, though, that a tensed verb does not always differ in its form from the basic stem. This is especially true in the present tense, where the form differs from the stem form only when the subject is third person singular (*he, she, it ...*). In [32], for example,

[32] They have gone.

have is the present tense of the perfect auxiliary. This can be confirmed by changing the subject NP to a third person singular NP (e.g. *she* or *Max*) and noting that *have* would then need to change to *has*. This shows that in [32] we are dealing with a tensed form of *have*. In [30] and [31], by contrast, the form of *have* is not affected by the subject – and this confirms that we are there dealing with the untensed (non-finite) stem form of *have*.

You may be confused by the fact that, while [28] and [32] contain a present tense, they both refer to past time. Bear in mind the lack of correlation between TIME and TENSE, mentioned earlier. There are more ways of referring to the past than using the past tense. **The use of the perfect auxiliary *have* is one way of referring to past time independently of tense.** As [28] and [29] show, the perfect auxiliary itself can be tensed for present or past.

The verb that follows *have* in the Vgrp always appears in its (non-finite) PERFECT PARTICIPLE FORM. This applies whether this following verb is a lexical verb or another auxiliary. Look again at [28]–[31]. *Forbidden, gone, given,* and *delayed* are the perfect participle forms of *forbid, go, give,* and *delay*.

As the perfect participle of *delay* illustrates, with many verbs (in fact, all regular and some irregular verbs) the perfect participle form is identical to the past tense form. However, no confusion should result from this: this form represents the (finite) past tense only if the verb is the first verb in the Vgrp. If a verb in that form is preceded by *have*, then that form represents the perfect participle. Here are some examples:

[33]	STEM FORM	PAST TENSE	PERFECT
Regular:	delay	delayed	have delayed
Irregular:	give	gave	have given
"	show	showed	have shown
"	go	went	have gone
"	put	put	have put
"	be	was/were	have been

***Have* can function both as the perfect auxiliary (modifying the head verb) or as the head verb itself**. [28]–[32] above illustrate its use as the perfect auxiliary. In [34] and [35], however, it functions as the head of the Vgrp:

[34] Tarzan *has* a bevy of apes at his disposal.
[35] Tony *will have* mayonnaise with his chips.

You can tell that *have* is not functioning as the perfect auxiliary in these examples because the constituents that follow it are not verbs (they are NPs). As the perfect auxiliary, *have* must precede another verb within a Vgrp.

Here are example sentences in which *have* functions both as auxiliary and as head verb:

[36] Aldo *has had* a little chat with the doorman. (present perfect Vgrp)
[37] By two a.m., I *had had* enough. (past perfect Vgrp)

Here is the phrase-marker analysis of the present perfect Vgrp *has given*:

[38]

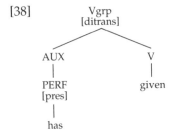

Now give the phrase-marker of the past modal perfect Vgrp *would have given* (given as **Discussion 1**, page 145).

3. *Progressive aspect (PROG)*

Try to identify the progressive auxiliary in the following Vgrps:

[39a] was smoldering (past progressive Vgrp)
[39b] is procrastinating (present progressive Vgrp)
[39c] would be trampolining (past modal progressive Vgrp)
[39d] have been cooking (present perfect progressive Vgrp)

What these examples all have in common is a form of the verb *be* (*was*, *is*, *be*, and *been*). *Be* is the PROGRESSIVE AUXILIARY. They also have in common the *-ing* inflection on the verb following *be*. Just as the perfect auxiliary *have* determines the form of the following verb (requiring it to adopt the perfect participle form), so **the progressive auxiliary requires the following verb to adopt the V-*ING* form. Call this the PROGRESSIVE PARTICIPLE.**

Before reading further, name the four forms of *be* that appear in [39].

In [a] and [b] *be* is the first verb in the Vgrp and is, therefore, tensed. In [a] it appears in its past tense form, in [b] in its present tense form. In [c], it follows the past tense modal *would*, so it appears in its basic stem form *be*. In [d] it follows perfect *have* and so appears in its perfect participle form.

Like *have*, *be* **can function either as an auxiliary or as the head verb itself**. As a head verb, it is the intensive verb, the COPULA, encountered in Chapter 4.

[40]   Kubla Khan *is* too extravagant.

In [41], *be* figures twice:

[41]   Nanny *is being* a nuisance again.

This is a present progressive Vgrp. *Is* is the present tense form of the progressive auxiliary *be*, and *being* is the progressive participle of the copula.

Now give the phrase-markers for [a] *was giving*, [b] *could be giving* and [c] *has been being*. (These are given as **Discussion 2**, pages 145–6.)

Before considering the fourth auxiliary option, Passive Voice, it will be useful to review all the options made available by M, PERF, and PROG:

[42a]   [i]   pres/past Vgrp (simple)
      [ii]   pres/past modal Vgrp
     [iii]   pres/past perfect Vgrp
     [iv]   pres/past progressive Vgrp
      [v]   pres/past modal perfect Vgrp
     [vi]   pres/past modal progressive Vgrp
    [vii]   pres/past perfect progressive Vgrp
   [viii]   pres/past modal perfect progressive Vgrp

As an exercise, give an actual example of each type of Vgrp listed in [42a]. Use *forget* as the lexical verb and, where necessary, the modal *will*. Assume that all the Vgrps have a third person singular subject. (**Discussion 3** (i)–(viii), page 146.)

---

4.   *Passive voice (PASS)*

All the Vgrps examined so far are said to be in the ACTIVE VOICE, because they do not contain the passive auxiliary. Vgrps containing the passive auxiliary verb are said to be in the PASSIVE VOICE. Compare the following active and passive Vgrps.

		ACTIVE	PASSIVE
[43a]	simple past:	stole	was stolen
[43b]	pres. progressive:	is stealing	is being stolen
[43c]	pres. perfect:	has stolen	has been stolen
[43d]	pres. modal:	will steal	will be stolen

Identify the passive auxiliary verb.

All the passive Vgrps contain a form of the verb *be*: *was* in [a], *being* in [b], *been* in [c], and *be* in [d]. *Be* **is the PASSIVE AUXILIARY VERB**.

Of course, *be* is also the progressive auxiliary. How are you supposed to distinguish between the progressive auxiliary and the passive auxiliary? **The difference between progressive *be* and passive *be* lies in the form taken by the following verb.** Following progressive *be*, a verb adopts the progressive participle form (V-ing – e.g. *stealing*). **Following passive *be*, a verb adopts the PASSIVE PARTICIPLE form (e.g. *stolen*).** Notice that the passive participle and the perfect participle of verbs always have the same form. Since the two participles are the same with every verb in the language, it is traditional not to distinguish between them. This participle form is traditionally called the PAST PARTICIPLE, though I have not adopted that term here since it misleadingly suggests that the form has something to do with past tense. But notice, in passing, that the passive option introduces no new form into the language; economically it just recombines forms which are anyway required for the formation of perfect and progressive Vgrps:

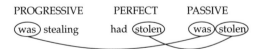

PROGRESSIVE	PERFECT	PASSIVE
(was) stealing	had (stolen)	(was)(stolen)

Since the eight (active) Vgrps enumerated in [42a] can all be passive, the passive option increases the total of possible Vgrps by another eight, to sixteen. Here are the remaining Vgrps (exactly the same as [i]–[viii] in [42a] but with PASS in the AUX).

[42b](*continued*)

     [ix] pres/past passive Vgrp
     [x] pres/past modal passive Vgrp
     [xi] pres/past perfect passive Vgrp
     [xii] pres/past progressive passive Vgrp
     [xiii] pres/past modal perfect passive Vgrp
     [xiv] pres/past modal progressive passive Vgrp
     [xv] pres/past perfect progressive passive Vgrp
     [xvi] pres/past modal perfect progressive passive Vgp

Again, using *forget* as the lexical verb and, where necessary, the modal *will*, give actual examples of the Vgrps named in [42b] [ix]–[xvi]. (**Discussion 3** (ix)–(xvi), page 146.)

Of course, the more complicated Vgrps occur more rarely, with [xvi], the most complicated, hardly occurring at all. Nevertheless, it is a possible Vgrp, available for use on the occasions it is needed.

A major difference between the passive auxiliary and all other auxiliaries is that the choice of passive affects not just the Vgrp but the whole sentence. If we want the progressive equivalent of [43]

[43] Everyone *dreads* Jim's stew.

we simply change the simple present Vgrp into a present progressive Vgrp:

[44] Everyone *is dreading* Jim's stew.

This is not enough with PASS. Changing just the Vgrp of [43] from active to passive gives [45], which is ungrammatical:

[45] *Everyone *is* dread*ed* Jim's stew.

The passive equivalent of [43] (repeated here) is [46]:

[43] Everyone dreads Jim's stew. (active)
[46] Jim's stew is dreaded by everyone. (passive)

Comparing the active and passive shows that **the object in the active becomes the subject of the passive**. Furthermore, **the**

subject of the active becomes a Prepositional Phrase introduced with *by*. Here is another example:

[47a] This earnest little wine will tantilise Fido. (active)
[47b] Fido will *be* tantilis*ed* by this earnest little wine. (passive)

What then are the passive counterparts of the following sentences?

[48a] Mrs Golightly has threatened the lodger.
[49a] Oddjob is ejecting the intruders.

If it is not immediately obvious how to do this, make the change
in stages: first make the Vgrp passive, then effect the other two
changes in the rest of the sentence. This gives:

[48b] The lodger has *been* threaten*ed* by Mrs Golightly.
[49b] The intruders are *be*ing eject*ed* by Oddjob.

In passive sentences, the (*by*) PP functions as a VP-(adjunct)
adverbial. As an adverbial, it is of course optional:

[47c] Fido will be tantalised.
[48c] The lodger has been threatened.
[49c] The intruders are being ejected.

We have seen that converting an active sentence into its passive counterpart involves making the object become subject.
Only verbs that can have objects, therefore, can appear in the
passive voice. Since INTRANSITIVE verbs do not take objects, or
indeed any complementation at all, sentences containing them
do not have a passive counterpart. In Chapter 4, MONOTRANSITIVE
and INTENSIVE verbs were distinguished: while both sub-categories can be complemented by an NP, as in [50a] and [51a],

[50a] Everyone present saw a doctor. (monotransitive)
[51a] Everyone present was a doctor. (intensive)

the complement NP functions as OBJECT only in the transitive
[50a]. In the intensive [51a] the complement NP functions as
SUBJECT-PREDICATIVE. So [50a] does have a passive counterpart,
but [51a] does not:

[50b] A doctor was seen by everyone present.
[51b] *A doctor was been by everyone present.

Since the direct object in the active becomes the subject in the
passive, **the direct object position with a monotransitive Vgrp**

won't be filled when the Vgrp is passive. Now, the term 'mono-transitive' means 'taking a direct object'. So you might ask: can we really still call such verbs 'monotransitive' in the passive, when they appear without an NP in the direct object position? Certainly we can. Even though *Jim's stew* appears as subject in the passive [46], you (as a speaker of this language) still understand it as being the (ex-)direct object of *dread*. Simply, it has moved – leaving a gap in the direct object position.

So the gap in direct object position in a passive sentence should be represented – for example, as in [52]:

[52]

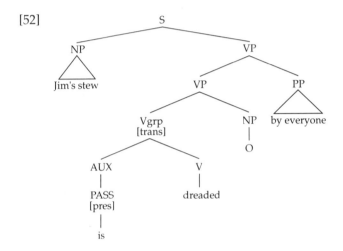

'O' denotes the gap. Note the VP-adverbial position of the PP *by everyone*.

Consider now the complex transitive active example [53a] and its passive counterpart [53b]:

[53a] This so-called music has driven Otto mad.
[53b] Otto has been driven mad (by this so-called music).

A complex transitive Vgrp, remember, is one that takes a direct object (*Otto* in [53a]) and a predicative (*mad*) that characterises that object – in other words, an object-predicative. But again, in the passive, the object has become the subject. So, paradoxically, the 'object-predicative' isn't describing the object but the subject! We can resolve the paradox by reference to the gap (O). Look at [53c]:

[53c]

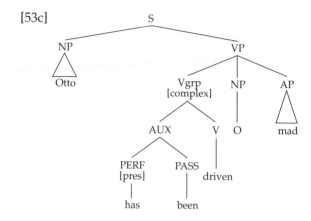

Since the Vgrp is [complex], the AP *mad* is (must be!) an object-predicative – even in this passive sentence. However, on inspecting the direct object position we find only 'O'. This tells us to look elsewhere for the NP that *mad* is characterising. Since AUX contains PASS, we know to look for it in the subject position.

Finally, let us consider the effect of PASS on DITRANSITIVE verbs. Recall that ditransitive verbs can take two objects in the active (direct and indirect). It is always the first object that becomes subject in the passive. So what are the passive counterparts of [54a] and [55a]?

[54a] The staff sent the general a pork-pie.
[55a] The staff sent a pork-pie to the general.

In [54a] the indirect object (*the general*) precedes the direct object, so *the general* becomes subject, leaving *a pork-pie* in object position:

[54b] The general was sent a pork-pie by the staff.

In [55a] *a pork-pie*, as direct object, precedes – so *a pork-pie* becomes subject, leaving the indirect object in the PP in its position:

[55b] A pork-pie was sent to the general by the staff.[1]

Give the phrase-marker for [54b]. Use the triangle notation as appropriate, but not for the Vgrp. **Discussion 4**, page 146.

---

1. In saying that it is always the first object that becomes subject in the passive, I am assuming that the passive counterpart of [54a] in which *a pork-pie* becomes subject is ungrammatical:

*A pork-pie was sent the general by the staff.

Negatives and auxiliary *do*

We have now reviewed all the options available under AUX but still have not said anything about **the auxiliary verb** *do*. This auxiliary is required in certain questions and in negative sentences with *not*. Here I consider negatives.

The rule for forming negative sentences with the NEGATIVE PARTICLE *NOT* is this:

The negative particle *not* is placed immediately after the auxiliary that carries the tense (i.e. the first auxiliary).

[56] Byron could not escape. (… couldn't …)
[57] Byron has not been escaping. (… hasn't …)

The rule makes crucial reference to the first auxiliary verb in the Vgrp. But what happens when the Vgrp is simple and there is no auxiliary present?

[58a] Byron escaped.

Here it is the lexical verb itself that carries the tense. In contrast to auxiliary verbs, lexical verbs do not, in present-day English, accept a following negative particle (*Byron escaped not*). In such cases, an auxiliary verb has to be supplied to carry the tense. **In negative sentences with *not*, auxiliary *do* is required to carry the tense in the absence of any other auxiliary.**

[58b] Byron did not escape. (… didn't …)

Since auxiliary *do* is now carrying the (past) tense, *escape* appears in its (non-finite, untensed) stem form.

The auxiliary verb *do* is empty of meaning. Its sole function is to carry the tense instead of the lexical head verb when required. In view of this, I shall represent *do* as immediately dominated by TENSE. The Vgrps of [56] and [58b] should be represented as in [59] and [60] respectively.

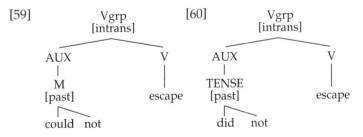

Note also **the use of *do* to carry the tense for** EMPHASIS **in positive sentences** (cf. *Byron DID escape*).

Like *have* and *be*, *do* can function as an auxiliary verb and as a head verb. Exercise 3 at the end of the chapter is concerned with this.

Fronting the auxiliary in questions

Compare again the following [a] and [b] examples:

> [61a] She has been laughing.   [61b] Has she been laughing?
> [62a] He spoke (he did speak).   [62b] Did he speak?

The rule for forming the question is this:

> **The auxiliary verb that carries the tense (i.e. the first auxiliary verb) moves in front of the subject.**

Again, the rule makes crucial reference to the first auxiliary verb. And again, ***do* is required to carry the tense in the absence of any other auxiliary**. It is *do* that moves in front of the subject. *Do* is required because, in contrast to auxiliary verbs, lexical verbs do not, in present-day English, move in front of the subject (**Spoke he?*).

This movement of the auxiliary is often called 'subject-auxiliary inversion'. In fact, however, that is not a good name for it, because it suggests that the subject and the (tensed) auxiliary verb exchange places, which they don't. The subject remains in its subject position (it remains the subject, in other words). It is the tensed auxiliary that moves to the front. That is why I am calling it 'AUXILIARY-FRONTING'. The question now is: **where does the tensed auxiliary move to?**

We have already encountered movement – in passive sentences. If you look back at the discussion of passives, you'll notice that phrases were moved only into positions already acknowledged, subject position and VP-adverbial position. This suggests that there should be a structural position in the phrase-marker that is, as it were, ready-willing-and-able to accept the fronted auxiliary. No such position has been mentioned yet. So I need to introduce it now. Look carefully at [63]–[64].

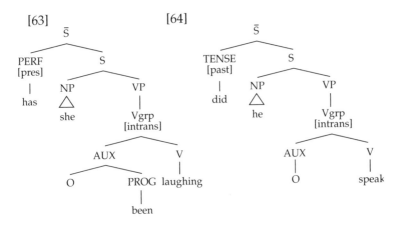

The new node is 'S̄'. This is called 'S-bar'. A fronted auxiliary is represented as a sister of the original sentence. The fronted auxiliary and 'S' are both dominated by S-bar.

It may seem that I have just invented this extra position (sister of S, daughter of S-bar) simply in order to find a place to put the fronted auxiliary. In fact, we shall see in later chapters that this position is real and is required for other purposes as well. So, **the position occupied by a fronted auxiliary is: sister of S and daughter of S-bar (S̄)**. This position has a name: the 'complementiser position'. I say more about it in later chapters. Strictly speaking, *every* sentence (S) should really be introduced by the complementiser position and dominated by S-bar, even when there is no fronted auxiliary. However, for simplicity, I shall only represent the complementiser position and S-bar when the position is filled.

As with passive, this fronting of the auxiliary has left a gap (O), this time under the AUX node. Thus, even though there is no tensed verb in the Vgrp in [63] and [64], we can tell that those are finite (tensed) Vgrps because they contain O. 'O' under AUX is the gap created by the fronting of an auxiliary verb and only TENSED auxiliaries can be fronted.

Now try phrase-markers for the following questions. Note that [66] is both passive and a question (needing two gaps).

[65] Has Buster been boiling the broccoli?
[66] Was Oleg arrested by the Squad?

(**Discussion 5**, page 147)

More on *have* and *be*

I have mentioned that *have* and *be* can function both as auxiliary verbs and as head verbs themselves. As you might expect, when FUNCTIONING as auxiliaries, they must BEHAVE like auxiliaries, moving in front of the subject in questions and accepting the negative particle ([67] and [68]). *Do*, which is normally required in the absence of an auxiliary, is ungrammatical with the auxiliary use of *have* and *be* ([69] and [70]).

[67a] **Are** they going?   [67b] They **aren't** going.
[68a] **Have** they gone?   [68b] They **haven't** gone.
[69a] *****Do** they **be** going?   [69b] *****They **don't be** going.
[70a] *****Do** they **have** gone?   [70b] *****They **don't have** gone.

Surprisingly, *have* can behave like an auxiliary even when it is functioning as a head verb. Both [71] and [72] are grammatical:

Functioning as a head verb, behaving like head verb:
[71a] Do we have any garlic?
[71b] We don't have any garlic.

Functioning as a head verb, behaving like an auxiliary:
[72a] Have we any garlic?
[72b] We haven't any garlic.

And *be* always behaves like an auxiliary whatever its function. Thus, only [73] is grammatical, not [74]:

Functioning as a head verb, behaving like an auxiliary:
[73a] Is Kubla extravagant?
[73b] Kubla isn't extravagant.

*****Functioning as a head verb, behaving like a head verb:**
[74a] *****Does Kubla be extravagant?
[74b] *****Kubla doesn't be extravagant.

[75] is the representation of [73a].

[75]

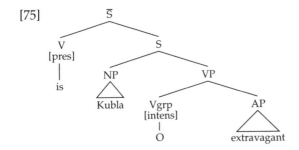

(The removal of *is* and its immediately dominating node leaves a gap in the Vgrp, symbolised by O.)

This completes our review of the finite Vgrp.

Discussion of in-text exercises

1.

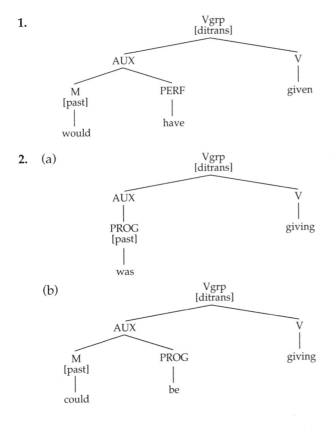

(c)

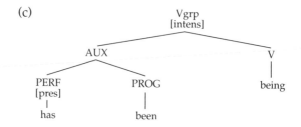

3.

ACTIVE	PASSIVE
[i] forgets/forgot	[ix] is/was forgotten
[ii] will/would forget	[x] will/would be forgotten
[iii] has/had forgotten	[xi] has/had been forgotten
[iv] is/was forgetting	[xii] is/was being forgotten
[v] will/would have forgotten	[xiii] will/would have been forgotten
[vi] will/would be forgetting	[xiv] will/would be being forgotten
[vii] has/had been forgetting	[xv] has/had been being forgotten
[viii] will/would have been forgetting	[xvi] will/would have been being forgotten

4.

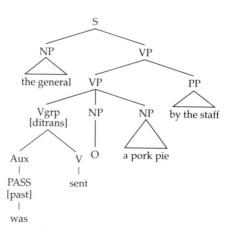

5.   [65]

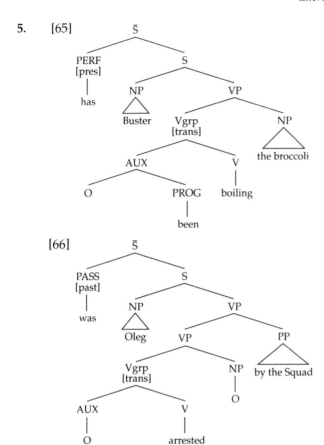

Exercises

1.   Using the modal *can* where necessary (and assuming a third person singular subject), construct the following Verb Groups:

(a)   The past modal passive of *see*.
(b)   The past perfect progressive of *see*.
(c)   The present perfect passive of *fly*.
(d)   The present progressive passive of *dictate*.
(e)   The present modal progressive of *slouch*.
(f)   The past perfect of *hit*.
(g)   The simple past of *sing*.
(h)   The present perfect of *sing*.
(i)   The past modal perfect of *have*.

2.   Using the triangle notation for all NPs, APs, and PPs (but representing the Vgrps in detail), draw phrase-markers for the following sentences:

(a)   The ingenious fellow had hidden the moussaka in his pocket.
(b)   Could this have been her famous purple wig?
(c)   The wildcats are being persecuted by flies.
(d)   Max and Adrian have been having another tedious conversation.
(e)   Did those feet walk upon England's green and pleasant land?
(f)   Was this written by you?

3.   As mentioned in the section on *do*, this verb can function as an auxiliary and as a head verb. Identify the Vgrps in the following sentences, classify the form of the Vgrps, stating whether *do* functions as a head verb and/or auxiliary. Where it functions as a head verb, give the sub-category of *do*.

(a)   The Café Royal will do nicely.
(b)   Have you done these exercises?
(c)   Did you do the broccoli?

Discussion of exercises

1.   (a) could be seen   (b) had been seeing
      (c) has been flown   (d) is being dictated
      (e) can be slouching   (f) had hit
      (g) sang   (h) has sung
      (i) could have had

2.   (a)

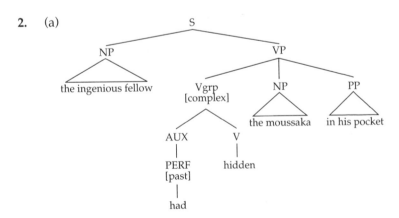

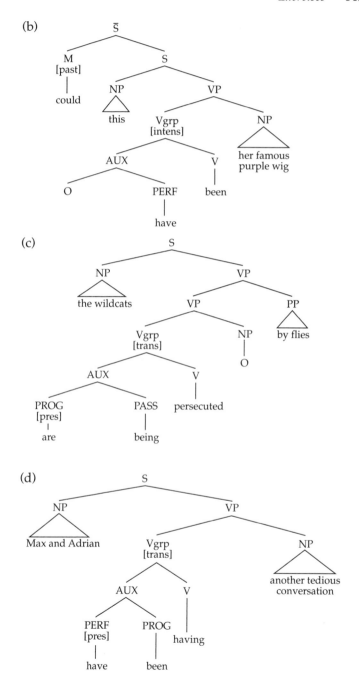

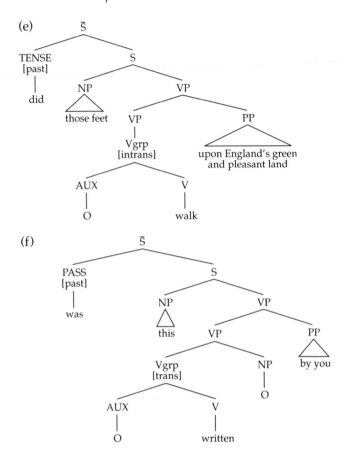

(e)

(f)

3.(a) The Vgrp is *will do*. This is **a present modal Vgrp**, with *do* as its [intransitive] head verb.

(b) *Have … done*. This is **a fronted present perfect Vgrp**, with *do* as its [transitive] head verb.

(c) *Did … do*. This is **a fronted past tense Vgrp**, with *do* functioning as auxiliary carrying the past tense and as the [transitive] head verb.

Further exercises

1.   For each of the italicised forms of the verb *be* in the following sentences, say whether it is an instance of the lexical

(copula) verb, the progressive auxiliary, or the passive auxiliary. Some of them admit of discussion. (10), in particular, is problematic. Can you say why?

(1) His behaviour may *be* peculiar.
(2) It *was* becoming noticeable.
(3) He *was* overheard by Polonius.
(4) The letter *was* found in his pocket.
(5) It *was* unexpected.
(6) Hamlet was *being* offensive.
(7) Ophelia was *being* driven mad.
(8) He had *been* going mad.
(9) He could have *been* her husband.
(10) They *were* very disturbed by the play.
(11) The play *was* unnerving.
(12) The play *was* unnerving the king.
(13) The wine *was* drunk by Hamlet.
(14) Hamlet *was* drunk by midnight.
(15) Yorick had *been* buried for years.
(16) Hamlet *was* buried the next day.

2. Turn to the first page of the Introduction to this book and identify examples of the following finite (tensed) Vgrps in the text on that page.

(a) Two examples of a simple present Vgrp.
(b) A complex (emphatic) present Vgrp.
(c) A present modal Vgrp.
(d) A present passive Vgrp.
(e) Two examples of a present modal passive Vgrp.
(f) A past passive Vgrp.
(g) A present modal perfect Vgrp.

Be warned, there are several non-finite Vgrps on that page. Note also that it is quite usual (though awkward!) to find adverbials placed in among the verbs of the Vgrp.

3. Give phrase-markers for the following sentences using the triangle notation for all NPs, APs, PPs and AdvPs (but not VPs or Vgrps). Set II (but not Set I) includes questions and passives.

Set I

(a)   She may have been watching the play.
(b)   They can't have brought up the children properly.
(c)   They were having a miserable time.
(d)   We don't lend our toothbrushes to anybody.
(e)   The exercises should not have been so easy.
(f)   They don't need drinks today.

Set II

(a)   Could she have put it behind the radiator?
(b)   You will have been seen by the doctor within five minutes.
(c)   Does Max never sit quietly?
(d)   Have all the applicants been interviewed already?
(e)   Shouldn't the equipment be being loaded now?
(f)   They will be drunk soon. (ambiguous)

4.   On page 126 I said that *dare* was 'less clearly' an auxiliary
      verb. There is considerable dialectal variation in this. In the
      light of the discussion of the differences between auxiliary
      and lexical verbs, consider how you yourself use *dare* and on
      the basis of that decide whether (or to what extent) *dare* is an
      auxiliary verb in your dialect.

Chapter 7

More on Noun Phrases

From the preceding chapters you will have gained a broad idea of how major phrases (NP, VP, Vgrp, AP, PP, and AdvP) are structured into sentences. The basic VP itself was shown to consist of a Vgrp complemented by NPs, APs, and PPs. Of these, only the internal structure of the Vgrp has been examined in any detail. In this chapter, I look in more detail at the internal structure of NP and the elements to be found within NP.

Certain aspects of the structure of NP are difficult to determine; the available tests do not always give clear results. I shall adopt an analysis in which **NP, in the basic case, has just two immediate constituents: DET (determiner) and NOM (nominal).** Here are two examples:

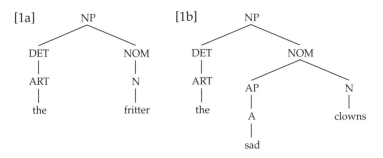

DET will always be simple, consisting of just one constituent or, as we shall see, nothing at all. Note that **DET *always* has NOM as its sister.**

NOM represents a level of NP-structure intermediate between the phrasal (NP) level and the lexical (N) level. NOM is the (intermediate) head of NP, and N is the head of NOM. Hence N is the ultimate head of NP. As [1a–b] show, NOM can be simple or complex. All modifiers of the head noun will fall under the NOM node.

I will start with those elements that can come under the DET node.

Determiners

These are a fixed set of 'grammatical' words which give information relating to definiteness and indefiniteness (roughly, whether the thing referred to by the NP is familiar to both speaker and hearer or not) and information about quantity and proportion.

The basic determiners are the ARTICLES (ART): the definite article (*the*) and the indefinite article (*a*). The articles are 'basic' in the sense that they provide a touchstone as to what counts as a determiner: **any expression that occupies the same position in NP structure as an article counts as a determiner.** How are you supposed to know whether an expression is occupying the same (determiner) position as an article? Well, if an expression can appear in sequence with an article (in other words, if an expression can 'co-occur' with an article) in an NP, then that expression must be analysed as occupying a different position and so cannot be the determiner.

There is a small set of words which seem to perform the same function as the articles and which cannot appear in sequence with them within an NP. These are therefore determiners themselves. They include:

DEMONSTRATIVES (DEM): *this, that, these, those*
Certain QUANTIFIERS (Q): *some, any, no, each, every, either, neither*
POSSESSIVES (POSS): *my, your, its, her, his, our, their, John's*

In addition, there are two rather odd quantifier expressions, *a few*, and *a little*, which I shall analyse as simple determiners without further analysis (using the triangle notation). I shall mention these again later.

[2], [3], and [4] are the phrase-marker representations of *those trampolines, some mistake,* and *my address*.

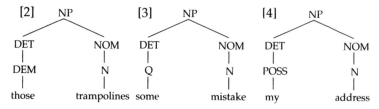

The determiner position is not always filled. Consider the subject NPs in the following sentences:

[5a] *Essays* should be typed.
[5b] *Smoke* gets in your eyes.

Although these italicised NPs contain just one word, they should still be analysed as having a DET + NOM structure, as in [6]:

[6]

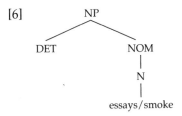

The reason for this 'unfilled determiner' analysis is this. In the first place both **these NPs** *could* **take a determiner** (*the smoke, the essays*). We need to allow for this possibility by making a determiner slot available, as in [6]. Furthermore, the unfilled determiner in these NPs has an affect on their interpretation. **An unfilled determiner gives the NP an indefinite and more general interpretation**. The subject of [5b], for example, is indefinite and more general than the definite NP *the smoke*. It is also more general than the indefinite NP *some smoke*.

Which head nouns allow for an unfilled determiner? The two types of noun are illustrated in [5a–b]: **plural count nouns** (as in [5a]) and **non-count (mass) nouns** (as in [5b]).

Not all single-word NPs merit this unfilled DET + NOM analysis, however. The two types of NP that do *not* are: **NPs consisting of just a pronoun** and **NPs consisting of a proper noun** (a name). An NP consisting of a proper noun like *Max* is not analysed as having an unfilled determiner position because proper nouns do not normally accept determiners anyway. Furthermore, lack of a determiner with a proper noun does not indicate indefiniteness or generality. On the contrary, proper nouns do not normally take determiners precisely because they are inherently definite. Pronouns, too, are inherently definite (e.g. *she, we, they, them, these*) or indefinite (*some, any, several*), quite independently of any determiner. We anyway saw, in Chapter 3, that the function of pronouns is to replace NPs as a whole, including DET. This is why pronouns do not accept a (further) determiner (cf. **the they, *some he*). These two types of NP should be assigned the following non-branching analyses:

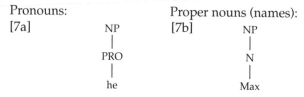

Pronouns:
[7a]

NP
|
PRO
|
he

Proper nouns (names):
[7b]

NP
|
N
|
Max

I have mentioned that no determiner can co-occur in sequence with any other determiner within an NP (i.e. within each NP, there can be only one determiner). Consider now the NP in [8]:

[8]   The book's colour.

This NP might appear to be an exception to this in containing an article (*the*) followed by a possessive (*book's*). Articles and possessives have both been categorised as determiners. It is not an exception, however. Can you see why it isn't and, if so, can you suggest an analysis for [8]?

You may have noticed that *John's* was listed among the possessive determiners. As you know, *John*, being a proper noun, counts not only as a noun but also as a full NP in its own right. So it appears that **a possessive determiner can consist either of a possessive pronoun (*my, your*, etc.) or a full NP + -s. This is called the possessive, or** GENITIVE, **-s.** The sequence *the + book + 's* in [8] is not a sequence of two determiners (article followed by possessive), since the article is actually contained inside a possessive determiner that consists of an NP (*the book*) + genitive *-s*. The correct analysis of [8], then, is [9]:

[9]

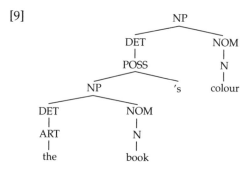

NP
DET   NOM
| |
POSS   N
| |
NP   's   colour
DET   NOM
| |
ART   N
| |
the   book

There is nothing to prevent the NP within such possessive determiners displaying all the structure that other NPs do - including the possibility of being determined by yet another possessive NP, as in [10] and [11]:

[10] Hieronimo's brother's behaviour.
[11] Hieronimo's brother's employer's behaviour.

In principle, there is no limit to the number of times this can be done. Draw the phrase-marker for [10] (given as **Discussion 1** on page 173).

Pre-determiners

Consider now the words *all*, *both*, and *half*. These resemble the determiners we have looked at. However, because they co-occur with and precede determiners, as in [12]–[14]:

[12] all the men
[13] both those trampolines
[14] half Jim's money

they cannot be categorised as determiners themselves. Instead, they are categorised as PRE-DETERMINERS (PRE-DET). Expressions like *double*, *treble* and so forth are also pre-determiners (cf. *double that amount*).

In deciding how pre-determiners fit into the structure of NPs, we must decide what they (pre-)determine. Give this a thought. Notice the following: within the NP *all the men*, there is a sequence that looks very much like a familiar constituent, namely *the men*. Furthermore, within *all the men*, the sequence *the men* can be replaced by a pronoun, as in *all those* or *all them*. What, then, would you suggest as a likely analysis of *all the men*?

The points just made suggest that *all*, as a pre-determiner, determines an NP consisting of *the* (DET) + *men* (NOM). So a pre-determiner should be represented as the sister of an NP within the overall NP:

[15]

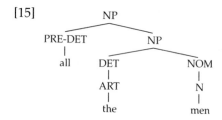

Now consider [16] and [17]:

[16] all men   [17] both trampolines.

Although they don't precede determiners in these NPs, *all* and *both* are still analysed as pre-determiners here. The determiner position itself is unfilled. The proposal that there is an unfilled determiner in [16], with *all*, is perhaps more plausible than in [17] with *both*. *All men* (*all DET men*) is both more indefinite and more general than *all the men*. However, *both the men* and *both men* differ neither in definiteness nor generality. Nevertheless, I shall continue to analyse *both* in [17] as a pre-determiner since, as [13] shows, it can co-occur with, and precede, the article.

The majority of determiners and all the pre-determiners are capable of functioning rather like pronouns:

[18] I've always wanted *those*.
[19] *Some* fell on stony ground.
[20] *John's* are turning blue.
[21] *All* is ruined.

I say 'rather like' pronouns because they differ from true pronouns in ways I discuss at the end of the chapter.

Among the determiners that cannot function as pronouns, there are some that correspond to forms that can. For example, the quantifier *no* cannot function as a pronoun (**I want no*), but corresponds to *none*, which can (*I want none*). And with the possessives, we find the following alternations:

DETERMINER:	my	your	her	our	their
PRONOUN:	mine	yours	hers	ours	theirs

Its cannot function as a pronoun; *his* can function as either determiner or pronoun.

It is predictable that pre-determiners, which pre-determine full NPs, should be able to co-occur with pronouns. Draw the phrase-marker of the subject NP in *All mine are at the cleaners* (given as **Discussion 2** on page 174).

Now review these sections on determiners and pre-determiners before tackling the following exercise. The phrases in [22a] and [23a]

[22a] Both the man's eyes   [23a] Both the men's behaviour

look much the same when considered simply as strings of words, but a little thought shows that they must differ in hierarchical structure. Give the different phrase-markers. (Don't forget that possessive NPs have all the structural possibilities that other NPs do.)

We want the representation of the hierarchical structure to reflect the fact that the function of *both* in [22a] extends over the whole of the rest of the phrase (i.e. *the man's eyes*); that it is prede-termining a constituent that has *eyes* as its head. [22a], after all, means 'both eyes of the man', not '*the eyes of both the man'. The function of *both* in [23a], on the other hand, extends only over *the men* (with *men* as its head); it has no function in respect of *behaviour* at all. [23a] means 'the behaviour of both the men', not *'both behaviour of the men'. This distinction is reflected in the difference between [22b] and [23b]:

[22b]

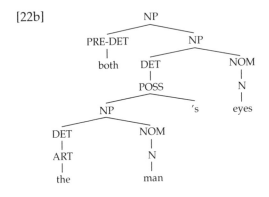

[23b]

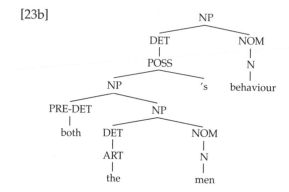

Notice that in [22b] *both* has the NP *the man's eyes* as its sister constituent. In [23b], it has *the men* as its sister constituent.

In distinguishing these examples, I introduced the idea of **the function of a constituent extending over a sequence of words. This phenomenon is more commonly referred to as SCOPE.** In these examples, we can say that the scope of *both* differs: in [22a/b] the scope of *both* is *the man's eyes*; in [23a/b] the scope of *both* is just *the men*. *Eyes* is said to be included in the scope of *both* in [22a/b], while *behaviour* is excluded from the scope of *both* in [23a/b].

This concludes our brief survey of determiners and predeterminers. Several expressions which resemble determiners have not been dealt with yet, for example *much, many, few,* and *little*. For reasons to be explained immediately, I treat these as QUANTIFYING ADJECTIVES and include them under the NOM node along with pre-modifying adjectives.

Pre-modifiers in NOM

Adjective phrases (APs) are the commonest pre-modifiers of the noun within the NOM constituent. These were introduced in Chapter 3. The position of pre-modifying APs in NP is illustrated in [1b] at the beginning of the chapter. Here I shall mention other possible pre-modifiers before discussing the structure of NOMs in which there are several pre-modifiers.

Quantifying adjectives

As mentioned, I include among the pre-modifiers in NOM the quantifying adjectives (QA) *much, many, few* and *little*. These items share important features with adjectives:

(i) Like adjectives, they co-occur with and follow determiners (*those many books, the little butter that I have, some few successes*) including an unfilled determiner: *many books* (= DET *many books*), *much garlic* (= DET *much garlic*).

(ii) Like adjectives, they may occur in the VP, functioning as subject-predicatives:

[24] His mistakes were $\left\{ \begin{array}{l} \text{many.} \\ \text{few.} \end{array} \right.$

[25] It wasn't much.
[26] It was little enough.

(iii) Like adjectives they are gradable: *very many books, too much garlic, so few ideas, very little tact*, where they are modified by DEG. The comparative and superlative forms of *many* and *much* are *more* and *most*; of *little, less* and *least*; of *few, fewer* and *fewest*. Notice that *more* in *more ferocious curries* is ambiguous. It could be either the comparative form of *many*, the quantifying adjective ('more curries that are ferocious') or it could be the comparative degree adverb mentioned in Chapter 3, modifying *ferocious*. This makes a difference to the constituent analysis (see Chapter 2, Exercise 3).

NUMERALS (the cardinal numerals *one, two, three* ..., and the ordinal numerals *first, second, third* ...) should be treated as quantifying adjectives within NOM, since they follow DET, including unfilled DET.

Quantifying adjectives are head of AP. APs with QAs as head always precede other APs in NOM. Here are phrase-markers for *very many mistakes* and *the one mistake*:

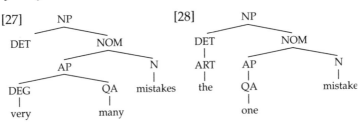

That many pages looks as though it might have the same structure as *those many pages*. It is different, though. Suggest contrasting structures for (a) *that many pages* and (b) *those many pages*. For the former, it might help to note the AP in *He was that high*. **Discussion 3 on page 174.**

Participle phrases (PartP)

The non-finite forms of verbs referred to in Chapter 6 as the progressive, perfect, and passive participles (V-part, for short) may appear as pre-modifiers within NOM:

PROGRESSIVE	PERFECT/PASSIVE
[29a] the leering manager	[30a] a faded dream
[29b] the sleeping guard	[30b] the departed nymphs
	[30c] sliced cake
	[30d] a forgotten valley

In this position, the perfect and passive participles can only be distinguished by appealing to the meaning. [30a and b] are perfect, referring to a dream that *has* faded and nymphs who *have* departed; [c] and [d], on the other hand, are passive, referring to cake that has *been* sliced and a valley that has *been* forgott*en*.

Since these forms are verbal rather than adjectival, they are not gradable: *the very leering manager, *rather sliced cake, *the slightly sleeping guard.* They may, however, be modified by general adverbs, as in *the rapidly congealing gravy.* Draw the phrase-marker for this NP (given as **Discussion 4 on page 174**).

Certain true adjectives look very much like verb participles: *charming, pleasing, (un)interested, relieved, surprising, unexpected.* However, since they are gradable, they are easily distinguished from participles: *rather pleasing, very interested.* Some of these, for example *unexpected*, do not even correspond to any known English verb anyway (cf. **unexpect*). As we saw in Further Exercise 1 in Chapter 6, the distinction between true adjectives and verb participles is sometimes blurred. For example, (10) in that exercise, *They were very disturbed by the play*, looks analysable as passive monotransitive. However, the presence of *very* is not consistent with that analysis (cf. *The play very disturbed them*). *Very* here suggests we are dealing with an AP complementing the (intensive) copula *be*.

Nouns

Nouns themselves may act as pre-modifiers of head nouns, as in *chess piece*, *roof maintenance*, and *computer game*. The relationship between a head noun and a pre-modifying noun is much closer than that between a head and any other pre-modifier. **The combination of modifier noun and head noun is referred to as a COMPOUND NOUN and is not treated as a phrasal constituent at all, but as a compound WORD.** Notice, for example, that in a sequence of modifiers that includes a noun modifier, it is the noun modifier that must appear last – it cannot be separated from the head noun.

[31] some expensive roof maintenance
[32] *some roof expensive maintenance

The compound noun *roof-maintenance* should be dominated by N as in [33]:

[33]

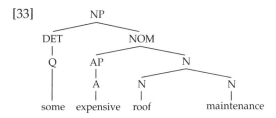

A complication arises from the fact that noun modifiers can themselves be modified. Consider [34]:

[34] Some Japanese print collectors.

You will notice that it is ambiguous. On one interpretation it means 'Japanese collectors of prints'. Draw the phrase-marker for that interpretation (given as [39] below).

On the interpretation just given, *Japanese* modifies the compound noun *print collectors*. On the other interpretation, *Japanese* modifies just *prints*, meaning 'collectors of Japanese prints'. On this interpretation, we have a constituent *Japanese print* modifying the head noun and the question arises what category it should be assigned to.

Since it is centred on a noun and has modification, it might seem that it should be assigned to NP or NOM. However, it displays few of the structural possibilities displayed by either NPs or NOMs. It cannot be plural, nor can it take determiners or pre-determiners:

[35] *Some [Japanese prints] collectors.
[36] *Some [those Japanese print] collectors.

It is also restricted in the kind of pre-modifiers it accepts. While *Japanese* (or *rare*) is fine as a modifier, I find that [37]

[37] Some beautiful print collectors.

is better interpreted as 'beautiful collectors of prints' and not as 'collectors of beautiful prints'; that is, for me at least, *print*, when acting as a pre-modifier itself, does not accept *beautiful* as a modifier. Finally, the modifying noun does not itself accept post-modification:

[38] *Some [Japanese print after Kunisada] collectors.

In view of all this, I shall categorise modifying nouns as N even when they are themselves pre-modified. Here, then, are the phrase-markers for the two interpretations of [34].

[39]

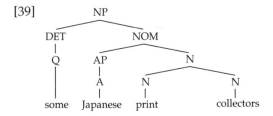

[40]

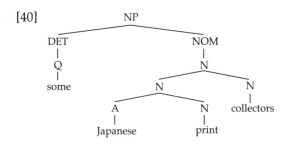

More on the structure of NOM

Before considering the structure of pre-modifiers in NOM, draw the phrase-marker for the NP in [41].

[41] All those hairy ape men

[42]

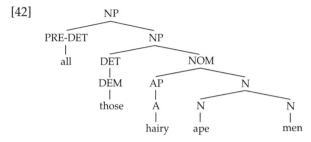

The claim made by this phrase-marker is that *all* pre-determines *those hairy ape men*, that *those* determines *hairy ape men*, that *hairy* modifies *ape men*, and that *ape* modifies *men*. This kind of configuration is called a NESTING STRUCTURE (as it were, *men* is nested in *ape men*, *ape men* is nested in *hairy ape men* and so on.) Given the distinction between pre-determiners, determiners, adjectival modifiers, and noun modifiers made in the preceding sections, the structure of [41] must be as represented in [42].

What about when we have a sequence of more than one AP within NOM? Consider [43a–b]:

[43a] A red car.   [43b] A new red car.

Before deciding how [43b] should be represented, give a phrase-marker for [43a].

The phrase-marker for [43a] will be exactly the same as that for *the sad clowns*, [1b] at the beginning of the chapter. So [*red car*] is a NOM in [43a]. And there is no reason to suppose that [*red car*] is not a NOM in [43b] as well. *New* is modifying *red car* considered as a syntactic unit. Furthermore, the NP in [43b] is itself analysable into DET plus NOM. You now have all the information to enable you to draw the phrase-marker for [43b].

The resulting phrase-marker should display a similar sort of nesting displayed by [42]. The difference is that we have two NOMs.

[44]

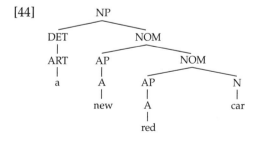

NOM is a recursive category. In other words, NOM can have NOM as one of its constituents. In fact, **each modifier must be dominated by a NOM.**

Now give the phrase-markers for the following NPs. (**Discussion 5**, page 175.)

[45] Some large greasy uneaten fritters.
[46] Those two very charming atomic scientists.

In a later chapter (Ch. 9), I refine this analysis. If you are interested in finding out now why it needs refining, see the Appendix at the end of this chapter.

Post-modifiers

In this section I look at just two of the categories that follow the head noun within NOM: Prepositional Phrases and certain types of Adjective Phrase.

Prepositional Phrases

In the NP *an expedition to the pub*, the head N is *expedition* and it is modified by the PP *to the pub*. In this case, we have a postmodifying (PP) sister to the noun, within NOM. As usual, the PP itself consists of P and NP. So:

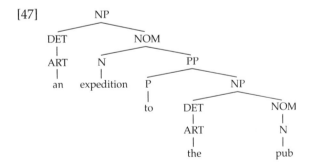

Just as *expedition* can be modified by a PP, so can *pub*. For example: *an expedition to the pub in the village*.

[48]

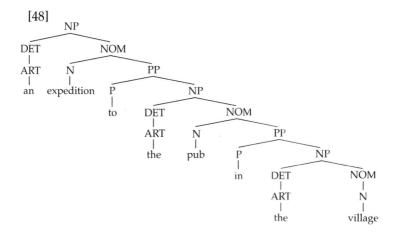

At first glance, [49] might appear to have the same structure.

[49]   An expedition to the pub for more cherry brandy.

However, unlike *the pub in the village* in [48], *the pub for more cherry brandy* does not form a constituent. Decide on the function of *for more cherry brandy*. Having done that, can you suggest an appropriate analysis for [49]? Use the triangle notation for each of the PPs.

It is clear that *for more cherry brandy* modifies a constituent that has *expedition* as its head (it's an expedition for more cherry brandy). So, *for more cherry brandy* must modify *expedition to the pub*. Now, *expedition to the pub* is a NOM and there is no reason why we should not take *expedition to the pub for more cherry brandy* as a NOM as well. [50], then, is an appropriate analysis.

[50]

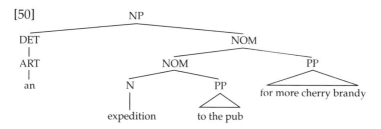

A complete analysis of this NP would require the structure of the PPs to be fully represented. I have summarised the structure as in [50] to bring out the parallelism with the APs in [44]. This arrangement of (post-modifying) PPs mirrors the arrangement of (pre-modifying) APs in [44]. Again, there are as many NOMS as there are modifiers of the head noun.

You may remember the NP *an agreement between workers on overtime* from a previous exercise. This is ambiguous, depending on whether *on overtime* modifies [*agreement (between workers)*] – 'an overtime agreement' – or just *workers* – 'workers who are on overtime'. Decide on the most likely function of the italicised PP in each of the following NPs. Is it (i) modifying a NOM consisting of the head N plus PP (as in [50]), or is it (ii) modifying the N within a PP (as in [48])? Only one of them could be analysed either way, making very little difference to the overall sense. Which is it? (**Discussion 6**, page 175.)

[51] Those observations on alchemy *by Newton*.
[52] An interpretation of that sentence *in Proust's novel*.
[53] Marlow's activities as a spy *on the continent*.
[54] A book of quotations *from Shakespeare*.
[55] A book of quotations *from Oxford University Press*.

All the NPs considered so far have included just pre-modifiers or just post-modifiers. **What happens when NOM includes both a pre-modifying AP and a post-modifying PP?** To repeat, there must be as many NOMs as there are modifiers. So, with a pre-modifier and a post-modifier, there are going to be two NOMs. There are two possibilities, then:

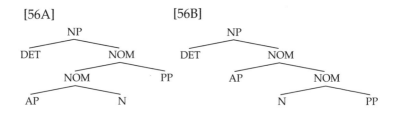

In the case of some NPs, it does not matter much which analysis we give (examples are given later). For others it does matter, and deciding which analysis is appropriate involves attending carefully to the meaning in each case. In each of the following it does matter. Try to decide which analysis is appropriate.

[57] The nuclear scientist from Germany.
[58] The bearded writer of many detective stories.
[59] An anonymous applicant for the job.
[60] Structural engineers in disgrace.
[61] The personal assistant in the hat.
[62] Their secret visits to the larder.
[63] Larry's neat summary of the argument.

Analysing [57] as in [56B] – *[nuclear][scientist from Germany]* –
would be incorrect. A nuclear scientist is a kind (or category) of
scientist. Since there *is* such a category, it is appropriate there
should be a linguistic expression to denote it. So [*nuclear scientist*]
is a constituent. In this example, the distinction between *nuclear*
and *from Germany*, and the closer relation between *nuclear* and
scientist, can be brought out clearly by noting that, while *The
[nuclear scientist] IS from Germany* is quite natural, *The [scientist
from Germany] IS nuclear* is bizarre. Assuming that the PP *from
Germany* means what the AP *German* means, the same bizarre
effect is achieved by the ordering *A nuclear German scientist*, in
which *nuclear* is again separated from the element with which it
seeks to form a constituent. Compare *A German nuclear scientist*,
which is fine. All this indicates that analysis [56A] is indicated for
[57].

Similar considerations suggest analysis [56A] for [60] and [61].
By contrast, analysis [56B] is required for [58], [59], [62], and [63].

As regards [63], for example, note the connection between that
NP and the sentence [64]:

[63] Larry's neat summary of the argument. (Noun Phrase)
[64] Larry neatly summarised the argument. (Sentence)

Give the phrase-marker for the sentence.

The argument is the direct object of the Vgrp *summarised*. As a
complement of the verb, it connects more tightly with the Vgrp
than does *neatly*, which is a VP-adverbial. It is reasonable to
expect this difference between *the argument* and *neatly* in their
relation to *summarised* in the sentence [64] to be reflected in the
Noun Phrase. [63], after all, is sentence [64] recast in the form of a
Noun Phrase:

[63]

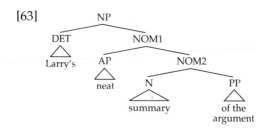

[64]

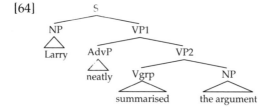

The overall structure is the same in the NP and the S; all that has changed are the categories. Notice that the NOMs in the NP match the VPs in the S. The same goes for the NPs in [58], [59], and [62], as you may check for yourself. The Appendix at the end of the chapter discusses a refinement suggested by this parallelism between S and NP.

Now compare the NPs in [57]–[63] above – in all of which the choice between the analyses (A) and (B) clearly matters – with the following NPs:

[65] The unknown scientist from Germany.
[66] The new railings in the park.
[67] That clever student in the hat.

With each of these, either analysis is possible. The NOM in [65], for example, could be analysed as (A) [[*unknown scientist*] [*from Germany*]] or (B) [[*unknown*] [*scientist from Germany*]]. However, the analysis which associates the more permanent and/or intrinsic property more closely with the head noun will generally seem slightly more natural. Thus the (A) analysis seems marginally more natural for [67].

The following NP includes three modifiers: *that clever student of maths in the hat*. Bearing in mind that there will be as many NOMs as there are modifiers, and that *student of maths* corresponds to the VP constituent [*studies maths*], give a COMPLETE phrase-marker for that NP. (**Discussion 7**, page 175.)

Adjective Phrases

A few adjectives (including *present*, *absent*, *responsible*, *visible*) may pre-modify or post-modify the head noun in NOM. To a greater or lesser extent, a difference in meaning is associated with the difference of position:

[68a] the present members	[68b] the members present
[69a] the responsible men	[69b] the men responsible
[70a] the visible stars	[70b] the stars visible

Post-modifying APs occupy the same position in the structure of NOM as post-modifying PPs.

Apart from these particular adjectives, there is a circumstance in which *any* AP must post-modify the head noun within NOM. This is when the AP itself contains material following the adjective head. For example:

[71] Responsible for the sauces.	[72] Happy in his job.
[73] Nervous of exams.	[74] Devoid of hope.

The constituent that follows the A in AP (a PP in all these examples) is referred to as the COMPLEMENT OF THE ADJECTIVE. So, **when a modifying AP includes a complement, it always post-modifies**:

[75]   The chef responsible for the sauces.
      (*The responsible for the sauces chef.)
[76]   A stuntman happy in his job.
      (*A happy in his job stuntman.)

[77]

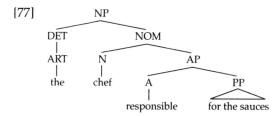

Modification of pronouns

I have said that pronouns replace full NPs. It is rather awkward, therefore, to find pronouns combining with an AP or PP *within* the structure of an NP.

[78a] Something surprising.   [79a] Someone in the crowd.
[78b] Anyone intelligent.   [79b] No-one from the
                                   slaughterhouse.

In the case of indefinite pronouns such as *something/one, any-thing/one, nothing/no-one* what has happened is that, historically, a determiner (*some, any, no*) and a head noun (*thing/one*) have coalesced into a single word (*some surprising thing > something surprising, any intelligent one > anyone intelligent*). The fact that such pronouns can only be post-modified (not pre-modified, as in **intelligent anyone*) is almost certainly connected with this historical fact. It means that we must allow for phrase-marker representations like [80a–b].

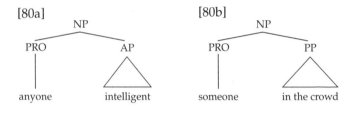

As [81]–[82] show, however, post-modification (particularly by a PP with *of* as head) is not restricted to such indefinite pronouns:

[81a] Some of the animals.   [81b] Those in the hold.

[82] $\left\{ \begin{array}{l} \text{All} \\ \text{Both} \\ \text{Half} \end{array} \right\}$ of the bottles.

Notice that all these pronouns are also determiners ([81]) or pre-determiners ([82]). If a pronoun cannot also function as a determiner or pre-determiner, it cannot be post-modified. (**They from the factory, *He of the men*). Notice also that *you at the back* and *we from the factory* are possible. This seems connected with the possibility of, e.g. *you men* and *we doctors*, in which *you* and *we* seem to be functioning as determiners (compare **they men, *he doctor*). The only determiner/pronouns that cannot be post-modified are the possessives: **His of the books, *John's of the suits*).

A possible analysis of these latter NPs would be one in which the 'pronoun' is in fact analysed *as* a determiner, as for example in [83]:

[83]

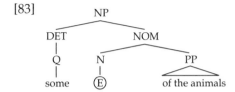

This analysis effectively claims that *some*, for example, only *appears* to have changed into the pronoun head of the NP because the real head noun (*animals*, perhaps) has been ellipted.

I shall not adopt **the elliptical head analysis** [83] for [81]–[82] because the simpler analysis in [80] is anyway available, and necessary for the NPs in [78]–[79]. On the other hand, given our analysis of numerals as QAs, an elliptical head analysis does seem indicated for:

[84] The two in the dungeons.

Give the phrase-marker. (**Discussion 8**, page 176.)

There are many facets of the structure of NPs which this chapter has not engaged with. Some of these will be dealt with in the chapters that follow. Furthermore, several problems have been skated over. You can get an inkling of what these might be by looking closely at NPs in any piece of writing and seeing to what extent the analyses proposed here can handle them satisfactorily. An important refinement to the analysis, which you and/or your tutor may want to incorporate, is discussed in the Appendix section at the end of this chapter.

Discussion of in-text exercises

1.

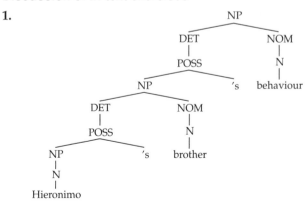

2.

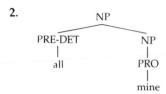

3.   As *He was that/this high* shows, *that* (and *this*) can function as
a **demonstrative degree adverb**. (Q: *How many pages?* A:
Very/that many pages.) In *that many pages*, *that* cannot be functioning as a determiner because it is singular and would
need to determine a NOM with a singular N as head; but
pages is plural. So *that many* is a Quantifying Adjective
Phrase with a demonstrative DEG. Compare its analysis
with that of *those many pages*.

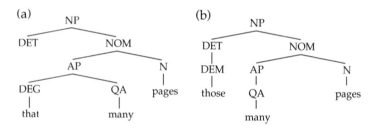

A slight implausibility in the analysis of (a) – with the
unfilled DET – is that, when *many* is modified by *that*, the
NP as a whole does not seem indefinite. Furthermore, the
determiner position *must* remain unfilled (compare *the very
many pages* with **the that many pages*). This might lead us to
question whether there really is an unfilled determiner in
the (a) phrase.

4.

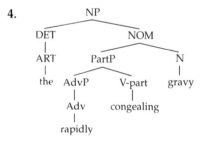

5.

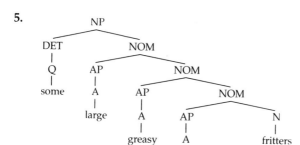

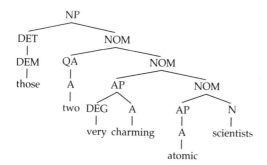

6. [51] Those [[observations on alchemy] [by Newton]].

[52] An [[interpretation] [of that sentence in Proust's novel]].

[53] Marlow's [[activities as a spy] [on the continent]].

Marlow's [[activities] [as a spy on the continent]].

(Both seem possible, and with little difference.)

[54] A [[book] [of quotations from Shakespeare]].

[55] A [[book of quotations] [from Oxford University Press]].

7. Of all the modifiers, it is *of maths* that relates most closely to the head N *student*, for the reason given. And since *clever* denotes a more permanent, inherent property than *in a hat*, I suggest:

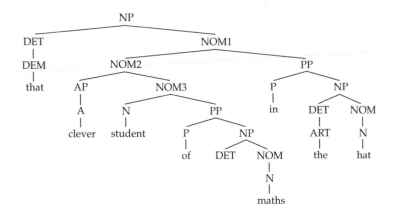

8. Numerals such as *two* have been analysed as quantifying APs, not as pronouns or determiners. This means that *two* cannot be regarded as the (pronominal) head of *the two in the dungeon*. And this in turn means that this NP must have an empty head noun.

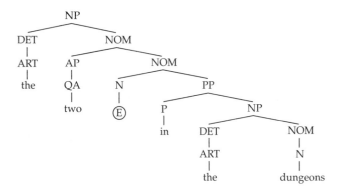

In *I saw two*, the object NP *two* has both an unfilled DET and an unfilled head N.

Exercises

1. Draw complete phrase-markers for the following NPs. 'Complete' means not using any triangle notation. Several of them involve an unfilled determiner. (c) is ambiguous

and should be assigned two phrase-markers. (f) and (g) contain co-ordinations. Remember that the mother and the two sisters of the co-ordinator *and* must all be of the same category. Before attempting the analysis of these, make sure of the level of the co-ordinated constituents. Is it a co-ordination at the lexical, (N), intermediate (NOM), or phrasal (NP) level?

(a) Experts at syntax.
(b) Those ten paintings of his garden by Monet.
(c) More ferocious curries.
(d) The dying king's final message.
(e) All Gulbenkian's contributions to charity.
(f) Some rather off-putting gestures and remarks.
(g) His partner in crime and lifelong cell mate.

2. In discussing determiners, I mentioned two expressions, *a few* and *a little*, proposing that they be treated as phrasal quantifiers functioning as DETERMINERS. Here are the phrase-markers.

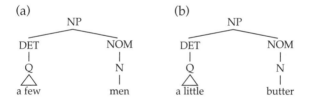

Later, in discussing pre-modifying adjectives, I mentioned the quantifying adjectives *few* and *little*. This exercise is about the difference between them. Can you think of any reason why *few* and *little* in (a) and (b) above should not be treated as quantifying adjectives within NOM? You might approach this question by drawing the phrase-markers that *a few men* and *a little butter* would have if *few/little* were treated as quantifying adjectives.

Discussion of exercises

1.(a)

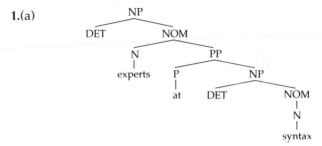

(b)

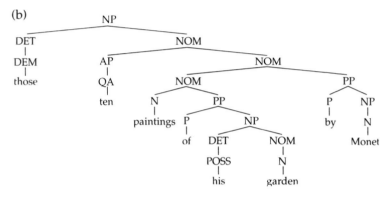

(c)(i)

(ii)

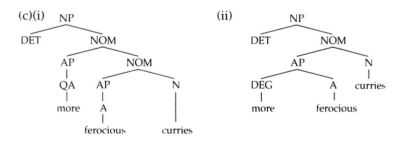

(d)

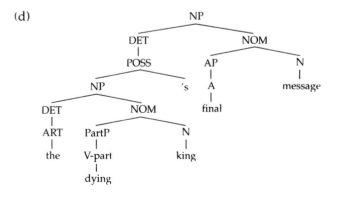

(e)

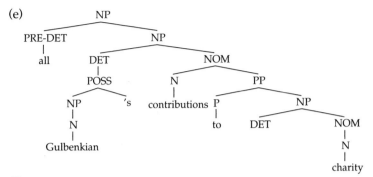

(f)

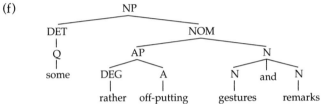

(g)

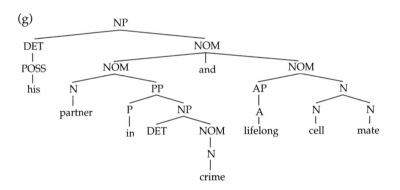

2. Look at phrase-markers (c) and (d), in which *few/little* in *a few men/a little butter* are treated as quantifying adjectives.

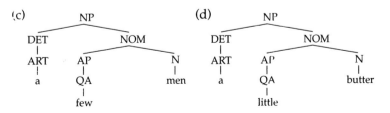

What is wrong with this analysis? Well, notice that the indefinite article is determining a NOM constituent that has *men* as its head in (c) and *butter* as its head in (d). We want to avoid this. The indefinite article *a* can only determine constituents that have a singular count noun as head; it cannot determine plural count nouns (**a men*) or mass nouns (**a butter*). This is why *a few* and *a little* must be treated as constituents, as phrasal determiners.

In *few men* (DET *few men*) and *the few men*, *few* does function as the quantifying adjective, as does *little* in *what little butter I have* and *very little butter* (DET *very little butter*). Since *few* (as QA) only modifies plural nouns, it cannot appear in a NOM determined by *a*. Similarly, since *little* (as QA) only modifies mass nouns, it cannot appear in a NOM determined by *a*.

Finally, notice that in *a little window*, where *little* does modify a count noun within a NOM determined by *a*, *little* is not a quantifying adjective, nor is *a little* a phrasal determiner. This is a third use of *little* – as the ordinary general adjective (meaning the same as 'small'). Note the ambiguity of *a little space*.

Further exercises

1. Draw complete phrase-markers for the following NPs. Some of these NPs might look as if they need the same analysis. However, I would never be so boring as to give two examples exactly the same.

Set I

(a) Melancholy thoughts.
(b) Some very clever chess moves.
(c) The boat's sudden move to the left.
(d) The word on the tip of my tongue.
(e) Some contributions to the fund from unknown sources.
(f) All performers absent from the rehearsal.

Set II

(a) Coffee and oranges.
    (Not ambiguous, but three analyses are possible. If you give only one of these, save ink and give the simplest.)

(b)   All the devil's tricks.
(c)   All the men's clothes. (ambiguous)
(d)   Three stars visible to the naked eye.
(e)   The king of England's short and turbulent reign.
(f)   These well dressed men and women. (ambiguous)

Set III

(a)   The few remaining pieces of kitchen furniture.
(b)   An author and composer of music from Newcastle.
(c)   Some of us at the back.
(d)   These two coins and the three in the pocket of your coat.
(e)   Three tall passengers angry about the altered height of the bulkheads.
(f)   Many of the more successful pancake tossers.

2.   This chapter concludes the survey of the structure of simple sentences. The remaining chapters deal with complex sentences (sentences that contain sentences as constituents). So this is an appropriate point to revise what has been covered thus far on simple sentences. Draw *complete* phrase-markers, then, for the following sentences. Leave yourself plenty of room. Again, several contain co-ordinations; before analysing them, satisfy yourself as to the category of the constituents co-ordinated in them.

(a)   Did the old man's secretary open the post on that particular day?
(b)   Obviously this calls for a thorough examination of the facts.
(c)   An acrobat happy in his job usually makes the circus management happy in theirs.
(d)   Extra hands have been hired for no good reason apparently.
(e)   Bruno and the spy at the embassy may have been the same person.
(f)   The driver of a passing limousine stopped and suavely offered them a welcome lift to the castle.
(g)   Could he be being investigated by the Feds or the Intelligence Agency?
(h)   Aren't any of the students or staff giving up anything for Lent?

(i)   The essays will be marked immediately by the lecturers but they won't be returned until the beginning of the next semester.

Appendix: NOM and the pro-form *one*

Here I introduce a refinement of the analysis provided in this chapter. Your tutor may ask you to adopt this.

Look again at the discussion on pages 169, especially the discussion of example NP [63] and its corresponding sentence [64], repeated here:

[1]   Larry's neat summary of the argument. (NP)
[2]   Larry neatly summarised the argument. (S)

In Chapter 5, we saw that in sentences like [2] there were two VPs, one within the other: VP1 [*neatly summarised the argument*] and VP2 [*summarised the argument*]. I gave evidence for this. This involved the expression *do so*. *Do so* replaces VPs. It *only* replaces VPs (not Vgrps, for example).

[3]   Larry summarised the argument neatly and Bill did so too.

We understand [3] in a way that demands that *do so* be thought of as replacing VP1 (*summarised the argument neatly*). In [4a–b] by contrast, *do so* must be understood as replacing just VP2, [*summarised the argument*]:

[4]   Larry summarised the argument neatly …
        … (a) but Bill did so clumsily.
        … (b) and so did Bill, though clumsily.

It is the ungrammaticality of [5] that shows that *do so* cannot replace just the Vgrp *summarised*:

[5]   *Larry summarised the argument and Bill did so the conclusion.

In the text I drew attention particularly to the parallelism between VP and NOM. For every VP in the S there is a corresponding NOM in the NP. Since *do so* provides a test for VP, you might ask whether there is a corresponding **test for NOM in NP** There is. **It involves the pronoun** *one*. In fact *one(s)* should really be called a pro-NOM, since it only ever replaces the intermediate category NOM (never full NP and never just N). Look:

[6]   Larry's neat summary of the argument and [this *one*], too.
        (*one* = NOM1: *neat summary of the argument*)
[7]   Larry's neat summary of the argument and [Bill's clumsy
        one].
        (*one* = NOM2: *summary of the argument*)
[8]   *Larry's summary of the argument and [Bill's *one* of the
        conclusion].
        (!!*one* = N: *summary*)

Just as *do so* could not replace the Vgrp *summarised* (but only a
VP), so *one* cannot replace just the N *summary* (but only a NOM).

So, *one* provides a test for whether we have a NOM or not. Feel
free to check the NOMs in any of the examples in the text of the
chapter. You will find that wherever there is a NOM, that
sequence of words can be replaced by *one*. So, if everything is
going so swimmingly, why is a refinement needed?

Well, take for example one of the first NPs considered in this
chapter, *the sad clowns*. Draw the phrase-marker. Then check it
against phrase-marker [1b] on page 153. That phrase-marker
only contains one NOM [*sad clowns*]. If that is correct, the *one* test
for NOMs suggests that we should only be able to replace [*sad
clowns*] by *ones*. We can do that:

[9]   Bill hired those sad clowns and you hired these ones.
        (*ones* = *sad clowns*)

However, we can also have:

[10] For heaven's sake, fire the sad clowns and hire some
        happy ones!

Before reading further, think carefully about why this is a problem for the analysis proposed in [1b] in the text and how we
might alter that analysis to make it consistent with the datum in
[10].

In [10], *ones* cannot be understood as replacing the NOM [*sad
clowns*]. If it were, [10] would be demanding that some happy
sad clowns be hired. Even if it is possible for a clown to be both
happy and sad, that is not what [10] means. [10] implies a contrast between happy ones and sad ones. So, in [10] *ones* is replacing just *clowns*. In analysis [1b], though, *clowns* by itself is just a
simple N, not a NOM. Now, we have seen that *one(s)* cannot
replace just simple nouns. If it could, [8] would not have been

ungrammatical. So this suggests that the analysis [1b] on page 153 is wrong. Certainly, *clowns* is a noun – but, because it is replaceable by *ones*, it must also be a NOM as well as an N. So the phrase-marker must look like [11], with an extra NOM (in bold) dominating N.

[11]

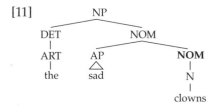

A contrast has emerged. This is the contrast between the NOM *sad clowns* in [11] – which contains an extra, non-branching, NOM node – and the NOM *summary of the argument* in [1] – which does not. In other words, in those two examples, *clowns* is, in its own right, a NOM as well as an N, but *summary* is just an N, not a NOM in its own right. How are you supposed to tell when the extra NOM node is required? Well, you can always test for it by replacement by *one*. However, while that will help you to get things right, it does not in itself *explain* the nature of the contrast. What you really need to know is WHY *one* can replace just *clowns* in *sad clowns* but not just *summary* in *summary of the argument*.

The answer lies in the different ways in which those two modifiers (*sad* and *of the argument*) relate to their respective heads. It comes down to this: *sad* is the modifier of a NOM (**a sister of NOM**), whereas *of the argument* is the modifier of an N (**a sister of N**). Put this way, this should remind you of the distinction, within VP, between **sister of VP (adjunct adverbial)** and **sister of Vgrp (complement)**. The point is that, within the NP, the PP *of the argument* relates to the head N *summary* in exactly the same way as, within the VP, the direct object NP *the argument* relates to the Vgrp *summarise*. They are both functioning as COMPLEMENTS of the head, whether that head is an N or a Vgrp. By contrast, there is no intuitive reason to suppose that *sad* relates to the head N *clowns* as a complement does to a Vgrp. This intuition is borne out by the fact that *the sad ones* is grammatical, which indicates that *sad* is not modifying an N, but a NOM. *Sad* relates to *clowns*, then, much as *neat* relates to *summary (of the argument)*; and this, essentially, is how ADJUNCTS relate to VP. Summarising, **the distinction between**

sister-of-Vgrp and sister-of-VP (which is the distinction between COMPLEMENT and ADJUNCT) is paralleled by the distinction between sister-of-N and sister-of-NOM.

As another example, consider [58] in the chapter, repeated as [12a]:

[12a] The bearded writer of many detective stories.

In this NP, *of many detective stories* relates to *writer* as a complement (i.e. as *many detective stories* relates to *wrote* in the VP *wrote many detective stories*). And, sure enough, **The one of many detective stories* is ungrammatical. *Bearded* is more peripheral in its relation to *writer*. So *of many detective stories* is a modifier of the head N itself (an N-modifier) and *bearded* is NOM-modifier (modifier of the NOM *writer of detective stories*). This predicts that *The bearded one* will be grammatical, which it is. In respect of this example, we have simply confirmed what was established in the chapter. The refinement being presented here concerns not [12a] so much as [12b]:

{12b] The bearded writer.

We have established that *bearded* is a NOM-modifier in [12a]. Clearly, *bearded* has exactly the same relation to *writer* in [12b] as it does in [12a]. So it must be a NOM modifier in [12b] as well. *One* can replace both *writer of many detective stories* in [12a] and just *writer* in [12b]. So [12b] must have the extra NOM node. It must have the same analysis as *the sad clowns* in [11] above.

So, the effect of the analysis proposed in this Appendix is this: the distinction between N-modifier and NOM-modifier is now a linguistically significant distinction (related to that between complement and adjunct) and is to be upheld consistently. **If a modifier can co-occur with the pro-NOM *one*, then it must be a sister of NOM (a 'NOM-modifier').** If a modifier relates to the head N as a NOM-modifier, it must *always* do so – regardless of whether or not there is another modifier present (i.e. regardless of whether the NOM branches or not).

Now that we have a consistent distinction between N-modifiers and NOM-modifiers, we are in a position to explain why some modifiers have to appear in a certain order while others can be ordered quite freely. For example *of geology* and *in hats* have to appear in the order given in [13a]:

[13a] Those students of geology in hats.
[13b] *Those students in hats of geology.

The explanation is that *of geology* relates to *student* as *geology* relates to *studies* in the VP *studies geology*. That's to say, it is a complement. As such, it is a N-modifier. N-modifiers must appear immediately adjacent to the simple N they modify. [13b] is ungrammatical because the N-modifier *of geology* is in a position where it has to modify, not a simple N, but the NOM *students in hats*. *In hats*, on the other hand, is as peripheral as an adjunct. It is a NOM-modifier, and so it tolerates being separated from the head noun by another modifier which, together with the head N, forms a NOM. NOM nodes allow for (create a slot for) the addition of further modifiers of the head N.

Consider now:

[14a] A painter with real talent from Germany.
[14b] A painter from Germany with real talent.

What conclusion can be drawn from the acceptability of both these orders, in the light of what has been said about [13a] and [13b]?

Since *from Germany* can modify *painter with real talent*, as in [14a], it must be a NOM-modifier. Now, *painter with real talent* could consist of N + PP or NOM + PP. But which? Put another way, is *with real talent* a (complement) N-modifier or an (adjunct) NOM-modifier? The fact that it can be separated from the head N – as in [14b], where it is modifying *painter from Germany* (a NOM) – indicates that it is an adjunct NOM-modifier, too. So both modifiers are NOM-modifiers, and this explains why they can occur in either order. This is entirely consistent with the fact that, in both [14a] and [14b], *one* can replace just *painter*.

Look again at the discussion of [51]–[55] in the main text of the chapter. Compare [51] in particular with [15].

[15]   Those observations by Newton.

In the light of the analysis proposed in this Appendix, draw the phrase-marker for [15]. The phrase-marker will be given in due course.

Now try phrase-markers for [16] and [17] (given in due course).

[16] Larry's neat summary.
[17] Larry's summary of the argument.

Now look at the discussion of [65]–[67] in the main text of the chapter. In [65], for example, which I repeat here as [18],

[18] The unknown scientist from Germany.

how many different strings of words can *one* replace in [18]?

In addition to being able to replace (a) *unknown scientist* and (b) *scientist from Germany* with *one*, we can also (c) replace just *scientist* with *one*: (a) *The one from Germany*, (b) *The unknown one*, (c) *The unknown one from Germany*. All three can mean 'The unknown scientist from Germany'. The fact that all three are possible indicates that *unknown* and *from Germany* are both NOM-modifiers and are equally peripheral. That is why, as noted in the main body of the chapter, we can analyse the NP either as [[*unknown scientist*] *from Germany*], as indicated by (a) – or [*unknown* [*scientist from Germany*]], as indicated by (b). Now draw the two possible phrase-markers, making sure both are compatible with (c).

Here are all the phrase-markers asked for above:

[15]

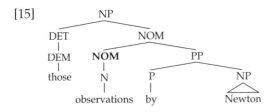

By Newton tolerates being separated from *observations* (as in *Those observations on alchemy by Newton*), so it must be a NOM-modifier. This is confirmed by the grammaticality of *Those ones by Newton*.

[16]

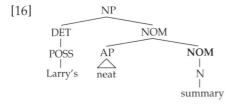

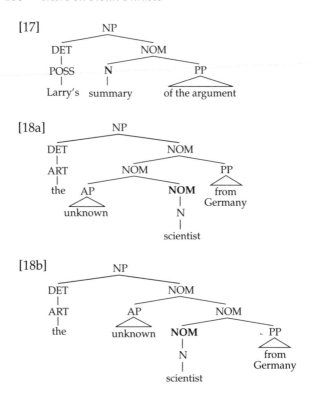

There is a final point to notice about *one*. Remember, it is a pro-NOM. We have seen that, as a NOM, it must, and does, co-occur with DET (cf. *the one*, *that one*). But what about the following NPs?

[19a] One from Poland.   [20a] One (as in *I've just eaten one*).

By contrast with *The one from Poland*, which is definite, [19a] and [20a] are indefinite. This suggests that *one* can be determined by an unfilled DET.

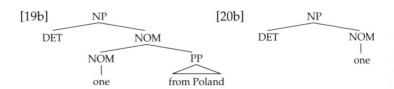

Notice that, in this one case, NOM does not dominate N, but dominates *one* directly. *One* must be immediately dominated by NOM and not by N, because it is a pro-NOM, not a pro-N (not a proNOUN).

Further Exercise

Decide, for each of the following italicised modifiers, whether they are (complement) N-modifiers or (adjunct) NOM-modifiers. Some are ambiguous. In this connection, notice that *A diplomatic appointment* can mean either 'an appointment which was (very) diplomatic' or 'the appointment of a diplomat'. Which of these interpretations does *A diplomatic one* have? Answering that will help you correlate the interpretative distinction with the distinction between N-modifier and NOM-modifier.

(a) Contributions *from unknown sources.*

(b) Contributions *to the fund.*

(c) The destruction *of the building.*

(d) The destruction *of April 1944.*

(e) The applicant *in the waiting room.*

(f) The applicant *for the job.*

(g) An adviser *to royalty.*

(h) A *royal* adviser.

(i) A *nuclear* scientist.

(j) A *charming* scientist.

(k) An *attentive* student.

(l) A *French* student.

(m) A *criminal* lawyer.

(n) A *stellar* observatory.

(o) A *pessimistic* engineer.

(p) A *structural* engineer.

Chapter 8

Sentences within Sentences

You are now familiar with the idea that a constituent may contain constituents of the same category of itself. You know, for example, that an NP may contain further NPs, that a NOM may contain further NOMs, a VP further VPs, and so on. This is called recursion. This and the next two chapters are mainly concerned with the description of sentences that have constituents which themselves have the structure of sentences, i.e. with sentential recursion.

You should not have much difficulty in picking out, from within the structure of the following sentence, a sequence of words that can itself be analysed as a sentence.

[1a] Georgette said she wouldn't burn the fritters.

You can confirm for yourself that the sequence you have identified really can be analysed as a sentence, just as described in previous chapters, by drawing a complete phrase-marker for it. The phrase-marker is given at the end of the chapter: **Discussion 1**, page 209. The sequence is, of course,

[1b] she wouldn't burn the fritters.

[1a] is a COMPLEX sentence: it contains a sentential structure functioning as a constituent. Compare it with the co-ordinate (COMPOUND) sentence [2]:

[2] He hired the acrobats and you hired those clowns.

The two sentential structures in [2] are independent of each other. Neither is a constituent of the other. They are at the same level in the overall structure of [2]. That is why that are described as CO-ORDINATE (with the emphasis on *co-*).

By contrast, the two sentential structures in [1a] are not at the same level of structure and are not independent of each other.

One of the sentential structures (namely [1b]) is included in, and contributes to the structure of, the other (namely [1a]). Stripped down to essentials, this other sentential structure is [*Georgette said S*], where the sentential structure *S* is functioning as direct object of [1a]'s verb (*say*). So, the two sentential structures in [1a] are not co-ordinated. Instead, [1b] is SUBORDINATE (with the emphasis on *sub-*) to [*Georgette said ...*], which must then be described as SUPERORDINATE (emphasis on *super-*) to *S*.

Subordinate sentential structures are traditionally called **subordinate clauses** (less traditionally, 'embedded sentences'). So this chapter is about subordinate clauses. The sentential structures that contain them are called **superordinate clauses**.

Now look at [3], which contains two subordinate clauses:

[3] They believe Georgette said she wouldn't burn the fritters.

As before [*she wouldn't burn the fritters*] is a structure that can be analysed as a sentence, so it is a subordinate clause. Again, it is subordinate to, and contributes to the structure of, [*Georgette said S*]. But now, in [3], [*Georgette said S*] is in turn subordinate to [*They believe S*], where *S* = [*Georgette said* [*she wouldn't burn the fritters*]]. We thus have three clauses here.

Every clause has a verb. So we can identify clauses in terms of their verbs, referring in [3] to the *burn*-clause, the *say*-clause and the *believe*-clause. [3] shows that a clause can simultaneously be SUBordinate to one clause and SUPERordinate to another. In [3] the *say*-clause is subordinate to the *believe*-clause but superordinate to the *burn*-clause. The *burn*-clause is subordinate to both the other clauses – to the *say*-clause directly and, indirectly, to the *believe*-clause.

A superordinate clause that is not subordinate to any other clause is referred to as the MAIN CLAUSE. In [3], then, the main clause is the *believe*-clause. **The verb of the main clause is the** MAIN VERB.

In phrase-markers, the main clause will be the topmost clause. If we want to concentrate just on what clauses a sentence contains and on how those clauses relate to each other in the structure, we can strip away all other details and use the triangle notation for clauses. I shall call any phrase-marker that does just this **an** ABBREVIATED CLAUSAL ANALYSIS **(ACA)**. The ACA of [3] is:

[4a]

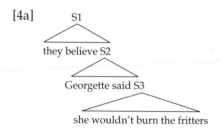

Alternatively, an ACA can take the form of labelled bracketings, as in [4b]:

[4b] $_{S1}$[They believe $_{S2}$[Georgette said $_{S3}$[she wouldn't burn the fritters]$_{S3}$]$_{S2}$]$_{S1}$

The representation in [4a] shows that [3] is a right-branching structure: it branches off regularly *from* the right. Though right-branching is preferred in the structure of English, not all structures are right-branching. To see this, identify the (single) subordinate clause in [5] and the two subordinate clauses in [6]. Which are the main Vgrps in [5] and [6]?

[5]   He reminded the men that he was in command at every opportunity.

[6]   The fact that you received no greetings from Mars doesn't mean that it is uninhabited.

Within the structure of [5], [7] can be identified as subordinate clause, and within the structure of [6], [8a] and [8b] can.

[7]   He was in command.

[8a] You received no greetings from Mars.   [8b] It is uninhabited.

Reminded is the main verb of [5] and *(doesn't) mean* is the main verb of [6].

It is important to note that, in [5], *at every opportunity* has its function in respect of the main verb *reminded*. *At every opportunity*, then, belongs in the main clause: *He reminded the men ... at every opportunity*. It cannot reasonably be considered as part of the subordinate clause, since, even if it is clear what *he was in command at every opportunity* is supposed to mean, that is clearly not part of the meaning of [5].

The abbreviated clausal analysis of [5], then, will be:

[9a]

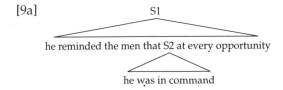

[9b] $_{S1}$[He reminded the men that $_{S2}$[he was in command]$_{S2}$ at every opportunity]$_{S1}$

So [5] is not right-branching. Now try an abbreviated clausal analysis of [6] above.

You may recall the subject-predicate analysis of this sentence from Chapter 2 Exercise 1(f): subject [*the fact that you received no greetings from Mars*], predicate [*doesn't mean that it is uninhabited*]. The first subordinate clause [8a], falls wholly within the main clause subject, while the second, [8b], falls wholly within the main clause predicate. So, although [6], like [3], contains two subordinate clauses, it differs from [3] in that each subordinate clause is subordinated directly to the main clause, independently of the other subordinate clause. As the following analysis shows, [6] is not a regularly right-branching structure either.

[10a]

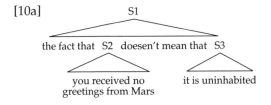

[10b] $_{S1}$[the fact that $_{S2}$[you received no greetings from Mars]$_{S2}$ doesn't mean that $_{S3}$[it is uninhabited]$_{S3}$]$_{S1}$

As noted, the subordinate clauses examined above can be straightforwardly analysed as sentences, exactly as outlined in previous chapters. So, in the rest of the chapter I concentrate, not so much on the internal structure of these clauses, but on how they fit into the structure of, and their functions within, their superordinate clauses.

Complementisers: *that* and *whether*

You will have noticed that the subordinate clauses in [5] and [6] were preceded by *that*. **That is a marker of clausal subordination; it serves to introduce subordinate clauses.** When it functions in this way (rather than as a determiner or pronoun), *that* **is a** COMPLEMENTISER (Comp).

As a complementiser, *that* fills the position occupied by fronted auxiliaries in questions, introduced in Chapter 6. Remember, **the complementiser position is defined as: daughter of S-bar (S̄) and sister of a following S.** The representation of the complementiser and subordinate clause in [5], then, is as in [11a]. This in turn can be further abbreviated as in [11b].

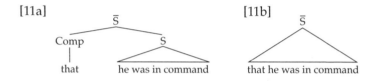

[11a] S̄ — Comp | that — S — he was in command

[11b] S̄ — that he was in command

From now on, I shall assume that **all subordinate clauses are introduced by a complementiser and dominated by S-bar.** We have seen, however, that the complementiser may not always be overtly present. In [5] and [6] it was overt. By contrast, neither of the subordinate clauses in [3] was overtly introduced by a complementiser – though both could have been, as in [12].

[12] They believe *that* Georgette said *that* she wouldn't burn the fritters.

When the complementiser position introducing a subordinate clause is not overtly filled, think of it as having been ellipted. As it were, it *is* there, but not explicitly. There are circumstances in which the complementiser simply cannot be ellipted. In my dialect at least, it cannot be ellipted in the first subordinate clause of [6a], for example – see [13] – but it can in the second – see [14].

[13] *The fact [●[you received no greetings from Mars]] …
[14] … doesn't mean [●[it is uninhabited]].

The subordinate clause within the VP [14] would be fully represented as in [15], with the complementiser position left unfilled.

[15]

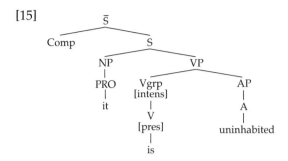

The 'complementiser position' introduced in Chapter 6 has that name, then, because it is the position occupied by the complementiser *that* (overt or not). That position was needed in Chapter 6 for fronted auxiliaries in questions. Interestingly, auxiliary-fronting is possible only in main clauses, never in subordinate clauses. (Put another way, auxiliary-fronting is what is called a 'main-clause phenomenon'.) The fact that **Comp *that* and fronted auxiliaries occupy the same position** suggests an explanation for this: auxiliaries cannot be fronted to a position filled by a complementiser (whether the complementiser is overt or not).

I will refer to clauses which can be introduced by *that* as ***that*-clauses.** Not all subordinate clauses are *that*-clauses, however. **Another expression that can occupy this complementiser position, introducing subordinate clauses, is** *whether.*

[16] Sarah asked [**whether** [those stupid sausages were ready yet]].
[17] Rashid doesn't know [**whether** [his disguise was successful]].
[18] [**Whether** [Rory should be promoted or fired]] was worrying them.
[19] [**Whether** [Jock will go up in that machine]] is doubtful.

The big difference between a *whether*-clause and a *that*-clause is this. In [16] Sarah is reported as *asking* something. So, without actually being used itself to ask a question, [16] does include allusion to a question, and it does so by means of the subordinate clause *[whether [those stupid sausages were ready yet]]*. (If [16] is true, then, Sarah in all probability said 'Are those stupid sausages ready yet?') Much the same goes for [17], where Rashid is reported as not knowing the answer to a question, the question represented by the clause *[whether [his disguise was successful]]*. These subordinate clauses are interrogative in character.

So, in addition to functioning (like *that*) as a marker of clausal subordination, **whether indicates that the subordinate clause is an** INTERROGATIVE CLAUSE. The *yes/no* questions considered in Chapter 6 are interrogative clauses. As MAIN interrogative clauses, they display auxiliary-fronting and are used to ask questions. *Whether*-clauses are SUBORDINATE interrogative clauses, subordinate counterparts to *yes/no* questions. They cannot display auxiliary-fronting to the complementiser position because that position is filled by *whether* (cf. **Sarah asked whether were those stupid sausages ready yet*). Incidentally, notice that the interrogative complementiser can take the form of *if*. It can in [16] and [17], but not in [18] or [19].

In addition to *that*-clauses and interrogative (*whether*-)clauses, **subordinate clauses can be introduced by subordinating conjunctions. These are generally** ADVERBIAL CLAUSES. Before dealing with these, I look at the functions of the clauses dealt with so far.

This would be a good point to try Exercise 1 at the end of the chapter.

The functions of *that*- and *whether*-clauses

I shall consider the following functions:

1. Subject – and extraposed subject.
2. Complement of Vgrp within VP.
3. Complement of A within AP.
4. Complement of N within NP.
5. Complement of P within PP.

Subject – and extraposed subject

Divide the following sentences into subject and predicate:

[20a] That the king was in his counting house disconcerted her.
[21a] That Goneril had a third eye has never been noted by the critics.
[22a] That Rashid's disguise was a success is undeniable.

Your analysis should show that subordinate *that*-clauses are functioning as subject in each case:

SUBJECTS:	PREDICATES:
[20a] that the king was in his counting house	disconcerted her
[21a] that Goneril had a third eye	has not been noted by the critics
[22a] that Rashid's disguise was a success	is undeniable

And in [18] and [19] above we had examples of an interrogative (*whether*-)clause functioning as subject (with *was worrying them* and *is doubtful* functioning as predicates).

Recall from Chapter 2 that **constituents functioning as subjects are always analysed as NPs.** So we shall analyse these subject clauses (otherwise known as 'clausal subjects') as dominated by NP. So, for example, [20a] will be represented as in [23], though I have summarised fairly liberally with triangles.

[23]

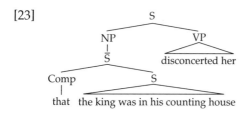

In support of having clausal subjects dominated by NP, notice that they can be replaced by pronouns (*it disconcerted her*, *this has not been noted by the critics*, *that's undeniable*).

Having a clause as subject makes for a very 'heavy' (complex) subject. If [20a]–[22a] seemed at all unnatural to you, you are almost certainly responding to this. In English we generally prefer to defer such complexity to the end of the sentence. So **a characteristic of** CLAUSAL SUBJECTS **is that they can be** EXTRAPOSED **from under the subject NP node to the end of the sentence, leaving behind the empty pronoun** *it*. Here are the extraposed versions of [20a]–[22a]:

[20b] *It* disconcerted her [that the king was in his counting house].

[21b] *It* has not been noted by the critics [that Goneril had a third eye].

[22b] *It* is undeniable [that Rashid's disguise was a success].

Give the extraposed versions of [18] and [19] above (given in due course).

The *it* that takes the place of the subordinate clause in subject position is special: it is quite empty of meaning and does not refer to anything. It simply serves as a 'dummy' subject. This is the *it* of *it is raining*, and is there just to give the verb *rain* a subject, needed in English though not in some other languages, e.g. Italian (*piove: it is raining*). Just as it makes no sense to ask 'What is raining?' (the only possible answer being 'rain'), it makes no sense to ask 'What disconcerted her that the king was in his counting house?' This is called **expletive** IT, to distinguish it from uses of *it* that do refer to things.

I shall represent these extraposed subjects as daughters of the main clause S, as in [24], for example.

[24]

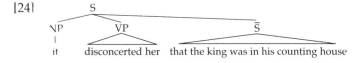

The extraposed versions [18] and [19] are:

[25] It was worrying them whether Rory should be promoted or fired.

[26] It is doubtful whether Jock will go up in that machine.

So, **the extraposed subject construction** has a clausal subject displaced to the end of the sentence and expletive *it* in the normal subject position, dominated directly by NP. But now look at the following:

[27a] It seems [that the recipe involves some dubious ingredients].

[28a] It happens [that dinosaurs are extinct].

With these, if you try putting the subordinate clause ('back'?) into the normal subject position, the result is totally unacceptable:

[27b] *[That the recipe involves some dubious ingredients] seems.

[28b] *[That dinosaurs are extinct] happens.

There is a handful of special verbs – including *seem, appear, transpire,* and *happen* – that cannot have clauses in the normal subject position. This raises the question whether the subordinate clauses in [27a]–[28a] can really be regarded as extraposed subjects. However, since [27a] and [28a] display the expletive *it* associated with the extraposed subject construction, I shall analyse them as such, with an analysis like that in [24]. Since this implies that the subordinate clauses *are* to be regarded as subjects, this group of verbs must be thought of as being [intransitive] in this use.

Notice, by contrast, that in [18]–[22], none of the verbs involved were [intransitive]. Those in [18], [20], and [21] were [transitive] and those in [19] and [22] were [intensive]. With these, extraposition of the clausal subject was OPTIONAL: the subordinate clause could appear either in the normal subject position or extraposed. In connection with our 'special' verbs, then, the generalisation seems to be that extraposition of a clausal subject is OBLIGATORY when the verb is [intransitive].

Now draw phrase-markers for the following sentences, using the triangle notation for all NPs and Vgrps. **Discussions 2 and 3**, page 209.

[29] That the squid sauce had been a mistake soon became clear.

[30] It is not my fault Max crushed your monocle.

Complement of Vgrp within VP

Look again at [21a] above. Did you notice that [21a] is a passive sentence? Give the corresponding active sentence.

The subordinate clause in [21a] is functioning as the subject of a passive Vgrp. We know that it is the object of an active Vgrp that becomes subject when the Vgrp is passivised. So the active counterpart of [21a] is:

[31] The critics have never noted [(that) Goneral had a third eye].

In [31] we have a *that*-**clause functioning as the complement of a transitive Vgrp (more specifically, its direct object)**. Here is another example:

[32]   Arnold claims [that the sea was calm that night].

In fact, this chapter has already included numerous examples of a subordinate clause functioning as the complement of a transitive Vgrp. Review the examples given so far and list the clauses functioning as complements of Vgrps.

The subordinate clause in [1a], both subordinate clauses in [3], that in [5a], the second subordinate clause in [6a], that in [16], and that in [17].

So, in addition to *note* (as in [31]) and *claim* ([32]), verbs that can take clausal direct objects include *believe* ([3]), the ditransitive verb *remind* ([5a]), *mean* ([6a]), *ask* ([16]) and *know* ([17]) and a host of others. Some of these can take both *that*-clauses and interrogative (*whether-*) clauses (e.g. *know, tell,* and *worry*), some can only take *that*-clauses (e.g. *claim* and *remind*), and some can only take interrogative clauses (e.g. *ask* and *wonder*).

We have seen that the ditransitive verb *remind* can take a clausal direct object. Other such ditransitive verbs are *tell, convince, warn, persuade, promise,* and *inform.*

[33]   I told him that his shirt was hanging out.
[34]   She finally convinced him he needed a shave.

That- and *whether-* clauses cannot function as indirect objects of ditransitive verbs for the simple reason that indirect objects must be able to refer to animate entities, whereas clauses (sentences) cannot. They don't refer even to concrete entities but denote propositions. Propositions are abstract and hence not animate.

Since *that-* and *whether-* clauses can function as the complements of verbs which also take NPs (including pronouns) as direct objects, as in [35]:

[35]

I have always { admitted / denied / thought / claimed / believed } it.

and since clauses functioning as objects in active sentences can become subject NPs in the passive, I shall analyse them as being dominated by an NP node, just like the clausal subjects considered in the last section:

[36]

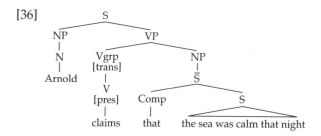

You should note, however, that not all verbs which can take clausal complements can take ordinary complements. *Hope* and *insist*, for example, cannot:

[37]   *I insist (hope) it.

Furthermore, not all object clauses can appear as subjects in passive sentences. For example:

[38]   *That his shirt was hanging out was told him.
[39]   *That he should abandon the monocle was insisted by the whole company.

Since not all transitive verbs can take clausal objects (e.g. *kick, boil,* and *engrave,* among many others), and not all transitive verbs that do take clausal objects can take simple (non-clausal) objects, the sub-categorisation label '[transitive]' is not much help here. There is a strong case for going beyond the sub-categorisations given in Chapter 4 and further sub-categorising verbs according to whether they can take clausal complements or not. Although this is, in fact, common practice, the basic subcategorisations introduced in Chapter 4 and used here will suffice for present purposes. This issue is discussed again in Chapter 10.

Now, using the triangle notation for all PPs, and (non-clausal) NPs, draw the phrase-markers for [33] above and [21b] above. The latter will need some thought: bear in mind (a) that its main verb is a passive [transitive] Vgrp, (b) that *by the critics* is a VP-adverbial and (c) that the subordinate clause is extraposed. **Discussion 4** for [33] and **Discussion 5** for [21b], pages 209–10.

In addition to functioning as direct objects in the complementation of Vgrp, *that-* and *whether*-**clauses can function as** SUBJECT-PREDICATIVES:

[40]   The consensus is that you should taste the stew first.

[41] The question is whether he should have accepted that offer.

Notice that, of all the intensive verbs, only the copula (*be*) can take a clausal predicative. *Taste*, *smell*, *sound* and *look* cannot. *Appear* and *seem* are, at least in one use, intensive verbs (*Julia seemed restless*, *Peter appeared happy*). However, when those verbs are followed by clauses, we are analysing those clauses, not as subject-predicatives, but as extraposed subjects. *That*-clauses can only follow *appear* and *seem* when those verbs have expletive *it* as subject. So [42], with its full (non-expletive) subject, is ungrammatical:

[42] *Julia seemed that she was restless.

In the extraposed-subject construction, remember, *appear* and *seem* are [intransitive].

With clausal subject-predicatives, there is no motivation for having the clause dominated by NP. We have already allowed that a range of categories can function as subject-predicatives (NP, AP, and PP), so there is no reason not to allow that $\bar{\text{S}}$ can as well.

Now draw the phrase-marker for [40], using the triangle notation for NPs and Vgrps. **Discussion 6**, page 210.

Complement of A within AP

We noted in Chapter 7 that, within AP, an A can be complemented by a PP (e.g. *nervous of exams*). Adjectives can also be complemented by a *that*-clause or a *whether*-clause. So: an AP can consist of the head A plus a clausal complement. Examples of such APs are:

[43a] Angry (that) they had not been chosen.
[44a] Aware (that) he had overstepped the mark.
[45a] Unsure whether he should sacrifice the pawn.

Such APs have all the usual range of functions for AP: subject-predicative – [43b] and [45b], and object-predicative – [44b], modifier of N, or NOM, within NP – [46].

[43b] The men seemed [angry [they had not been chosen]].
[44b] She made him [aware [that he had overstepped the mark]].

[45b] Hassan was [unsure [whether he should sacrifice the pawn]].

[46] Drivers [anxious [that they had made mistakes]] complained.

Like PPs, clauses complementing adjectives are represented as the sister of A in AP:

[47]

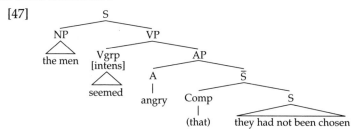

Using the triangle notation for NPs, Vgrps, and the embedded S, draw a phrase-marker for the sentence in [44b]. **Discussion 7, page 210.**

By way of revision, it would be a good idea to draw a *complete* phrase-marker for the sentence [46]. You'll need to leave yourself plenty of room. **Discussion 8, page 211.**

A final point to notice here is the distinction between:

[48]   It is certain that her hair is dyed.

[49]   William is certain that her hair is dyed.

Can you explain the difference? (Look again at pages 197–8).

Only one of them contains an AP with a clausal complement of the A. The other contains an extraposed-subject clause. It is only in [49] that [*certain that her hair is dyed*] is an AP. Since, [48] has the expletive *it* as subject, [*that her hair is dyed*] is an extraposed subject and the AP just consists of the adjective *certain*. Note that [48] is paraphrased by *That her hair is dyed is certain*.

Complement of N within NP

Consider the following NPs:

[50a] The fact that you received no greetings from Mars.

[50b] The question whether they should establish a Website.

Both of these NPs contain a clause complementing the N, a *that*-clause in [50a], an interrogative clause in [50b]. A feature of **noun-complement clauses** (useful in distinguishing them from other clauses that can appear in NPs) is that they can only complement ABSTRACT nouns like *fact, rumour, idea, news, question, claim, suggestion, rule, message, indication*, etc. Thus we have the NPs in [51] but not those in [52]:

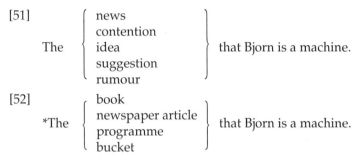

[51]   The   { news / contention / idea / suggestion / rumour }   that Bjorn is a machine.

[52]   *The   { book / newspaper article / programme / bucket }   that Bjorn is a machine.

The clause is said to 'complement the noun' because it is in the same relation to the N within NP as clauses that complement the Vgrp in VP. The same, incidentally, goes for clauses complementing A in AP. Compare the following.

[53a] His absence [INDICATES that he disapproves]. (VP)
[53b] His absence is [INDICATIVE that he disapproves]. (AP)
[53c] His absence is [an INDICATION that he disapproves]. (NP)

The bracketed string in [53b] is simply an AP version of the VP in [53a]. And that in [53c] is the NP version of that VP. Having noticed the parallelism between these, we must regard the clause as a COMPLEMENT of the A in [53b] and of the N in [53c] because it is clearly functioning as complement of the Vgrp *indicates* in [53a]. And, since the clause complementing the Vgrp in [53a] is represented as a sister of that Vgrp, the clausal complement of the A in AP is represented as the sister of the head A. And the same goes for the clausal complement in NP. As a sister of the head N it will be dominated by NOM, as in [54]:

[54]

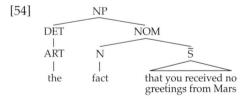

In Chapter 9 you will encounter another kind of clause (the relative clause) appearing within the structure of NP. Relative clauses have a different relation to the head N, however, and this will be reflected in how they are represented in phrase-markers. While **the distinction between noun-complement clauses and relative clauses** need not concern you in this chapter, it will become important in the next, and that is why I mention it here.

NPs containing complement clauses have the functions usually expected of NPs. When NPs with a *that*-clause complement function as subject-predicatives, however, a possible confusion with extraposed-subject *that*-clauses arises again. All the following sentences include a *that*-clause that follows a noun, but only in two of them does that clause function as noun-complement clause within an NP. Identify them.

[55] It is a disappointment that his monocle was not stolen.
[56] One small difficulty is the fact that dinosaurs were extinct by then.
[57] It was a message that the party had been cancelled.
[58] It is a well known fact that beavers build dams.
[59] It is our contention that you could dispense with that stupid monocle.

Since extraposed-subject (ES) clauses only ever occur with expletive *it*, and since *it* does not figure in [56], you can be sure that in [56] we are dealing, not with an ES-clause but with a noun-complement clause, within the NP *the fact that dinosaurs were extinct by then*. The others all have *it* as subject. The question is whether that *it* is EXPLETIVE or not. If this is not intuitively obvious, you can check by seeing whether the *it* in normal subject position can be replaced by the subordinate clause. If it can, you are dealing with an ES clause. This works with [55], [58] and [59]:

[55a] That his monocle was not stolen is a disappointment.
[58a] That beavers build dams is a well known fact.
[59a] That you could dispense with that stupid monocle is our contention.

In [57], by contrast, *it* does actually refer to something (a piece of paper or a 'phone call perhaps). Notice that replacing *it* with the subordinate clause yields [57a],

[57a] *That the party was cancelled was a message.

which, even if grammatical, is not a true paraphrase of [57]. So, in [57], *a message that the party was cancelled* is an NP with a noun-complement clause.

Complement of P within PP

In illustrating an interrogative clause functioning as a noun-complement clause, I gave *The question whether they should establish a Website*. This sounds less natural to me than [60], in which I have introduced a preposition. See also [61] and [62].

[60]   The question *of* whether they should establish a Website (was raised).

[61]   Sarah's concerns *about* whether anyone had enough time were ignored.

[62]   Sergeant Gourmet was worrying *about* whether the rations would arrive.

These show that **an interrogative clause can function as the complement of a preposition within PP**. In [60]–[61], the PP is modifying a noun. In [62], the PP is functioning as the complement of the Vgrp (*was worrying*). These PPs will have the following representation:

[63]

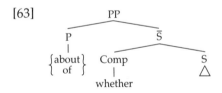

Having noticed that an interrogative clause can complement P within PP, we should ask: **can a *that*-clause complement a P within PP?** Compare:

[64a]   *After that she left.   [64b] After she left.

[65a]   *Until that the tree   [65b] Until the tree falls down.
          falls down.

[66a]   *Before that the food   [66b] Before the food gets cold.
          gets cold.

[67a]   *Since that you came.   [67b] Since you came.

The ungrammaticality of the [a] examples suggests the answer is No. But, in that case, what is going on in the [b] examples? This is a tricky question. In the next section, I adopt an analysis which effectively says that *after* **(etc.) is itself functioning as a kind of complementiser introducing the clause**. On the assumption that Comp cannot be filled twice over, this approach offers an explanation for the ungrammaticality of e.g. **After that she left.*

Adverbial clauses

What distinguishes adverbial clauses from *that-* and *whether*-clauses is that they take SUBORDINATING CONJUNCTIONS as complementisers. Here are some examples of expressions that have been analysed as subordinating conjunctions: *before, after, until, since, although, unless, if, because, once, as, now, so.*

The first four of these are the prepositions (also capable of taking an NP object) mentioned in the last section. I shall also take certain word sequences as phrasal complementisers without further analysis (using the triangle notation): *now that, so that, except that, as if, in case, in order that, as soon as.*

It is the subordinating conjunction – and the extra meaning it carries with it – that allows the clause to function as an adverbial. For example, in

[68a] Things will be rather dull *if Hieronimo leaves.*

it is the subordinating conjunction *if* that makes the clause function as a CONDITIONAL adverbial clause, as does its negative counterpart, *unless.*

[68b]

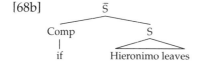

Because makes for an adverbial clause of REASON, and *after, before,* etc. make for TEMPORAL adverbial clauses.

As in Chapter 5, there is a distinction to be made between (adjunct) VP-adverbials and S-adverbials. In [68a], it is a VP-adverbial. Further examples of sentences with a clausal VP-adverbial are:

[69] I'm pleased [because [I actually prefer burnt fritters]].
[70] We hired a substitute for the night [in case [you felt too ill]].

[71]   The sedan chair was moving [as if [it was propelled by rockets]].

Examples with clausal S-adverbials are:

[72]   [Unless I'm gravely mistaken], you are King Kong.
[73]   [Since you ask], my name is Ozymandias.
[74]   That's my toothbrush, [in case you were wondering].

Using the triangle notation for NPs, Vgrps, PPs, and APs, give phrase-markers for [70] (note that *for the night* is a VP-adverbial, so this example has two VP-adverbials) and [72]. They are given as **Discussions 9 and 10** respectively, page 211.

A final word on *after, before, since,* and *until.* A disadvantage of treating those words as subordinating conjunctions (as a kind of complementiser) is that it amounts to saying that, when they introduce an NP (as in *after her departure, since the war*), they are prepositions (and hence head of PP) – but, when they introduce a clause, they are a kind of complementiser (in S-bar). This may seem implausible. The question comes down to this: is [*after she left*] a PP or a clause (S-bar)? Might it not be better to assign *after* etc. to a single category, regardless of the category of the constituent that it introduces and/or which functions as its complement? In Further Exercise 6, you are asked to look at some examples intended to make you think further about *after, before,* etc.

This problem arises most obviously with those four words rather than with the other subordinating conjunctions because, of all the subordinating conjunctions, only those four can introduce an NP. *If, because, unless,* etc. only ever introduce S, so there is less motivation to think of them as prepositions.

This completes our survey of *that-, whether-,* and adverbial clauses. In the next chapter we look at another general kind of clause: Wh-clauses. The fact that sentences can contain clauses – which can in turn contain further clauses – means that sentences may be indefinitely lengthy and complex. Nevertheless, it should by now be clear that, however complex, sentences and their constituents always have a well defined meaning, structure and function. To repeat a point from Chapter 2, if you satisfy yourself that your analysis gives each constituent a well-defined and recognisable meaning, structure and function, you should have little difficulty in analysing even the most complex sentences.

Discussion of in-text exercises

1.

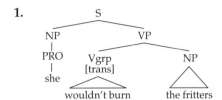

2.

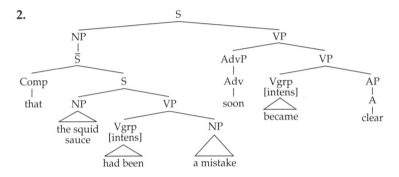

3.

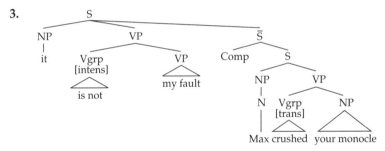

4.

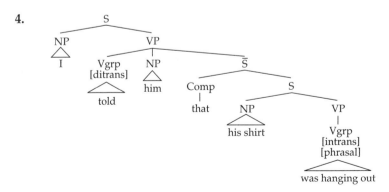

5.

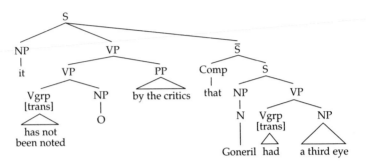

6.

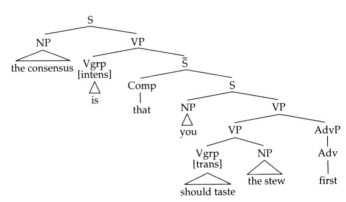

7.

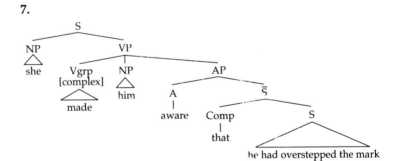

8.

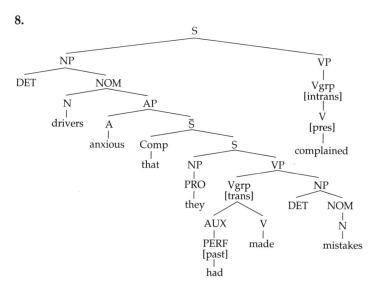

N.B. In terms of the analysis discussed in the Appendix in Chapter 7, the AP would be represented as a sister of, and N (*drivers*) dominated by, an extra non-branching NOM node.

9.

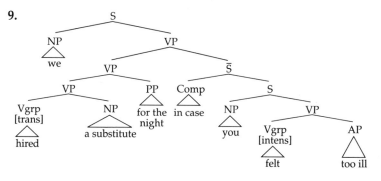

10.

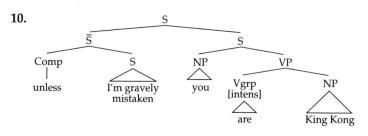

Exercises

1.   Give abbreviated clausal analyses (ACAs) of the following sentences. (c) and (d) contain two subordinate clauses each. Remember to check whether these are contained one within the other or whether they are independent of each other. Include any complementiser in with the subordinate clause triangle (which should then be labelled as $\overline{S}$ (S-bar).

Here are some hints on how to proceed. First decide how many clauses there are. You can do this by counting the Vgrps (one per clause, remember). Then identify the main verb and everything associated with it in the main clause. Draw the main clause triangle and label it 'S1'. All the other clauses will be subordinate to S1 – and hence below it (and contained within it). Then deal likewise for the subordinate clauses.

(a)   They did not suspect they were being observed at all.
(b)   That the ejector seat didn't work was quite forgotten.
(c)   I don't think the fact that the moped has an ejector seat is a great selling point personally.
(d)   Your suggestion that Max might refuse a second zabaglione just shows you don't know Max.

2.   Give ACAs of the following and give the function of all subordinate clauses.

(a)   Until you mentioned it, it had not struck me that the book would make an excellent film.
(b)   I am surprised Rory has learned so much because he is usually asleep.
(c)   As soon as the princess has ascended, I just knew the palanquin would not budge.
(d)   The fact that you endorse Omar's feeling that life is too short doesn't imply you should get drunk every day.
(e)   It appears that the new chef thought he could slip away before the missing *bombes surprises* were noticed.
(f)   If you are wondering if Max is turning up tomorrow, the general rumour is that, since he's getting married, he won't be in for the rest of the month.

Discussion of exercises

1.(a)

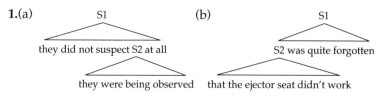

(c)

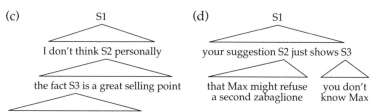

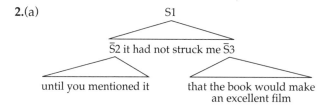

Alternatively:

(a) $_{S1}$[They did not suspect $_{S2}$[they were being observed]$_{S2}$ at all]$_{S1}$.

(b) $_{S1}$[$_{S2}$[That the ejector seat didn't work]$_{S2}$ was quite forgotten]$_{S1}$.

(c) $_{S1}$[I don't think $_{S2}$[the fact $_{S3}$[that the moped has an ejector seat]$_{S3}$ is a great selling point]$_{S2}$ personally]$_{S1}$.

(d) $_{S1}$[Your suggestion $_{S2}$[that Max might refuse a second zabaglione]$_{S2}$ just shows $_{S3}$[you don't know Max]$_{S3}$]$_{S1}$.

2.(a)

S1

$\bar{S}2$ it had not struck me $\bar{S}3$

until you mentioned it   that the book would make an excellent film

$_{S1}$[$_{S2}$[Until you mentioned it]$_{S2}$ it had not struck me $_{S3}$[that the book would make an excellent film]$_{S3}$]$_{S1}$.

S1 = main clause.
S2 = VP-adverbial (in S1).
S3 = extraposed subject.

(b)

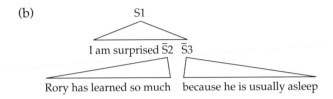

$_{S1}$[I am surprised $_{S2}$[Rory has learned so much]$_{S2}$ $_{S3}$[because he is usually asleep]$_{S3}$]$_{S1}$

S1 = main clause.
S2 = complement to A (*surprised*).
S3 = VP-adverbial (in S1). N.B. Were S3 an adverbial in S2 rather than in S1, S2 would be [*Rory has learned so much because he is usually asleep*] – possible, but presumably not what was intended!

(c)

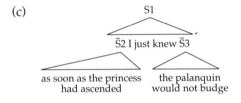

$_{S1}$[$_{S2}$[As soon as the princess had ascended]$_{S2}$ I just knew $_{S3}$[the palanquin would not budge]$_{S3}$]$_{S1}$

S1 = main clause.
S2 = VP-adverbial.
S3 = complement to Vgrp (*knew*): direct object.

(d)

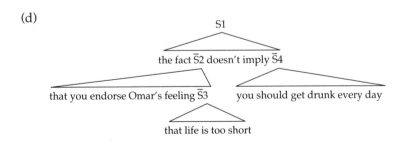

[*S1*The fact *S2*[that you endorse Omar's feeling*S3*[that life is too short]*S3*]*S2* doesn't imply*S4*[that you should get drunk everyday]*S4*]*S1*.

S1 = main clause.
S2 = complement to N (*fact*).
S3 = complement to N (*feeling*).
S4 = complement to Vgrp (*doesn't imply*): direct object.
N.B. It does not matter in what order the subordinate clauses are numbered.

(e)

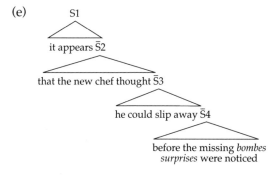

S1[It appears*S2*[that the new chef thought*S3*[he could slip away *S4*[before the missing *bombes surprises* were noticed]*S4*]*S3*]*S2*]*S1*.

S1 = main clause.
S2 = extraposed subject.
S3 = complement to Vgrp (*thought*): direct object.
S4 = VP-adverbial (in S3).

(f)

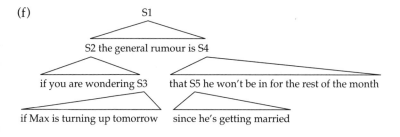

$_{S1}[_{S2}[$If you are wondering $_{S3}[$if Max is turning up tomorrow$]_{S3}]_{S2}$ the general rumour is $_{S4}[$that $_{S5}[$since he's getting married$]_{S5}$ he won't be in for the rest of the month$]_{S4}]_{S1}$.

S1 = main clause.
S2 = S-adverbial in S1.
S3 = complement to Vgrp (*are wondering*): direct object.
S4 = complement to Vgrp (*is*): subject-predicative.
S5 = VP-adverbial in S4.

Note the two *if*s. That in S2 is the conditional *if*, making S2 a conditional adverbial clause. That in S3 is the interrogative complementiser, an alternative to *whether*, making S3 an interrogative clause.

Further exercises

1.   Give Abbreviated Clausal Analyses (either by means of trees or by means of bracketings) of the following sentences. For each subordinate clause, say what its function is. Look at Exercise 1 above for hints on how to proceed. The first few contain just one subordinate clauses. Later examples contain more.

(a)   He told me Rory was an abstract expressionist at our first meeting.

(b)   That anyone would actually like his paintings came as a surprise.

(c)   The big idea here is that we all become rich and famous as quickly as possible.

(d)   The announcement that Frank has resigned will be made after the plane takes off.

(e)   It's well known that Max thinks syntax is good for the brain.

(f)   Before the exhibition opened, the gallery had been certain his paintings would sell extremely well.

(g)   That Savonarola came to power is a direct consequence of Lorenzo's insistence that his sermons were harmless.

(h)   Once it was certain that all the paintings were copies, the exhibition closed.

(i)   The gallery's defence was that they didn't realise they were copies until it was too late.

(j)   In case you were hoping that I would be grateful for the gift of all these masterpieces, I am aware the exhibition only closed because no-one else wanted them.

2.   Draw **complete** phrase-markers for the following sentences:

(a)   Do you think she's good at syntax?
(b)   This is a proposal that we should support the workers.
(c)   Whether Frank and Bill would be promoted wasn't entirely clear.
(d)   His friends were certain he would not pass the test.
(e)   It was unfortunate the first lecture was cancelled.
(f)   Is it so obvious that she doesn't like the paintings?
(g)   The exhibition closed because all the paintings were copies.
(h)   Max was under the impression that Cynthia was glad he had arrived.

3.   Consider the following sentences carefully. How do you suggest the function of the subordinate clauses should be described? This possibility has not been mentioned in the chapter, but it is related to functions that have been mentioned. Suggest a phrase-marker representation for (1) consistent with the discussion in this chapter.

(1)   He thought it a shame that no-one had crushed the monocle.
(2)   She considered it odd that so few had signed the petition.
(3)   She declared it in the worst taste that they'd left nothing for Mr Manners.

4.   A syntactic possibility not mentioned in the chapter is that interrogative (*whether-*) clauses can function as adverbials. Make up a sentence that includes an adverbial *whether-*clause.

5.   Another possibility not mentioned is illustrated by the following:

(1)   The thought occurred to him that he should have done the washing up.
(2)   The claim was made that syntax is actually good for the brain.
(3)   A rumour is spreading that the Prime Minister has resigned.

In the light of the discussion in this chapter, how *exactly* would you describe the function of the subordinate clause in these? Precisely how does it differ from anything explicitly described in the chapter?

6.   *After, before, since,* and *until* were treated as subordinating conjunctions and dealt with in the section on adverbial clauses. But look now at (1)–(4) below and try to identify what is interesting (and mildly problematic for the present treatment) about the form and function of the italicised constituent. (5)–(7) are given for comparison.

(1)   The discussion *after you left* was fascinating.
(2)   During his long wait *until the pubs opened,* Gomez knitted quietly.
(3)   The weeks *before the fighting started* were known as 'The Phoney War'.
(4)   His behaviour *since he got married* is unaccountable.

(5)   *The discussion *unless you go* is fascinating.
(6)   *His behaviour *as if you weren't there* dismayed us.
(7)   *The lack of activity *although war had been declared* was unnerving.

7.   We have seen that, when a *that*-clause functions as the complement of a verb, Comp *that* is always omissible (need not be overt): *They complained (that) they couldn't see.* By contrast, when *that*-clauses function as subjects (as in e.g. *That he might lose the match never even occurred to Ramon*), Comp *that* must be overt. Can you suggest a reason for this difference?

Chapter 9

Wh-Clauses

In Chapter 1, I used replacement by a single word to show that a sequence of words should be analysed as a constituent. As pointed out there, Wh-words (*who, what, which, whose, why, when, where, how*) can be used in this way. For example, given

[1]   Vince is taking Violetta's icon to Athens.

we can replace *Vince* with *who* – as in [2], *Violetta's icon* with *what* – as in [3], *Violetta's* with *which* or *whose* – as in [4], and *to Athens* with *where* – as in [5]:

[2]   ***Who*** is taking Violetta's icon to Athens?
[3]   Vince is taking ***what*** to Athens?
[4]   Vince is taking ***whose/which*** icon to Athens?
[5]   Vince is taking Violetta's icon ***where***?

Similarly, *by plane* and *secretly* could be replaced by **how**, *shortly* or *on Tuesday* could be replaced by **when**, and *for restoration* and *so that it can be restored* could be replaced by **why**.

Clauses that include a Wh-word are called Wh-CLAUSES. Wh-words can appear in main clauses and in subordinate clauses. As you can see from [2]–[5] **including a Wh-word in a MAIN clause has the effect of making it into a kind of question: a Wh-question.** The *yes/no* questions of Chapter 6 question whether something is the case or not. Wh-questions, by contrast, question some particular constituent. Hence Wh-questions are commonly called **constituent questions**.

I begin by describing main Wh-clauses – Wh-questions, in other words – and then go on to discuss subordinate Wh-clauses.

Wh-questions

Compare [3] above, repeated here, with [6]:

[3]   Vince is taking what to Athens?
[6]   What is Vince taking to Athens?

When the Wh-question takes the form in [3] there is nothing special about its analysis. It can be analysed exactly as [1] would be – except that, where [1] has the NP *Violetta's icon*, [3] will have an NP consisting of the Wh-pronoun *what*.

The real interest of Wh-questions – and Wh-clauses in general – is illustrated in [6]. It will help you to focus on the differences between between [3] and [6] if you first draw a phrase-marker for [3]. (Assume that *take* is a [monotransitive] verb, and that the PP *to Athens* is therefore a VP-adverbial.) The phrase-marker will be given shortly.

Now, [6] differs from [3] in exactly two ways. Identify the two differences.

You will agree that, in both [3] and [6], *what* is understood as functioning as the direct object of the Vgrp (*is taking*). The first difference is that in [3] *what* is actually in the direct object position, whereas in [6] it has been fronted. Secondly: [6], but not [3], exhibits fronting of the tensed auxiliary. So the two differences are: (i) fronting of the Wh-phrase, (ii) fronting of the auxiliary carrying tense.

What sentences correspond to [4] and [5] as [6] corresponds to [3]?

You will have discovered for yourself that in [4] we cannot front just the Wh-word itself (cf. **Whose/which is Vince taking icon to Athens?*). In [4] *which* and *whose* are functioning as determiners. Only full phrasal categories can be fronted. So it is the full NP containing that Wh-determiner (*which icon* or *whose icon*) that has to be fronted:

[7] $\left\{ \begin{array}{l} \text{Whose icon} \\ \text{Which icon} \end{array} \right\}$ is Vince taking to Athens?

[8]   Where is Vince taking Violetta's icon?

The auxiliary-fronting displayed by these examples will be familiar to you from Chapter 6. What is new here is **the fronting of the Wh-phrase. This is called 'Wh-fronting'.**

As with the movement of an object to the subject position in passive sentences – and, more generally, as with all other movements

– **Wh-fronting leaves behind a gap (O) of the appropriate category**. I show this in due course. But first we have to decide where the Wh-phrase moves to.

Recall that fronting of a tensed auxiliary in *yes/no* questions is fronting to the Comp position: daughter of S-bar, sister of S. But if the fronted auxiliary occupies that Comp position, where does the Wh-phrase get fronted to? Clearly, it moves in front of the fronted auxiliary.

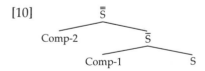

[9]   What is Vince • taking • to Athens?

That tells us where in the linear (horizontal) order it appears, but it doesn't tell us what structural position it occupies (in the vertical hierarchy). Is the Wh-phrase in the Comp position *as well as* the fronted auxiliary? Well, the last chapter suggested we don't get auxiliary fronting in *that*- and *whether*-clauses because auxiliaries cannot be moved to a position that is already filled (overtly or otherwise). The fact that a sentence can exhibit both auxiliary-fronting *and* Wh-fronting suggests that the Wh-phrase does not move to the same Comp position that auxiliaries move to. This in turn suggests that it moves into another Comp position. So we need a second Comp position.

Current thinking suggests that this second Comp is a *higher* Comp. In other words, it introduces S-bar, just as the already familiar Comp position introduces S. This higher Comp must be dominated by a node that also dominates S-bar. I shall call this node 'S-double-bar' ($\overline{\overline{S}}$). So, **this higher Comp position, the landing site for fronted Wh-phrases, can be defined as: daughter of S-double-bar, sister of S-bar**:

[10]

```
              S̿
          ⟋        ⟍
     Comp-2          S̄
                 ⟋      ⟍
            Comp-1        S
```

(It is not necessary to number the two Comp positions, but I have done so here for ease of reference in what follows.)

We can now give a representation of [6]. Essentially, it will be like the representation of [3], except for the two frontings and the $\overline{\overline{S}}$ and $\overline{S}$ nodes. So let's remind ourselves explicitly of the points made so far. [6] displays fronting of a Wh-NP from the direct object position to the Comp-2 position just defined. The object position following the Vgrp must therefore have an NP gap. And the auxiliary carrying tense (Prog *be*) has been fronted to the familiar Comp-1 position, leaving a gap under AUX. Earlier you were asked for a phrase-marker for [3]. It is given in [11a]. Compare it with [11b], the phrase-marker for [6]:

[11a]

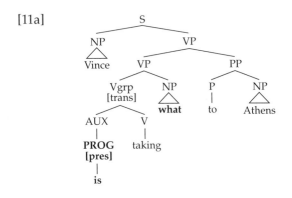

[11b]

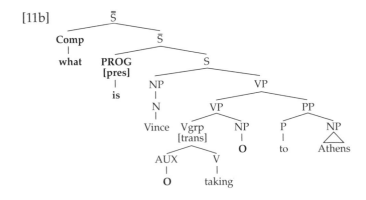

In fact, [11a] and [11b] would look more similar were we to include the S̿ and S̄ nodes in [11a]. In that case, the two Comp positions in [11a] would be empty. This indeed is how [3] should, strictly speaking, be represented. The frontings don't *create* those Comp positions. Rather, fronting is only possible in the first place because those positions are already there, ready to accept the fronted expressions. However, for simplicity, I shall not demand

– in the case of main clauses – that the two Comp positions be represented in unfronted sentences.

We now have two Comp positions:

Comp-1 (lower): Daughter of $\bar{S}$ and sister of S

Filled, in subordinate clauses, by *that, whether,* and subordinating conjunctions.

Filled, in main clauses, by fronted tensed auxiliaries.

Comp-2 (higher): Daughter of $\bar{\bar{S}}$ and sister of $\bar{S}$

Filled, in both main and subordinate clauses, by fronted Wh-expressions.

The major contrast between *that/whether* (and subordinating conjunctions) and the Wh-expressions that occupy the Comp-2 position is this: *that/whether,* etc. are SIMPLY complementisers (complementisers and nothing else): they belong to no other syntactic category, they are not fronted from within the clause they introduce, and hence have no function *within* that clause. By contrast, the Comp-2 Wh-expressions are always fronted; so, in addition to introducing the clause, they do have a function within that clause, indicated by the position of the gap they 'leave behind'. These fronted Wh-expressions in the Comp-2 position must, then, belong to categories capable of having clausal functions: NP, AP, PP, AdvP. The fact that *What* in the Comp-2 position is an NP is captured by there being an NP gap in the clause it introduces.

Now give the (Aux- and Wh-) fronted versions of the following sentences:

[12a] You are giving what to Bill?
[12b] Julia will give the pen to who(m)? (two possible Wh-frontings here)
[12c] He drank that beer how quickly?
[12d] Max is how tall?

These examples show the variety of phrases that can be fronted. In [12a] it is, again, a (direct object) NP. In [12b] we have two options. In very formal styles, the whole PP (*to whom*) can be fronted and (in my dialect) the Wh-pronoun must then be in the objective case (*whom*). In ordinary conversational style, however, just the Wh-NP is usually fronted. This will leave the preposition (and the PP of which it is head) in place but with an NP gap. In my dialect, when the NP is fronted from within the PP it need not (except in very formal style) be in the objective case. As regards [12c–d], *how* is a degree adverb and degree adverbs cannot be fronted alone. So, as you will have discovered for yourself, the whole AdvP *how quickly* must be fronted in [12c], as must the AP *how tall* in [12d].

> [13a] What are you giving • to Bill?   (• = NP)
> [13b] (i) Who(m) will Julia give the pen to •? (• = NP)
>   (ii) To whom will Julia give the pen •?   (• = PP)
> [13c] How quickly did he drink that beer •?   (• = AdvP)
> [13d] How tall is Max •?   (• = AP)

Notice that the verb in [13d] is the copula *be*. Recall that, although the copula is a full verb, it behaves (when tensed) like an auxiliary. In other words, it fronts to the Comp-1 position in questions. This, together with the fact that the whole AP (*how tall*) has to be fronted, means that very little is actually left in the clause (the S) itself. In fact, only the subject (*Max*) is left in its original place!

Take time now to draw a phrase-marker for each of the five sentences in [13]. Use the triangle (∆) notation for NPs, APs and AdvPs. Leave yourself plenty of room. **Discussion 1**, page 236.

Now look again at [2]–[5] at the beginning of this chapter. [3]–[5] are unfronted questions. Such unfronted questions are commonly called **echo-questions** – they are used to echo – and ask about – something said earlier. But they all have normal (non-echo) alternative forms displaying auxiliary- and Wh-fronting, namely [6]–[8]. But what about [2], repeated here as [14]?

> [14] Who is taking Violetta's icon to Athens?

[2]/[14] is itself the only possible form for that particular question, and it doesn't sound noticeably echoic. [2]/[14] is distinctive because there it is the subject constituent that is questioned. The point is that, as subject, the Wh-phrase appears at the beginning of the sentence anyway. So, the first question raised by this example is: **should a Wh-SUBJECT be represented as being in the subject position or as fronted into the Comp-2 position?** In short, does [14] display Wh-fronting, like [6]–[8], or not?

Both answers are possible (and have been given). For convenience, I shall make the following general assumption: **without exception, Wh-expressions appearing at the front of clauses are**

to be represented as occupying the Comp-2 position. In moving to the Comp-2 position, however, a subject will not cross any other expression, so the movement makes no difference to the order of words.

The next question is: **does [14] display auxiliary-fronting?** Again, given our assumption that the Wh-phrase is up in Comp-2, auxiliary-fronting makes no difference to the order of words. And again, I adopt the strategy of assuming that **auxiliary-fronting to Comp-1 does occur in all (non-echo) questions**. (If you are interested in thinking further about this question, look at Further Exercise 3).

In the light of the above answers (in bold) to these two questions, draw a phrase-marker for [14]. Use the Δ-notation for NP and PP. **Discussion 2**, page 238.

A word now about *where, when, how,* and *why*. Generally these are regarded as Adverb Phrases (AdvPs). But, as mentioned at the beginning of the chapter, they don't only stand in place of AdvPs, but also PPs, APs, and even clauses. I have adopted a representation whereby you are not required to state the category of the Wh-phrase in the Comp-2 position. But you do still have to decide on the most likely category of the gap it has left behind. In this connection, suggest complete phrase-markers for the following. **Discussion 3**, page 238.

[15]   How have you been lately?
[16]   Where did Lisa put the liquor?

To conclude this survey of Wh-questions, notice that a Wh-phrase can be fronted, not just from the immediately following (main) clause, but also from a subordinate clause. Here are two examples. In each, establish where exactly the gap corresponding to the fronted Wh-phrase should be. Giving Abbreviated Clausal Analyses might help here.

[17]   Whose poem did Stevens suggest would be ideal for the lecture?
[18]   Who did Leopold think Haydn had said he admired?

Possible answers to these questions are:

[19a] Stevens suggested $_{S2}$[*his own poem* would be ideal for the lecture]$_{S2}$.
[19b] Leopold thought $_{S2}$[Haydn had said $_{S3}$[he admired *Mozart*]$_{S3}$]$_{S2}$.

So, in [17] there is a subject gap in *S2*. In [18] the gap is even further away – two clauses away – in the direct object position in *S3*. Notice though that, while the Wh-phrase has been fronted from within a *subordinate* clause, it is still the *main* clause that displays auxiliary-fronting in these Wh-questions.

Subordinate Wh-clauses

The big idea in this chapter is that Wh-clauses are introduced by a fronted Wh-phrase occupying the Comp-2 position (daughter of S-double-bar, sister of S-bar). It corresponds to a gap of the appropriate category in the position from which it was fronted.

This goes for all Wh-clauses, whether main or subordinate. The one structural difference between a main and a subordinate Wh-clause is that only main Wh-clauses display auxiliary-fronting as well as Wh-fronting (auxiliary-fronting being a 'main clause phenomenon'). In the rest of this chapter, I deal with two main types of subordinate Wh-clause, interrogative clauses and relative clauses.

Subordinate Wh-interrogative clauses

The distinction between main Wh-interrogative (Wh-questions) and subordinate Wh-interrogative clauses is exactly the same as that between main *yes/no* interrogatives (*yes/no* questions) and subordinate *yes/no* interrogatives. See Chapter 8, pages 195–6.

The following all contain subordinate Wh-interrogative clauses:

[20] Martha was enquiring why he wore it on his foot.
[21] How he would fare on the trapeze preoccupied him.
[22] It is my affair what I wear at night.
[23] Marcel was not certain who he had sent the flowers to.
[24] The immediate problem was where they could hide those fritters.
[25] The little matter of who is going to pay for all this has yet to be resolved.

The subordinate clauses in each of these sentences have functions familiar to you from previous chapters. So, first identify the subordinate clauses and, for each, state what its function is.

As Wh-clauses, all these subordinate clauses have a Wh-phrase fronted from a position within the clause, leaving a gap. Identify the position of the gap and (relatedly) state the function of the Wh-phrase.

[20a] [why [he wore it on his foot •]] – dO of [trans] Vgrp, *was enquiring*.
    Why: adjunct adverbial.
[21a] [how [he would fare on the trapeze •]] – subject.
    How: adjunct adverbial.
[22a] [what [I wear • at night]] – extraposed subject.
    What: direct object of trans Vgrp, *wear*.
[23a] [who [he had sent the flowers to •]] – complement of A (*certain*) in AP.
    Who: complement of P, *to*.
[24a] [where [they could hide those fritters •]] – sP of intensive Vgrp, *was*.
    Where: oP of complex Vgrp, *could hide*.
[25a] [who [• is going to pay for all this]] – complement of P (*of*) in PP.
    Who: subject.

As mentioned, these subordinate Wh-clauses have exactly the same structure as the Wh-questions considered in the last section. Remember that the fronted Wh-phrase occupies the higher Comp-2 position. Since these interrogative clauses are subordinate and therefore don't display auxiliary fronting, the lower Comp-1 position will be empty. Here is the phrase-marker for [23]:

[26]

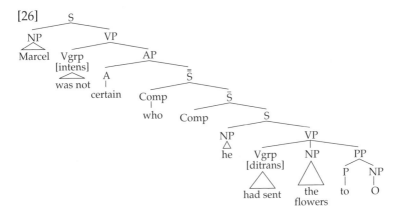

Phrase-markers for [20] and [22] are given in **Discussion 4**, page 239.

Relative clauses

It would be understandable if you had formed the impression that any clause that is a Wh-clause is an interrogative clause. This is not so. **Relative clauses are Wh-clauses, but they are not interrogative**. In contrast to interrogative clauses, they can only be subordinate. This is because **relative clauses only function as modifiers**. Although they can modify a range of categories, I shall focus on their modifying function within NP.

Have a good look at the following NPs, all of which contain Wh-clauses. These are relative clauses. Identify the relative clause in each, and the function of the Wh-phrase within the clause.

[27]   The trampolines which they had bought.
[28]   The fool who lent you a fiver.
[29]   A friend whose car we borrowed.
[30]   The usher who I showed my ticket to.
[31]   The place where you left your wallet.

When Wh-forms occur in a relative clause, they are traditionally referred to as **relative pronouns** (in contrast to their occurrence in interrogative clauses when they are traditionally referred to as 'interrogative pronouns'). These relative clauses have the same structure as the subordinate Wh-interrogative clauses discussed in the previous sections, with Wh-fronting into the higher Comp-2 position, from within the clause:

[27a] [which [they had bought •]]   (*which* = dO)
[28a] [who [• lent you a fiver]]   (*who* = subject)
[29a] [whose car [we borrowed •]]   (*whose car* = dO)
[30a] [who [I showed my ticket to •]]   (*who* = complement to P in PP)
[31a] [where [you left your wallet •]]   (*where* = aA)

What concerns us here, then, is not their (by now familiar) internal structure but how they fit into the structure of sentences – more specifically, how they fit into the structure of the NPs in which they function as modifiers. In this connection, **compare**

relative clauses with noun complement (*that*-)clauses, introduced in the last chapter. Among the following NPs, the [a]
examples contain noun complement clauses, while the [b]
examples contain relative clauses.

[32a] The conclusion [that Mars was inhabited].
    [32b] The conclusion [which Gomez disputes].
[33a] The thought [that he should have done the washing up].
    [33b] The thought [which occurred to him].
[34a] The claim [that syntax is good for the brain].
    [34b] The claim [with which he concluded his lecture].

The obvious contrast here is that the noun complement clauses
in [a] give us central information about the head noun, telling us
the actual content of the conclusion, thought, or claim (what
exactly the conclusion etc. was), while the relative clauses tell
something else about it, something more peripheral. From [32b],
for example, we don't know what conclusion Gomez disputes,
only that it is the one he disputes.

Recall that noun **complement** clauses are so-called because the
clause relates to the noun exactly as a clause complementing a
Vgrp relates to a Vgrp. Compare the [a] NPs above with the
[bracketed] VPs in the following sentences:

[35] He [concluded that Mars was inhabited].
[36] He [thought he should have done the washing up].
[37] Surely he [couldn't claim that syntax is good for the
    brain].

**As complements, NOUN-COMPLEMENT CLAUSES are sisters to
the head N within NOM, just as verb-complements are sisters
to the Vgrp within VP.** Here, then, is a reminder of how NPs
with complement clauses are represented:

[38]   NP WITH NOUN COMPLEMENT CLAUSE:

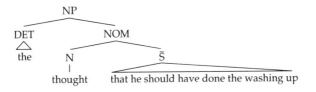

Noun complement clauses, remember, are introduced by the Comp-1 complementiser *that* (dominated by S-bar). Since nothing has been fronted from within it, the clause itself is complete (no gaps). By contrast, you know that the relative clause is a kind of Wh-clause: the Wh-phrase is in the Comp-2 position (dominated by S-double bar) and has been fronted, leaving a gap.

The points just made serve to distinguish noun complement clauses and relative clauses quite clearly, at least as regards their internal structure. But we still haven't answered the question of how relative clauses fit into the structure of NPs. Well, relative clauses clearly don't relate to the head noun as noun complement clauses do. They are NOT complement clauses and so cannot be represented as sisters of the head N. I have anyway mentioned that relative clauses give more peripheral information about the head N. To reflect this, RELATIVE CLAUSES **are represented, not as sisters of the N, but as sisters of NOM within a higher NOM**:

[39] NP WITH RELATIVE CLAUSE:

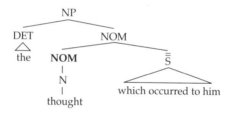

So, in addition to differences in their internal structure, noun-complement clauses and relative clauses are distinguished by their position in the structure of NPs: **noun-complement clauses are N-modifiers (sisters-of-N), relative clauses are NOM-modifiers (sisters-of-NOM)**. If you tackled the Appendix of Chapter 7, the distinction will be familiar to you, as will the following discussion.

Evidence supporting this distinction between N-modifiers and NOM-modifiers comes from the pro-form *one*. You will need to read what follows carefully. *One* **is a pro-NOM**: it stands in place of NOMs. It cannot replace a noun by itself unless that noun is the *only* constituent of a NOM. So we must interpret *one* as replacing, not just the noun itself, but the NOM that dominates it. Now, if a noun-complement clause is the sister of the N itself (an N-modifier), a NOM is created only by the *combination* of N AND complement clause together. So we predict that the pro-NOM *one* should *not* be able to replace just the N in the context of a following complement clause. By contrast, if a relative clause is the sister of NOM (a NOM-modifier), we predict that, even if that NOM contains nothing other than an N, it should still be replaceable by the pro-NOM *one*. **In short, we predict that [*one* + complement clause] will be ungrammatical, but [*one* + relative clause] will be fine**. These predictions are fully borne out:

[40a] *The one that Mars is inhabited.
[40b] The one which Gomez disputes.
[41a] *The one that he should have done the washing up.
[41b] The one which occurred to him.
[42a] *The one that syntax is good for the brain.
[42b] The one with which he concluded his lecture.

[43a] *I accept all the conclusions, including the one that Mars is inhabited.
[43b] I accept all the conclusions, including the one which Gomez disputes.

Notice that, if N-complement clauses are sisters-of-N in parallel with V-complements (sisters-of-Vgrp), then the structural position of relative clauses (sister-of-NOM, daughter-of-NOM) parallels the structural position of adjunct adverbials (sister-of-VP, daughter-of-VP). In other words, **you can think of relative clauses as adjuncts in the structure of NP**. (For more detail on the distinction beween N-modifiers and NOM-modifiers, see the Appendix of Chapter 7.)

Now give a complete phrase-marker representation for the NP in [32b] above, *The conclusion which Gomez disputes*. **Discussion 5**, page 240.

___

Omission of the Wh-phrase

In most cases, the fronted Wh-form in a relative clause can be omitted (by ellipsis). Look again at [27]–[31] above, and decide for yourself which of those it can be ellipted from. Under what two circumstances can it not be ellipted? You can check your findings against [32b]–[34b] above.

___

[44] The trampolines /\ they had bought (were dangerous).

[45] *The fool ∧ lent you a fiver (is here).
[46] *A friend ∧ car we borrowed (wants it back).
[47] The usher ∧ I showed my ticket to (has framed it).
[48] The place ∧ you dropped your wallet (is too far away now).

See also: *The conclusion Gomez disputes (was indeed absurd), *The thought occurred to him (cheered him up), *The claim with he concluded his lecture (surprised them).*

The fronted Wh-form cannot be ellipted (1) when it functions as subject ([45] and [33b]) and (2) when other material has been fronted with it ([46] and [34b]). Generally, ellipsis is possible only when it does not interfere with the interpretation or with ease of comprehension. For example, the fronted Wh-subjects in [45] and [33b] cannot be ellipted because this would create the misleading first impression that *lent/occurred* are the main verbs, whereas in fact each is the verb of a subordinate clause. In the absence of the Wh-form, the mistake would only become apparent when the real main verb (*is, cheered*) made its appearance.

That *again*

Now look at the following NPs:

[49] The fool *that* lent you a fiver.
[50] The thought *that* occurred to him.
[51] The trampolines *that* they had bought.
[52] The conclusion *that* Gomez disputes.

In these NPs, the subordinate clause is introduced by *that*. What should we make of these? Are they relative (Wh-)clauses or noun-complement (*that*-)clauses? Try to decide.

Relative clauses always include a gap. In genuine *that*-clauses, by contrast, *that* has not been fronted so the clause itself is complete. Now, the clauses in [49]–[52] are clearly not complete: [• *lent you a fiver*], [• *occurred to him*], [*they had bought* •], [*Gomez disputes* •]. This indicates that, despite the presence of *that* rather than a Wh-form, these are relative clauses. Compare the relative clauses in the following [a] examples with the noun complement clauses in the [b] examples:

[53a] This is *a proposal that we should support.*
[53b] This is *a proposal that we should support the opposition.*

[54a] *The news that she had given John* shocked them all.
[54b] *The news that she had given John a good kick* shocked them all.

Furthermore, we have seen that there is nothing to prevent any NOM being modified by a relative clause, including NOMs that have *fool, thought, trampoline,* or *conclusion* as the head N. By contrast, *trampoline* and *fool* are not nouns of the (abstract) sort that can take noun complement clauses. This too indicates that all these are relative clauses.

The traditional approach to *that* in relative clauses is simply to say that, in this kind of relative clause, Wh-forms can be replaced by *that*. On this approach, *that* is regarded as an alternative 'relative pronoun', and the NP [*the conclusion **that** Gomez disputes*] will be represented exactly like [*the conclusion **which** Gomez disputes*] (see Discussion 5), but with *that* in Comp-2 instead of *which*. This approach has the merit of simplicity so, for convenience, I shall adopt it here. In the light of this, draw contrasting phrase-markers for the italicised NPs in [53a] and [53b]. **Discussion 6**, page 240.

An alternative analysis, better supported by the evidence, would insist that *that* is – as always – the Comp-1 complementiser and is permitted to make an overt appearance in (the Comp-1 of) a relative clause only when the Wh-phrase in Comp-2 has been ellipted.

Restrictive vs. non-restrictive clauses

All the relative clauses considered so far are RESTRICTIVE relative clauses. The other kind of relative clause is described as NON-RESTRICTIVE (or APPOSITIVE). The internal structure of these two kinds is identical. **The difference between restrictives and non-restrictives lies in the way they relate to the head noun within the overall NP.** In the following sentences, all the subject NPs contain relative clauses. Those in the [a]s are restrictive, those in the [b]s are non-restrictive.

[55a] The books which John has consulted are out of date.
  [55b] The books, which John has consulted, are out of date.
[56a] The dogs which have rabies are dangerous.
  [56b] The dogs, which have rabies, are dangerous.

As you can see, non-restrictives are distinguished in writing from restrictives by being marked off by commas. The difference between them, though, does not consist in the presence vs. absence of commas, so you need to ask yourself what the commas in the [b] examples are telling you about the relation between the main clause and the relative clause. This can be brought more clearly by showing that certain relative clauses can only be used non-restrictively in certain contexts:

[57a] *The dogs which are mammals need special treatment.
   [57b] The dogs, which are mammals, need special treatment.
[58a] *Triangles which have three sides have interesting properties.
   [58b] Triangles, which have three sides, have interesting properties.

The oddity of the (restrictive) [a] examples is due to the fact that RESTRICTIVE **relative clauses specify more exactly which of the things picked out by the head noun are being mentioned**. In [55a], for example, the relative clause tells us *which* books are out of date. It is described as 'restrictive' because it serves to restrict the mentioned set of books to the SUB-SET that John has consulted. It is that more highly specified (sub-)set that are said, in [55a], to be out of date. But the relative clauses in [57] and [58] cannot be used to pick out a more highly specified set of dogs or triangles, because all dogs are mammals – and all triangles three-sided – anyway. So, you cannot (as in [58a]) use *which have three sides* to pick out a sub-set of triangles. Of course, there is nothing to stop us parenthetically adding the extra information that triangles have three sides (or that dogs are mammals). And this is precisely what the non-restrictive clause allows us to do. NON-RESTRICTIVE **relative clauses serve to add extra information, without restricting the set of things (triangles, dogs, books ...) being mentioned**.

To compare [56a] and [56b]: [56a], with the restrictive clause, does not imply that all the dogs are dangerous; only the rabied ones are said to be dangerous. But [56b], with the non-restrictive clause, does imply that all the mentioned dogs are dangerous, adding the further information that they also have rabies. The big difference, then, is that, while [56a] makes just *one* statement – a statement about the rabid dogs to the effect that they dangerous – [56b] makes *two* statements, both of them about the dogs, one to the effect that they are dangerous, another to the effect that they have rabies.

The representation of NPs containing a restrictive relative clause has already been given. As a reminder, that in [56a] is given here as [59]:

[59] NP with restrictive relative clause (see also [39] above):

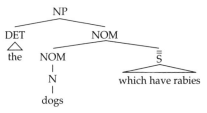

Notice that in the restrictive [59], the determiner is the sister of a constituent that includes the relative clause, namely the NOM [*dogs which have rabies*]. This means that the restrictive clause falls within the scope of the determining function of the definite article (in other words, *the* is determining, not *dogs*, but *dogs which have rabies*). So, in [56a], there is no NP of the form *the dogs* that is the subject of the VP *are dangerous*. This seems right: we have agreed that, in [56a], no statement is made about the dogs as such, only about a sub-set of them, the rabid dogs.

What about [56b] – with the non-restrictive clause? Well, we agreed (I hope) that in [56b] two statements were made, both of them about the dogs. Here, the subject of the main clause predicate VP (*are dangerous*) is indeed *the dogs*. So, if the non-restrictive clause is a modifier, it must be seen as a modifier, not just of *dogs*, but of *the dogs*, which is an NP in its own right. **As the modifier of a complete NP, the non-restrictive relative clause must be represented as the sister of that NP within a higher NP**, as in [60]:

[60] NP with non-restrictive relative clause:

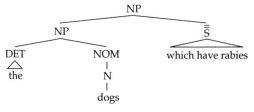

We get a second statement here (the additional statement that the dogs have rabies) because the *which* of the non-restrictive clause is a pronoun that replaces, and hence refers to, the NP *the dogs*.

Notice a couple of further differences between restrictive and non-restrictive relative clauses: in contrast with restrictives, the Wh-phrase in non-restrictives cannot be ellipted and it cannot be replaced by *that*.

In conclusion, it is worth stepping back briefly to review the kinds of clauses that can appear within NP. There are three: (a) noun complement clauses, (b) restrictive relative clauses, and (c) non-restrictive relative clauses. Restrictive relatives are more peripheral than noun complement clauses, and non-restrictive relatives are more peripheral still. This three-way distinction corresponds with the general structure of NPs. There are three levels of NP structure: (a) the lexical (lowest) level of N itself, (b) the intermediate level of NOM, and (c) the phrasal (highest) level of the NP.

Noun-complement clauses: modifiers of N (within NOM).
Restrictive relative clauses: modifiers of NOM (within NOM).
Non-restrictive relative clauses: modifiers of NP (within NP).

Discussion of in-text exercises

1.(a)

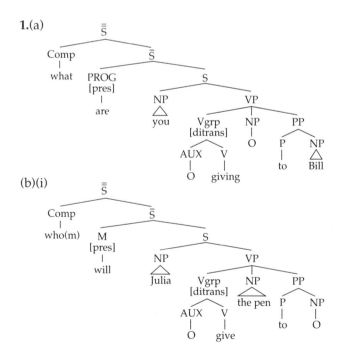

(b)(i)

(b)(ii)

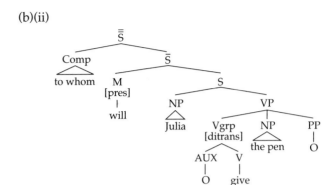

(c)

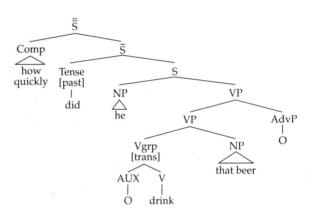

(d)

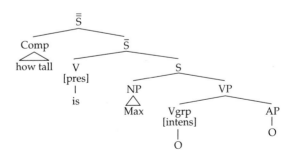

2.

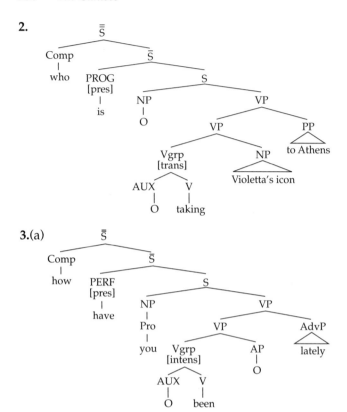

3.(a)

Since most answers to that question take the form of APs (*well, brilliant, healthy, awful, much better, too busy*) I have assumed that *how* corresponds to an AP gap. But a PP gap is possible (*in good spirits*).

(b)

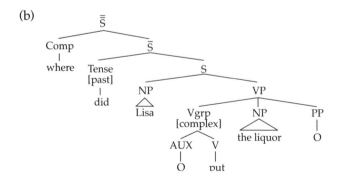

As indicated, *put* is a complex transitive verb, generally taking an NP and a PP. So I have represented *where* as corresponding to a PP gap.

4.

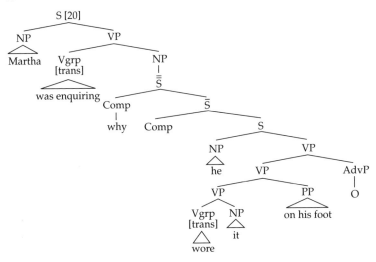

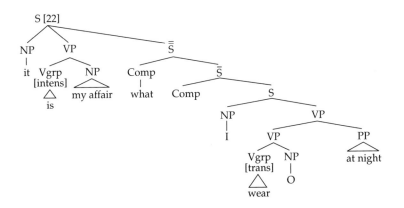

5.

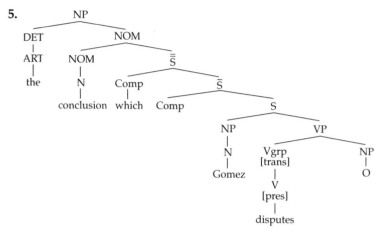

6.(a)

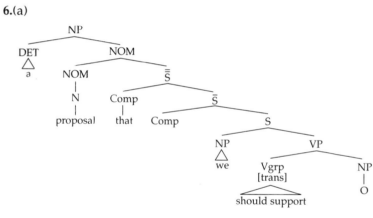

(b)

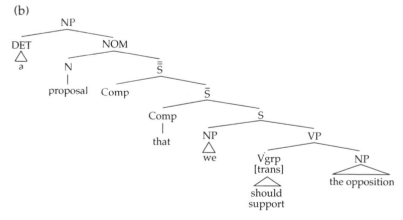

Exercises

1. Replace the italicised constituent in the following sentences by an appropriate Wh-word, and give the Wh-question that results from Wh- and auxiliary fronting.

(a) We shall feed the cat *smoked salmon* today.
(b) He got to London *by hitch-hiking*.
(c) *The man at the front* called out.
(d) A recidivist is *a persistent offender*.
(e) He can get *very* arrogant.
(f) Grishkin showed up in *dark glasses*.
(g) Tessa pocketed the fried egg *because it was too greasy to eat*.
(h) You are acting in the capacity *of Vice-Chancellor*.
(i) Mary suggested *Lomax* should be fired.

2. For each of the following, embed the (i) clause as a relative clause in an NP of the (ii) clause, giving the sentence that results. For example, (i) and (ii) would yield (iii):

    (i) You mislaid some stilton last Christmas.
    (ii) The stilton has just strolled into the bedroom.
    (iii) The stilton which you mislaid last Christmas has just strolled into the bedroom.

(a)   (i) I had been trying to extract a cork.
    (ii) The cork suddenly launched itself at Widmerpool.
(b)   (i) Some officer issued this ridiculous order.
    (ii) I am going to override the officer.
(c)   (i) Crusoe said he had been marooned on an island.
    (ii) The island has never been discovered.
(d)   (i) I had borrowed a passenger's toothbrush.
    (ii) The passenger was seething.

3. For each of the following sentences decide whether the relative clause that follows it could be (a) only restrictive, (b) only non-restrictive, or (c) either, when included in the italicised NP. Then draw phrase-markers for sentences (a) and (b) including the relative clauses. (Use the Δ notation for Vgrps, PPs and simple NPs).

(a)   *Napoleon* died in exile.
            who inaugurated the penal code.
(b)   I haven't owned *a pig* in my life.
            which could fly.
(c)   I prefer (i) *cats* to (ii) *cats*.
            (i) which have stripes.
            (ii) which have spots.
(d)   *The acrobat* ate ravenously.
            who I had just hired.
(e)   The source of the Nile was discovered by Speke.
            which I have visited.

4.   Give Abbreviated Clausal Analyses of the following sentences. For each subordinate clause, state what type of clause it is (*that*-clause, interrogative, or relative) and its function. Example: *The books from the library that John has consulted are out of date.*

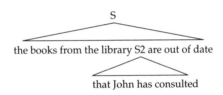

S2: restrictive relative clause – modifier of NOM (*books from the library*).

(a)   I never understood how the theory worked until I read your book.
(b)   Why Max didn't answer the accusation that he had cheated is a mystery.
(c)   Why Max didn't answer the poor man that he had cheated is a mystery.
(d)   The acrobat, who is injured, is anxious that the high-wire should be strengthened before anyone is allowed on it again.

Discussion of exercises

1.(a) What shall we feed the cat today?
(b)   How did he get to London?
(c)   Who called out?
(d)   What is a recidivist?
(e)   How arrogant can he get?
(f)   What did Grishkin show up in?
(g)   Why did Tessa pocket the fried egg?
(h)   In what capacity are you acting? (What capacity are you acting in?)
(i)   Who did Mary suggest should be fired?

2.(a) The cork which I had been trying to extract suddenly
launched itself at Widmerpool.
(b)   I am going to override the officer who issued this ridiculous
order.
(c)   The island on which Crusoe said he had been marooned has
never been discovered. (or: The island which Crusoe said he
had been marooned on ...)
(d)   The passenger whose toothbrush I had borrowed was
seething.

3.(a) Non-restrictive only. Since *Napoleon,* a proper name, already
uniquely identifies a particular individual, it is impossible to
restrict the range of reference of this NP further.
(b)   Restrictive only. If we included the clause as non-restrictive,
the whole sentence would be equivalent to *I haven't owned a
pig and a pig could fly* which hardly makes sense. In the context of this (negative) sentence, the expression *a pig* does not
pick out a particular individual pig. Only if it did pick out a
particular pig could we then add the further information
about that pig that it could fly.
(c)   (i) and (ii) must both be restrictive. If either or both of them
were non-restrictive, the resulting sentence would be contra-
dictory, as indeed (c) is without the relative clauses.
(d)   Both restrictive and non-restrictive are possible here.
(e)   Non-restrictive only. Like *Napoleon, the source of the Nile*
already uniquely identifies a fully specified entity.

(a)

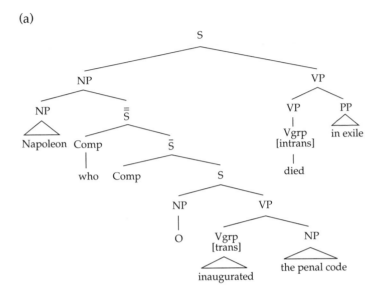

(b)

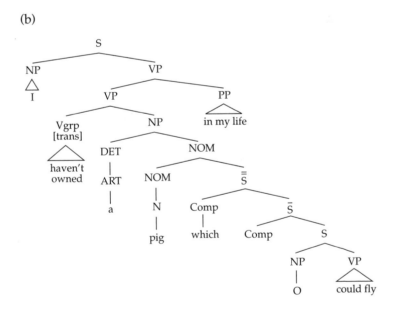

4.(a)

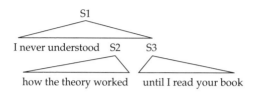

S1: Main clause.
S2: Wh-interrogative clause: Complement (dO) of Vgrp (*understood*).
S3: Adverbial clause.

(b) and (c)

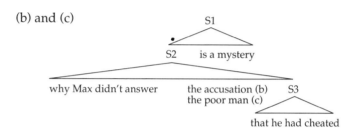

S1: Main clause.
S2: Wh-interrogative clause: subject of S1.
(b) S3: *That*-clause: complement to noun (*accusation*). *Cheat* is [intrans] here.
(c) S3: Restrictive relative clause: modifier of NOM (*poor man*). *Cheat* is [trans] here, with a gap in dO position.

(d)

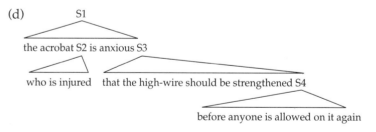

S1: Main clause.
S2: Non-restrictive relative clause: modifier of NP (*the acrobat*).
S3: *That*-clause: complement to A (*anxious*).
S4: Adverbial clause.

Further exercises

Questions and interrogatives

1.   Draw complete phrase-markers for the following.

Set I

(1) Which salami shall we buy?
(2) Where have I put my glasses?
(3) Where did they have the picnic?
(4) Who's been eating my porridge?
(5) What drinks are we serving to the visitors?
(6) Which of these books does John recommend?
(7) Do you know what they ate?
(8) What do you think they put in that soup?

Set II

(9a) I don't know who he found an amusing companion.
(9b) I don't know whether he found an amusing companion.
(10a) Who did Granny say should play?
(10b) Who did Capablanca say I should play?
(11a) Who is a phonologist?
(11b) What is a phonologist?

Set III

(These need care.)
(12) Which exam was it certain Julia would pass?
(13) Who did John ask which films they had seen?
(14) Who has been sacked?
(15) Who were they given to?

2.(a) (1) and (2) below will have different phrase-markers (as an exercise, you could give them). But those phrase-markers do not in themselves explain the difference between the questions that (1) an (2) would be used to ask. Try doing that. You may find this easier after tackling (b).

    (1)   Did you discover who was giving the lecture?
    (2)   Who did you discover was giving the lecture?

(b) In (2), we can replace *discover* with *say, know, hope*, and *assume*, but in (1) we can only replace it with *say* and *know*, not *hope* or *assume*. Explain this difference between *discover / say / know* and *hope / assume*.

3. In connection with Wh-subject questions such as that in (2)

(1) Vince is taking the icons to Athens.
(2) Who is taking the icons to Athens?

I assumed that auxiliary-fronting always occurs in Wh-questions, even though it doesn't change the order of words. But was that the right decision? And how could we know? Well, here is a small piece of evidence. Change the Vgrp in (1) from *is taking* to *takes*. Then (3) but not (4) is the Wh-question that corresponds to (2).

(3) Who takes the icons to Athens?
(4) *Who does take the icons to Athens?

(4) is only grammatical if *does* is emphatically stressed. How does this bear on the question of whether auxiliary-fronting occurs in Wh-subject questions? Does it confirm or disconfirm the analysis adopted in the chapter?

Relative clauses and other matters

4. Draw complete phrase-markers for the following NPs:

(1) The chef who I fired.   (2) The spy who loved me.
(3) A style I think appropriate. (4) The place where we had the picnic.
(5) The reason why it spits.   (6) The woman in whose care we left you.

5. Draw complete phrase-markers for the following sentences:

(1a) The man they cheated is furious.
(1b) The reason they cheated is clear.
(2a) I have an idea we should think about.
(2b) I have an idea we should think about exams.

(3a) The fact that I communicated with Mona is irrelevant.
(3b) The fact that I communicated to Mona was irrelevant.

6. I have discussed only relative clauses appearing in the structure of NPs. A difference between restrictive and non-restrictive relatives is that, while the former only ever function as modifiers within NP, non-restrictives can modify a range of categories. Decide on the constituents (and their categories) that the non-restrictive relative clauses are modifying in (1)–(3). Then, bearing in mind that they modify full phrasal categories, draw a complete phrase-marker for (1).

    (1)   He was very rude, which I never am.
    (2)   Lomax argued for trampolines, which surprised me.
    (3)   Hedda got out with the aid of a trampoline, which seemed a sensible way of doing it.

7. The following sentences illustrate a function of certain Wh-clauses not explicitly discussed in this chapter. Decide on their function and then draw the phrase-markers for (1) and (2), not forgetting that Wh-phrases are fronted phrases:

    (1)   Lola merely smiled when I proposed marriage.
    (2)   They pitched the tent where they always pitch the tent.

8. Give Abbreviated Clausal Analyses of the following sentences. Indicate the gaps. For each subordinate clause, state what type of clause it is (*that*-clause, *yes/no* interrogative, Wh-interrogative, or relative (restrictive or non-restrictive)) and give its function. For all Wh-clauses, identify and give the function of the Wh-phrase that introduces it (whether that Wh-phrase overt or not). For examples, see the answers to Exercise 5 above.

    (1)   The man who broke the bank at Monte Carlo is now my butler.
    (2)   Which animals Bertram feeds is his decision.
    (3)   We should find out who the visitors to the restaurant during those hours were.
    (4)   It's hardly surprising you can't get your teeth into the fritters Jim cooks.

(5) Whether we are going for a picnic again is a question that he is always asking.

(6) I'm nervous that the hoops that have been alight will topple over when the hippos jump through them.

(7) Watson, who was never very quick, is still wondering if Holmes' theory that the governess is the guilty party can possibly be right.

(8) Did you ask how many players knew what instrument Miss Scarlet was murdered with?

(9) None of the people who went to Narnia when it was first created ever explained how they got there.

(10) Marcel often wondered whether Gilberte ever asked Swann what the boy she'd seen in the garden was called.

9. The following are ambiguous. For each, draw a phrase-marker for each interpretation. Abbreviate them as far as possible (but not so far as to obscure the distinction between the interpretations.)

(a) I had forgotten how bitter beer tastes.
(b) When did you say he should go?
(c) The news that Max had left Greta was alarming.
(d) He asked the man who he had seen.

Chapter 10

Non-finite Clauses

I conclude this survey of English constituent types and their functions by looking at the different types of non-finite clause. All the sentences and clauses considered so far in this book have been finite. In other words, they all had a finite Vgrp, with the first verb of the group tensed (present or past). **A non-finite clause is a clause with a non-finite (tenseless) Vgrp**. Main clauses, remember, are always finite. So **non-finite clauses can only be subordinate**.

I look first at the form of non-finite clauses and then at their functions. As regards their form, they can be grouped into four main types, corresponding to four types of tenseless Vgrp. However, there is more to the difference between finite and non-finite clauses than just the presence vs. absence of tense in the Vgrp. So a point about the general form of non-finite clauses needs to be made at the outset.

Not only do non-finite clauses lack tense in the Vgrp, they may also overtly lack one or more major constituents. Non-finite clauses frequently lack an overt subject, for example. In a finite clause, the finite (tensed) Vgrp must have an overt subject to agree with in terms of number (singular/plural). Non-finite Vgrps are not subject to this constraint. When a non-finite clause lacks an overt constituent, this indicates either

(i) the reference of that constituent is general (indefinite, non-specific), or

(ii) its reference is identical to a constituent in a higher (superordinate) clause.

Consider, for example, the italicised non-finite clauses in [1] and [2]. Their Vgrps (*chatting* and *wasting*) are tenseless and they lack an overt subject.

[1]   [*Chatting with the construction workers*] is a good way of [*wasting time*].

[2]   Hedda enjoys [*chatting with the construction workers*].
[3]   Hedda doesn't tolerate [*Anna chatting with the construction workers*].

There is a clear difference between the non-finite clauses in [1] and those in [2] and [3]. Although not overt, the subject of the non-finite clause in [2] is just as specific as that in [3] (with the overt subject). This is because it is understood as identical with the subject of the main clause, *Hedda*. What Hedda enjoys is *Hedda* chatting with construction workers (Anna, it seems, it another matter!). The subjects of the non-finite clauses in [1], by contrast, are not specific. [1] mentions chatting with the construction workers (and wasting time) *in general*, regardless of who does it.

We need a short-hand term for this contrast between constituents that are non-overt because general and nonspecific and those that are non-overt because understood as identical to a constituent in a higher clause. **When a non-overt element is specific and understood as identical to an overt constituent in a higher clause, the higher overt element is said to** CONTROL **the non-overt element.** So the subject of the non-finite subordinate clause in [2] is controlled by the main clause subject. By contrast, neither of the non-overt subjects in [1] has a controller in the main clause. **A non-overt constituent that is** NOT CONTROLLED **is described as** FREE.

Try Exercise 1 at the end of the chapter before reading further.

Henceforth I shall refer to non-overt constituents as 'covert constituents'. Covert constituents can be indicated in the same way as gaps, by 'O'. That will do for covert constituents that are free. For covert constituents that are controlled, we need to indicate that they are controlled and what they are controlled by. Using subscript numbers for this, we can indicate that the covert subject of the subordinate clause in [2], for example, is controlled by *Hedda* by adding a subscript '1' to both 'O' (O_1) and the subject NP node in the main clause (NP_1). This is called an index, so giving the same index to two nodes is 'co-indexing'.

The form of non-finite Verb Groups

As regards their form, the four types of non-finite Vgrps are classified according to the (untensed) form taken by the first verb in the Vgrp. The term 'non-finite' covers 'infinitive' Vgrps and 'participle' Vgrps.

INFINITIVE Vgrps:

I: Bare infinitive
      (only simple)

II: *To*-infinitive
       (simple or complex)

PARTICIPLE Vgrps:

III: Passive participle
     (only simple)

IV: *-ing* participle
       (simple or complex)

I. Bare infinitive Vgrps

This just consists of the (untensed) stem of a lexical verb. It is called 'bare' because it lacks the infinitive particle *to*. Examples of sentences with bare infinitive clauses are:

[4]   She made him [*darn* her socks].
[5]   All you have to do is [*squeeze* the trigger slowly].

These non-finite (untensed) forms can be distinguished from simple present tense forms (as in *I darn her socks every week*) by the feature [−tense], to be read as 'minus tense', on the V node, as in [6]. This feature will appear in all non-finite Vgrps.

[6]   Vgrp
          [trans]
            |
            V
         [−tense]
            |
          darn

II. To-infinitive Vgrps

[7]   We declined his invitation [*to taste* the wine].
[8]   He is thought [*to be hiding* in Brazil].
[9]   Gomez is unlikely [*to be beaten* by a six year old].
[10] [For Max *to have been beaten* at chess] seemed hardly believable.

The auxiliary possibilities mentioned in Chapter 6 – PROG, PERF, PASS – remain possibilities in the *to*-infinitive Vgrp. However, since modals (M) are always tensed, modals do not appear in any non-finite (tenseless) Vgrp. Like the verb that follows M, the verb following the infinitive particle *to* has the basic stem form. In several aspects, then, it is appropriate to think of *to* as replacing the M option. So, even in a simple Vgrp such as that in [7], I shall analyse *to* itself as the sole representative of an untensed auxiliary element. The AUX node will carry the [−tense] feature.

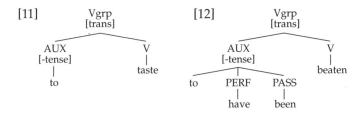

III. Passive participle Vgrps

Like bare infinitives, these can only be simple. As the description 'passive' implies, these contrast with the bare infinitives (active in meaning) in having a passive meaning. These simple Vgrps will be distinguished from bare infinitives by the feature [pass] on the V node. Here are some examples:

[13] [The palanquin *loaded*], we took a rest.
[14] [*Loaded* to capacity], the palanquin lurched on.
[15] [I saw [your book *reviewed* in the paper].
[16] I want [those accusations *investigated*].

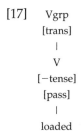

[17]   Vgrp
       [trans]
         |
        V
     [−tense]
      [pass]
         |
     loaded

Remember that only verbs taking objects in the active (monotransitive, ditransitive, and complex transitive verbs) can be passive, since passive entails making an object into the subject, leaving a gap in object position. In [13], [15], and [16] this subject is overt (*the palanquin, your book, those accusations*). In [14] it is not overt but controlled by the main clause subject (*the palanquin,* again). In the subordinate clause of [14], then, there will be both a subject- and an object-gap.

IV. -ing *participle Vgrps*

Like *to*-infinitive Vgrps, these can be complex. They have the same structure except that, instead of the first verb being preceded by *to*, it takes the -*ing* affix.

[18] He had difficulty in [*getting up* in the mornings].
[19] Judith was busy [*stuffing* the peppers].
[20] [Murtlock *having been hospitalised*], I conducted a bedside interview.

I shall analyse all -*ing* participle Vgrps as having an AUX node with the [−tense] feature. In simple Vgrps like that in [18], this AUX node will be unfilled.

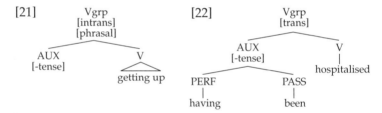

I have called these non-finite Vgrps '-*ing* participle' rather than 'progressive participle'. While the participles discussed under III above clearly are passive, -*ing* participles cannot be regarded as progressive. The reason for this is that there are verbs (called stative verbs), such as *know* and *own*, which cannot appear in the progressive ([23a], [24a]) but can appear in non-finite -*ing* participle clauses ([23b], [24b]):

[23a] *I am knowing the Beethoven trios intimately.
[23b] Knowing the Beethoven trios intimately helps a lot.
[24a] *He was owning this mangrove swamp.
[24b] Owning this mangrove swamp meant nothing to him.

Furthermore, progressive *be* cannot precede perfect *have*. This means that perfect *have* cannot assume the -*ing* form demanded by a preceding progressive. See [25a]. But perfect *have* can assume the -*ing* participle form in non-finite clauses – as in [25b].

[25a] *Buster is having sold the swamp.
[25b] Having sold the swamp, Buster departed.

So much then for the form of non-finite Vgrps themselves. I now turn to more general aspects of non-finite clauses.

Complementisers and non-finite clauses

As in finite clauses, there are two complementiser positions in non-finite clauses. These are filled by **the (unfronted) Comp-1 complementisers:** *for* and *whether*, and **(fronted) Comp-2 Wh-phrases**. As before, I shall represent all subordinate clauses as introduced by Comp-1 and dominated by S-bar but, for simplicity, I shall only represent the Comp-2 position and S-double-bar when strictly necessary.

Comp-1: for *and* whether

Only *to*-infinitive clauses can be introduced by the Comp-1 complementisers *for* and the (*yes/no*) interrogative *whether*.

For only figures overtly in (*to*-infinitive) clauses with overt subject. See [26]–[28]. Even then – as [29] shows – *for* is not always possible, in which case the Comp-1 position will be empty.

[26] [For Angelo to get all the blame] seems unfair.
[27] The police issued orders [for the vehicles to be removed].
[28] It will be difficult [for me to get there on time].
[29] The magician expected [(*for) the rabbits to disappear].

Notice, incidentally, the pronominal subject in [28]: although it is subject, it takes the accusative case form. I mention this again below.

The phrase-marker for the non-finite clause in [26] is given as **Discussion 1**, page 272.

Yes/no interrogative clauses (*whether*-clauses), by contrast, are always *to*-infinitive and never have an overt subject. Generally, the covert subject is controlled by the subject of the superordinate clause, as in [30] and [31]. Notice, though, that when the *whether*-clause is itself functioning as subject, as in [32], the covert subject is free:

[30] King Louis was doubtful [whether to support the Pope].
[31] Olsen asked the Captain [whether to cut the engines].
[32] [Whether to permit such activities] is a tricky question.

Comp-2: fronted Wh-phrases

Non-finite Wh-clauses can be interrogative or relative. First, **interrogative clauses**. As with the *yes/no*-interrogative clauses just looked at, Wh-interrogative clauses can only be *to*-infinitive and have a covert subject.

[33] Sarah asked me [how many guests to expect].
[34] He told me [where to put it] in no uncertain terms.
[35] The Orsini never had doubts about [who to vote for].
[36] It was not clear [who to nominate].

Notice a difference here between *tell* and *ask*. In [33], with *ask*, the subject of the interrogative clause is controlled by the main clause subject (*Sarah*). In [34], with *tell*, by contrast, it is controlled by the indirect object (*me*).

Since the subject in these clauses must be either free (as in [36]) or controlled by a constituent in the superordinate clause, the subject is the one constituent that cannot be fronted to the Comp-2 position of the subordinate clause. Here is a phrase-marker for the subordinate clause in [33].

[37]

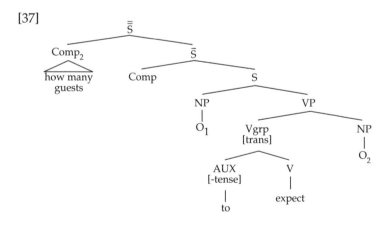

Assuming that *Sarah* in the main clause of [33] has the index '1', I have co-indexed the covert subject with *Sarah*. And, to keep track of all these 'O's, I have also co-indexed *how many guests* with the direct object gap. Given that *how many guests* has here been fronted from the dO position, it is reasonable to think of it as being the controller of that position (controlling the interpretation of the gap).

Non-finite **relative clauses** are less readily identifiable as Wh-clauses (with fronting) than the Wh-interrogative clauses just considered. This is because **the fronted Wh-phrase is never overt in the non-finite relative clause**. As the following show, all forms of non-finite Vgrp are permitted in relative clauses except the bare infinitive:

[38a] The instrument [to use] is a #9 scalpel.
[39a] A book [for you to review] is in the post.
[40a] There are no WCs on the overnight train [now leaving Platform 3].
[41a] A cat [fed on smoked salmon] will start demanding champagne.

Although there is no overt Wh-phrase in these, we know they must be relative clauses (a) because they are functioning as modifiers within NP (more specifically as NOM-modifiers) and (b) because – in addition to any covert constituent they may have in virtue of being non-finite – they always have a further gap. This gap is created by the fronting of a covert Wh-phrase (to Comp-2). In the following, I indicate (in [b]) the covert constituents (by •), and (in [c]) give the closest finite clause, each of which is an overt relative clause.

[38b] [• to use •]	[38c] which one should use
[39b] [for you to review •]	[39c] which you might/should review
[40b] [• now leaving Platform 3]	[40c] which is now leaving Platform 3
[41b] [• fed • on smoked salmon]	[41c] which has been fed on smoked salmon

In [38] the subject of *use* is free and the object is controlled by a fronted Wh-phrase (covert in [b], overt in [c]). In [39] the gap in the object position is due to the fronting of a covert Wh-phrase. The same goes for the subjects in [40] and [41]. The object gap in [41] is due to its being a *passive* participle clause, with object promoted to subject (from whence it is Wh-fronted). Here is the phrase-marker for the subject NP of [38a].

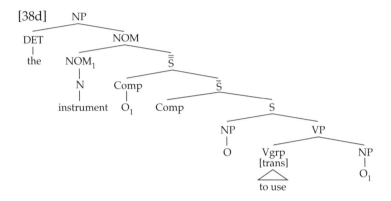

[38d]

Notice that, in addition to co-indexing the object NP gap and the higher Comp, I have co-indexed that Comp and the NOM *instrument*. This means that the NOM and the object gap are co-indexed. This captures the fact that the direct object of *use* is understood as being an NP having *instrument* as head.

Now give phrase-markers for the subject NPs of [39a] and [41a]. **Discussion 2**, page 272.

The functions of non-finite clauses

The functions of non-finite clauses will be familiar to you from previous chapters. They are illustrated (some of them many times) in the examples given so far in this chapter. Before reading further, then, take time to go through all the examples of sentences containing non-finite clauses thus far and decide on the function of that clause in each. List them by function (i.e. when you encounter a particular function for the first time, establish a new list). They are listed in **Discussion 3**, page 273.

In the rest of this chapter I simply list those functions, giving further examples where necessary. Occasionally it will be necessary to comment on particular issues and problems, but I have kept these to a minimum. Complementation of the Vgrp by non-finite clauses requires more discussion and this has been reserved until the end.

Subject and extraposed subject

This function is illustrated in [1] (the first clause), [10], [23b], [24b], [26] and [32]. In [28] and [36] the subject clause is extraposed. As with the finite clauses of Chapter 8, a non-finite clausal subject should be dominated by NP. *-ing* participle clauses with overt subject cannot be extraposed. Compare [42a–b] with [43a–b].

[42a] Stripping wallpaper is a wretched business.
[42b] It's a wretched business stripping wallpaper.
[43a] Oscar attempting the double somersault should amuse you.
[43b] *It should amuse you Oscar attempting the double somersault.

The phrase-marker for [42a] is given as **Discussion 4**, page 273.

Complement of A in AP

This function of non-finite clauses was illustrated in [9], [19], and [30]. This is an intriguing construction. There are several types of adjective complementation by *to*-infinitive clause, depending on the head adjective itself. Here I shall distinguish two main types, exemplified by

[44a] Max is reluctant to try it.
[44b] That piano is impossible to move.

Adjectives that pattern [a] like **reluctant** are: *anxious, eager, keen, hesitant, unwilling, happy* and *liable*. Those that pattern [b] like **impossible** are: *easy, hard, difficult, tough, tiresome, boring, enjoyable, disgusting,* and *delicious*. Focusing on the interpretation of the covert constituents, what is the difference between these?

With the [a] adjectives the higher subject controls the covert SUBJECT of the adjective complement clause. By contrast, with the [b] adjectives, the higher subject controls the OBJECT of that clause. The lower subject with the [b] adjective cannot be controlled: it must either be free, as in [44b], or overt, as in [45].

[45] That piano is impossible for the dancers to move.

Sentences with [b]-type adjectives correspond to ones in which the object figures overtly (in a clause functioning as extraposed subject).

[46]   It would be impossible [to move that piano].
(cf [47] [To move that piano] would be impossible.)

It could be argued, then, that the [b]-construction actually
involves, not a complement of A in AP, but extraposition of the
clausal subject. In the absence of expletive *it* in [44b], however, I
shall treat the clause there as an A-complement. Draw phrase-
markers for [44a]–[44b]. **Discussion 5**, pages 273–4. See also
Exercise 2 and the Further Exercises.

Complement of P in PP

Only *-ing* participle clauses can complement a preposition within
PP. Examples are the second clause in [1] and that in [18] and
[35]. In each of those, the PP itself is functioning as a noun-complement in NP. But PPs with a non-finite clausal complement
have other functions too. Give the function of the relevant PP in
the following.

[48]   John reparked the car in his absence *by* leaving the hand-
brake off.
[49]   *With* the troglodytes approaching, Argon capitulated.
[50]   This resulted *in* Murtlock being hospitalised.
[51]   He was hopeless *at* writing letters.
[52]   We became zombies *through* watching TV.

The PPs in [48], [49] and [52] are functioning as adverbials, that
in [50] as complement of the [prep] Vgrp (*resulted*), and that in
[51] as complement to A (*hopeless*) in AP.

Assuming that PP always consists of P and NP, clauses having
this function should be dominated by NP. Phrase-markers for
[51]–[52] are given as **Discussion 6**, page 274.

Adverbial

We have seen that non-finite clauses can function as the complement of a preposition in a PP functioning as an adverbial. They
can also function as adverbials in their own right. Examples
already given are: [13], [14], [20], and [25b]. As the following
show, the subject must be overt if not controlled by the superordinate subject.

[53a] *The count having invited us,* we cancelled other plans.
[53b] *Having furnished ourselves with garlic,* we set off.
[54a] We hung around *for the count to appear.*
[54b] We helped ourselves to wine *to relieve the boredom.*
[55a] *The wine finished,* we dozed fitfully in our chairs.
[55b] We returned, *disappointed by our evening.*

The phrase-marker for [55b] is given as **Discussion 7**, page 275.

Mention should be made here of non-finite adverbial clauses introduced by (Comp-1) subordinating conjunctions. Examples are:

[56] I will come [*if* needed].
[57] This mixture will explode [*unless* kept below freezing].
[58] [*Although* feeding twice a day], he still seems hungry.
[59] I can do this [*without* using my hands].
[60] Max brandished the weapon [*as if* to frighten them].

Modifier of NOM in NP

Examples were given in [38a]–[41a]. As mentioned, these are all relative clauses with a covert Wh-phrase. Here are further examples containing (italicised) NPs which, in addition to including a non-finite relative clause, also include a pre-modifying adjective:

[61a] He was *the last person to be executed on the guillotine.*
[62a] Boswell found him *a difficult walker to keep up with.*
[63a] *The least likely person for us to appoint* would be Max.

The interest of these lies in the interdependence between the two modifiers of the head N. In the most closely corresponding finite relative clause, the premodifying adjective in [61]–[63] clearly belongs within the postmodifying relative clause:

[61b] … the person who was last executed on the guillotine.
[62b] … a walker who was difficult to keep up with.
[63b] The person who we are least likely to appoint ….

In these, the non-finite clause functions as complement of the adjective, so *last to be executed …, difficult to keep up with,* and *most likely to succeed* are APs. It is surprising, then, to find the adjective wholly outside the non-finite clause in the [a] examples. Since the adjective is only there in virtue of its relation to the non-finite clause, it seems reasonable to suppose that it modifies a NOM composed of head noun and non-finite clause as in [64]:

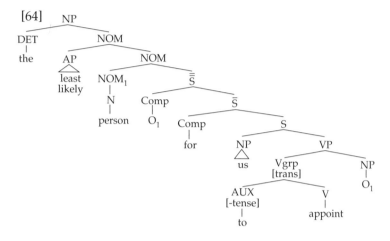

Complement of N in NP

Examples were given in [7] and [27] above, *his invitation [to taste the wine], orders [for the vehicles to be removed]*. Here are further examples:

[65] We simply ignored [his appeals for us to join the folk-dance].

[66] [His ability to think straight] was severely impaired by the experience.

[67] [His proposal to show us the holiday snaps] was treated politely.

Which constituent controls the covert subject in the infinitive clauses of [66] and [67]?

The bracketed NPs in [66] and [67] are NP versions of the following clauses:

[68] He was able to think straight.

[69] He proposed to show us the holiday snaps.

In these, the covert subject of the infinitive clause is controlled by the subject of the superordinate clause. In the NPs in [66] and [67] this subject has assumed the form of a (personal, genitive) determiner. So the covert subject of the infinitive clauses in [66] and [67] is controlled by the determiner of the NP within which they appear. Contrast this, however, with the control pattern in [7] above, *We declined his invitation to taste the wine.* The phrase-marker for that whole sentence is given as **Discussion 8**, page 275.

Complement of Vgrp

As mentioned, complementation of the Vgrp by non-finite clause requires more discussion. What follows is intended to give just an initial impression of this rich and controversial area of English grammar.

Since Chapter 4 we have operated with a useful six-way sub-categorisation of verbs which has the effect of assigning more specific functions to their complements (direct and indirect object, subject- and object-predicative, prepositional complement). It is not clear, however, that this sub-categorisation system (and the functions associated with it) is appropriate in cases of complementation by non-finite clause.

For example, while there are straightforwardly monotransitive verbs (taking an NP as direct object) that can also take a non-finite clause as complement (e.g. *believe* as in [70a–b]), there are other verbs that can take a clause but not an NP (e.g. *hope* and *condescend* as in [71a–b]).

[70a] I believe his story/William.
[70b] I believe William to have been in the garden.
[71a] Michaelangelo condescended to decorate the ceiling.
[71b] *Michaelangelo condescended the decoration of the ceiling.

Can we then think of the clause in [71a] as a direct object exactly?

Again, *promise* and *ask* are ditransitive verbs, taking an indirect object NP and a direct object NP (as in [72a], [73a]). This might lead us to analyse [72b] and [73b] as ditransitive and to take the non-finite clause as the direct object:

[72a] I promised [Herzog] [my spaghetti machine].
[72b] I promised [Herzog] [to wear the wig].
[73a] I asked [Astrid] [a question].
[73b] I asked [Astrid] [to make no comment].

So far, so good. There are good reasons, though, for analysing VPs with *force* and *dare* as having the same constituent structure as those with *promise* and *ask*.

[74] I $\left\{\begin{array}{c}\text{forced}\\\text{dared}\end{array}\right\}$ [Astrid] [to wear the wig].

Yet neither *force* nor *dare* can take two NPs in complementation (i.e. they are not obviously ditransitive) – and it is anyway not obvious that *Astrid* in [74] (and even in [73b]) is understood in the way we understand 'indirect object'.

Rather than give further examples of specific problems to do with the functions of complements in the various sub-categories, I should mention here a more general consideration. In order to capture the full complexity of what you know about verbs and their complements, they really need to be sub-categorised in a way quite independent of, and much more detailed than, the six subcategory feature labels used so far. To give just one example: subcategorising *kick, believe, say* and *watch*, as '[transitive]' hardly does justice to the differences between them as regards the complements they can and cannot take. Certainly, all four can take a direct object NP (*kicked the chessboard, believed the story, said the prayer, watched the fun*). But, unlike *say* and *believe, kick* and *watch* cannot take a *that*-clause.

[75] *Gomez kicked that he had lost the match.
[76] She believed that William was in the out-house.
[77] She said that Rashid had the perfect disguise.
[78] *Talulla watched that the clown was putting on his make-up.

Furthermore, leaving *kick* aside (since it cannot take any clause), *believe* can take a *to*-infinitive clause with overt subject, but *say* and *watch* cannot.

[76a] She believed William to be in the outhouse.
[77a] *She said Rashid to have the perfect disguise.
[78a] *Talulla watched the clown to put on his make-up.

However, *watch* can take an *ing*-participle clause, which *believe* and *say* cannot.

[76b] *She believed William being in the outhouse.
[77b] *She said Rashid having the perfect disguise.
[78b] Talulla watched the clown putting on his make-up.

A fully detailed and explicit sub-categorisation system, one that did justice to the intricacy of your knowledge of this aspect of the English language, would need to sub-categorise each verb for at least the following:

[79] (a) whether it takes a clause as complement;
      (b) if so, whether it may or must be interrogative;
      (c) whether it can be finite or non-finite;
      (d) if non-finite, which of the four types of non-finite clause are permitted;
      (e) whether an NP can intervene between the finite and the non-finite verbs;
      (f) if so, what the function of that NP is;
      (g) what constituent, if any, controls the covert constituents (if any) in the non-finite clause.

Answering these questions for the several thousand English verbs would be ambitious by any standard and beyond the scope of this chapter. Even so, as I hope the discussion of *kick*, *say*, etc. shows, it would result in an approach to the sub-categorisation of verbs rather different from that employed so far, one independent of the functions dO, iO, sP and oP. This is not to say there is no correspondence between verb complementation by non-finite clause and the six-way sub-categorisation of previous chapters. There is, as with *ask* and *promise*. Consider also the complements of the [intensive] copula *be* in the following, which clearly parallel subject-predicatives in function.

[80] The noise you can hear is [Tessa slurping her coffee].
[81] All he ever did was [lounge about and clean his ears].

When a non-finite clause complements a Vgrp, then, I shall not attempt to assign that clause a more specific function (dO, iO, sP, oP) in terms of the sub-categorisation of the verb that it complements. This means that the sub-categorisation features on the Vgrp can be dispensed with. And, since we have questioned whether such complement clauses do function precisely as direct objects, I shall not demand that they be dominated by an NP node.

For **verbs complemented just by a non-finite clause without overt subject**, it suffices to note that only *to*-infinitive and *-ing* participle clauses are admitted. The covert subject is always controlled by the superordinate subject. Further examples are

[82]–[83]. Notice the distinction in meaning between the *to*-infinitive (which implies that Jeeves didn't kiss her) and the *ing*-particle (which implies that he did).

[82a] Jeeves didn't remember to kiss her.
[83]   Jeeves didn't remember kissing her.

[82b]

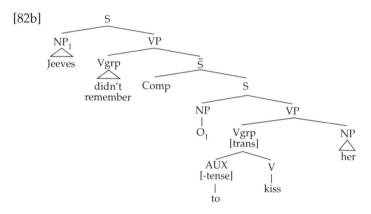

Matters are not so straightforward when an NP intervenes between the superordinate verb and the non-finite verb of the subordinate clause. In the following, the relevant NP is italicised.

Vgrp + NP + *to*-infinitive.
  [84] I'd prefer *the butler* to taste it first.
  [85] She encouraged *Muldoon* to buy her the diamonds.
  [86] Machiavelli believed *him* to be the ideal prince.
  [87] I'd like *the Right Honourable Member* to try it for a week.

Vgrp + NP + *-ing* participle.
  [88] He had heard *Victoria and Albert* singing that duet.
  [89] I caught *the clowns* helping the elephants onto the trapeze.

Vgrp + NP + bare infinitive.
  [90] Marcel made *Celeste* peel him a grape.
  [91] He watched *Matilda* polish off the toast.

Vgrp + NP + passive participle.
  [92] She found *the icon* buried in the wall.
  [93] She kept *Raleigh* imprisoned in the tower.

The question raised by these examples is (f) in [79] above: is the italicised NP subject of the SUBordinate (lower) clause or object of the SUPERordinate (higher) clause. Take [91] for example: is *Matilda* subject of *polish off* or is it object of *watched*? Perhaps you have an intuitive view on this? It makes a difference to the constituent analysis of the higher VP. If **(I)** that NP is the subject of the lower Vgrp, then it must be included within the structure of the lower clause. In that case the higher VP will consist just of a Vgrp and a non-finite clause (with overt subject) functioning as its **one complement**. On the other hand, if **(II)** the NP is object of the higher verb, then it must be a constituent in the structure of the higher VP (a sister of the higher Vgrp). In that case, it won't be included in the structure of the lower clause. The higher Vgrp will then have **two complements**, a direct object NP and a non-finite clause (with covert subject).

I. Subject of lower Vgrp   **II. Object of higher Vgrp**

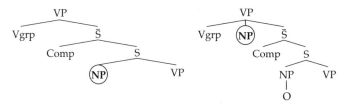

This uncertainty arises for several reasons, three of which I shall mention here.

(i) When functioning as the complement of Vgrp, non-finite clauses rarely allow an overt complementiser. *Prefer* is among the very few verbs, in British English at least, to do so – and then only for some speakers.

[94] I'd prefer [*for* the butler to taste it].

Since the function of the complementiser is to introduce the subordinate (lower) clause, it very clearly marks the division between the higher and the lower clause. In [94] (and [84] above), then, *the butler* falls squarely within the lower clause and must be regarded as its subject. However, in the (much more usual) absence of an overt complementiser, no such obvious clue as to the function of the NP is provided.

(ii) If you replace the italicised NPs in [84]–[93] by pronouns, those pronouns must appear in the accusative case (*me, him, her, us, them*, rather than *I, he, she, we, they*). This might appear to suggest that those NPs must be functioning as objects rather than as subjects (cf. *She loves him and he loves her*). Against this, however, it could be, and has been, argued that it is not just objects that take accusative case form, but also subjects of non-finite Vgrps. And the following examples, in which the accusative pronoun clearly is functioning as subject of its clause, bear this out.

[95] [For *him* to attempt it] would be ludicrous.
[96] The noise you can hear is [*them* slurping their drinks].

In such terms, the fact that the NP is accusative is consistent with either analysis.

(iii) The fact that the relevant NP may be understood as the subject of the lower verb does not help us either – for this could be explained in either of two ways. On the one hand, we could take the fact that the NP is *understood* as the subject of the lower verb as indicating that it actually *is* the subject of the lower verb (Analysis I). What could be more straightforward? On the other hand, however, it is quite possible to say that, while it actually is the object of the higher verb, that higher object controls the covert subject of the lower verb. This gives Analysis II, in which the fact that it is *understood* as the subject of the lower clause is consistent with its actually *being* object in the higher clause.

These structures have been subject to varying analyses – and much discussion. The one point of agreement is that they cannot all receive the same analysis: it depends on the verb that heads the higher VP. But different grammatical theories make different decisions as to how many sub-categories of verb are involved in [84]–[93], which verbs belong to which sub-categories, and even as to what considerations are relevant in deciding these questions.

For the purposes of this chapter, I shall simplify matters by dividing verbs taking non-finite clausal complements into just two types: those which head VPs with Analysis I (i.e. verbs taking just a single (clausal) complement, with overt subject) and those which head VPs with Analysis II (i.e. verbs taking two complements, a direct object NP and a clausal complement with covert subject).

Type I verbs include: *assume, believe, consider, desire, dread, expect, feel, hear, know, like, observe, prefer, regret, suppose, watch*.

Type II verbs include: *advise, ask, coax, compel, dare, encourage, force, promise, persuade*.

The rest of this chapter discusses ways of deciding which type a given verb belongs to. In reading what follows, try to decide for yourself which type each of the following belong to: *teach, claim, love, forbid, find, hate, invite, beg, prove, recommend, prevent, urge*. The answers are given as **Discussion 9** (page 275) but I recommend you not to look at Discussion 9 until the end.

Type I verbs take just clauses as complements. Clauses (finite or non-finite) only denote the kind of thing that can be true or false. In other words, clauses denote PROPOSITIONS. It is propositions that are thought, said, considered, supposed, believed, wanted, desired or dreaded. You think (say, consider, suppose, believe, want, etc.) certain propositions to be true; you regret (dread, imagine, like, prefer) certain propositions being true. Accordingly, all the verbs alluded to in this paragraph are Type I verbs, taking just a clause (with overt subject) as their (single) complement.

A proposition just isn't the kind of thing you can advise, ask, coax, dare, encourage, persuade (etc.). So these verbs, and others like them, cannot be thought of as taking just a clause (which denotes a proposition) as complement. Hence they cannot be Type I verbs; they must be Type II.

It is consistent with this general picture that the vast majority of Type I verbs can also be complemented just by a finite *that*-clause (cf. *He believed [that Cesare was the ideal prince]*). By contrast, Type II verbs are not in general capable of taking just a *that*-clause (compare **He persuaded [that Cesare was the ideal prince]* with *He persuaded [us] [that Cesare was the ideal prince]*).

Propositions are abstract. Type II verbs call for objects that are not only concrete, but animate. Even more specifically, their objects must be AGENTS; in other words, they must be capable of having volition. You cannot advise, persuade volitionless things to do something. So, these Type II verbs require an agentive NP as (dO) complement in addition to the non-finite clause.

In this connection, consider:

[97] The tree lost it leaves.
[98] I advised the tree.

[97] expresses something which can be believed without making any special assumptions about trees. [98], by contrast, does require a special assumption, the fairy-tale assumption that a tree could exercise the volition required to follow advice. So, [97]

shows that no special assumption is required for *the tree* to be subject of *lost its leaves*, while [98] shows that special assumptions are required for it to be object of *advise*. Now consider [99], in which the function of the italicised NP is in question.

> [99] I advised *the tree* to lose its leaves.
> [100] I expected *the tree* to lose its leaves.

[99] requires exactly the special assumption about trees that [98] did. This suggests that in [99] *the tree* is functioning as it did in [98] – as object of *advise*. Certainly, *the tree* **is understood** as the subject of *to lose its leaves* – but this is because, while functioning as object of *advise*, it **controls** the covert subject of *to lose its leaves*. Were we to represent *the tree* as actually being the subject of *to lose its leaves*, we would fail to capture the contrast (regarding special assumptions) between [97] and [98] – and the contrast between [99] and [100].

Another way of testing this involves **expletive *there***, as illustrated in [101b]:

> [101a] Five gorillas are in the outhouse.
> [101b] There are five gorillas in the outhouse.

In contrast to expletive *it* (which can function as subject or object), **expletive *there* can only function as subject, never as object**. Since the NP following a Type II verb functions as its object, expletive *there* can only follow Type I verbs, not Type II verbs – and we get the following contrast:

> [102–I]   Gulliver expected there to be more food.
> [102–II] *Gulliver advised there to be more food.
> [103–I]   I prefer there to be plenty of exercises.
> [103–II] *I persuaded there to be plenty of exercises.
> [104–I]   He dreaded there being reporters in the lobby.
> [104–II] *He forced there to be reporters in the lobby.

With just one verb, *promise*, there is an even more compelling reason for assigning it to Type II. In the light of the discussion of control in this chapter, can you identify that reason?

With all other verbs of Type II, the covert subject of the lower clause is controlled by the object of the higher clause. This was one of the reasons given for wondering which position (subject or object) the intervening NP actually occupied. But with *promise*, the covert subject of the lower clause is controlled, not by the overt object of the higher clause, but by the subject. *Promise* thus very clearly demands both an object and a clause with a quite distinct (covert) subject. Compare *promise* and *beg* (which are both Type II) in Exercise 1 below. Further Exercise 6 deals with an intriguing further difference between the two types of verb.

To conclude, then: [105a], with the Type I verb *expect*, should be represented as in [105b], and [106a], with the Type II verb *persuade*, as in [106b].

[105a] They expected the bear to dance.
[106a] They persuaded the bear to dance.

[105b]

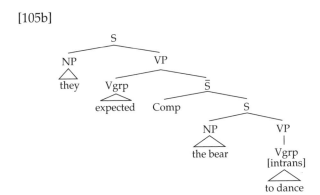

[106b]

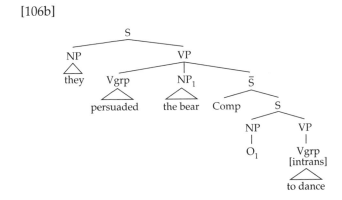

Discussion of in-text exercises

1.

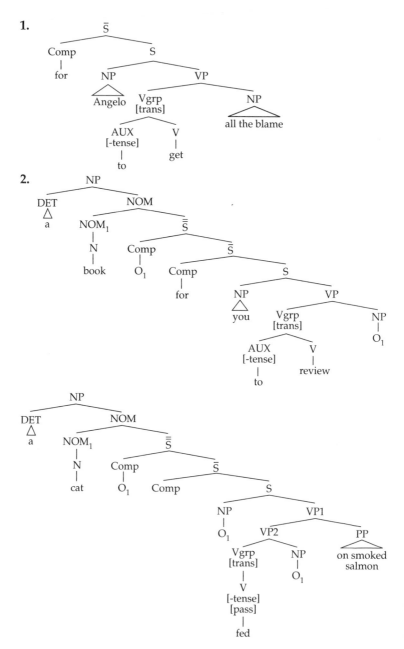

2.

The co-indexings ensure that VP1 is interpreted in the same way as *feed a cat on smoked salmon.*

3. Subject: [1] (1st), [10], [23b], [24b], [26], [32].
    Complement of P: [1] (2nd), [18], [35].
    Complement of Vgrp: [2], [3], [4], [8], [15], [16], [29], [31], [33], [34].
    Complement of Vgrp (sP): [5].
    Complement of N: [7], [27].
    Complement of A: [9], [19], [30].
    Adverbial: [13], [14], [20], [25b].
    Extraposed subject: [28], [36].
    Modifier of NOM: [38a]–[41a].

4.

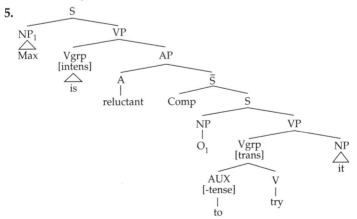

(The subject of the non-finite clause is free.)

5.

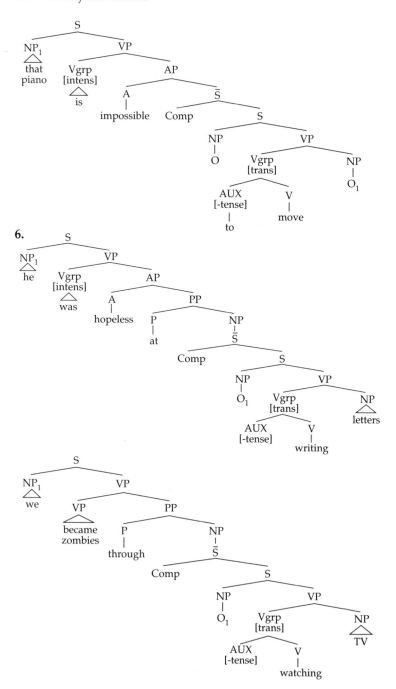

6.

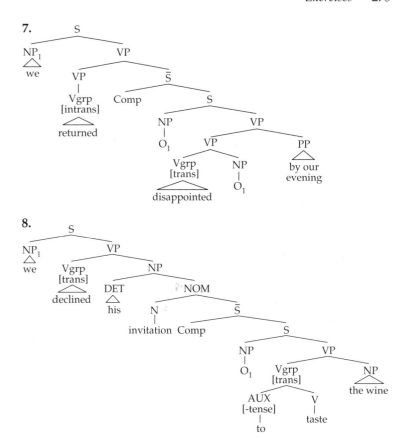

A noun complement clause, remember, is represented as the sister of the head noun. The control pattern here seems to be determined by the meaning of the head noun (*invitation*). Cf. *He invited us to taste the wine.*

9. Type I verbs: *claim, love, find, hate, prove, prevent.*
   Type II verbs: *teach, forbid, invite, beg, recommend, urge.*

Exercises

1.(a) Identify any covert constituents in the bracketed non-finite clauses of the following sentences (ignoring the lack of tense).

(b)   State whether they are controlled or free, and if controlled, identify the controller.

Example: *Louis was wondering [whether to support the Pope]*.

(a) Subject, (b) controlled by main clause subject (*Louis*).

(i)   I want [to be alone].
(ii) I wanted [John to be alone].
(iii) Morgan promised Bill [to give it a good review].
(iv) Morgan begged Bill [to give it a good review].
(v)   [Getting to the top] finished Hedda off.
(vi) [Giving it a swift kick] sometimes works.
(vii) The trombone is too old [to play].
(viii) Max is too stubborn [to talk].
(ix) Max is too stubborn [to talk to].
(x)   Svengali was too clever [for them to entrap].
(xi) It should be clear [how to do this].
(xii) John was not clear [how to do it].

2.   Under complement of A in AP we considered

(i) This piano is impossible to move.

Notice that we could refer to the piano by means of the pronoun *it*:

(ii) It is impossible to move.

But now (ii) is ambiguous. The ambiguity is created by two distinct factors. Say what these are before reading further.

Firstly, the *it* of (ii) is ambiguous. Out of context we cannot tell whether it is the expletive *it* associated with an extraposed subject, or whether it is a referring expression (referring e.g. to a piano). Secondly, *move* can be either transitive or intransitive. Bearing these points in mind, draw a phrasemarker for each interpretation of (ii).

3.   Assign each of the following verbs to Type I or Type II. You will find this easier if you construct sentences of the form [NP – finite verb – NP – non-finite verb], taking into account the discussion in the chapter.

mean, understand, tell, want, order, warn, imagine

4.(a) Draw Abbreviated Clausal Analyses of the following sentences:
 (b)   Indicate covert constituents by means of 'O'. If they are controlled, co-index them with their controllers.
 (c)   For each clause, give its form and function.

 Example: *Having shaved your head, will you ask the wigman if he's ready to fit you?*

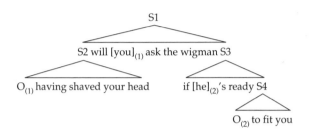

 S1: finite *yes/no* interrogative, main.
 S2: non-finite (*-ing* participle), adverbial.
 S3: finite interrogative, complement of Vgrp (*will … ask*).
 S4: *to*-infinitive, complement to A (*ready*).

 (i) The Doge of Venice appears to have been eager to join the Crusade.
 (ii) Which authors does the professor hope to lecture on this term?
 (iii) Plans to recover the disabled vehicles abandoned during the night are under consideration.
 (iv) The first chef to be informed of it congratulated Melvin on having rescued the steaks without damaging them.
 (v) It seems that, having been taught by Mozart himself, Joachim knew the quintet to be well within his capacities.
 (vi) To be frank, I am sure the trainees would say they didn't consider it part of the job to answer calls from time-wasters wanting a bit of company.

Discussion of exercises

1. (i) Subject, controlled by main clause subject (*I*).
 (ii) No covert constituents.
 (iii) Subject, controlled by main clause subject (*Morgan*).

(iv) Subject, controlled by main clause indirect object (*Bill*).

(v) Subject, controlled by main clause object (*Hedda*).

(vi) Subject, free.

(vii) Subject, free. Object, controlled by main clause subject (*the trombone*).

(viii) Subject, controlled by main clause subject (*Max*).

(ix) Subject, free. Object of P in PP, controlled by main clause subject (*Max*).

(x) Object, controlled by main clause subject (*Svengali*).

(xi) Subject, free.

(xii) Subject, controlled by main clause subject (*John*).

2.   With *it* as a referring expression, the clause complements A, and the covert object of the transitive verb *move* is controlled by the main clause subject (the referring expression *it*). See (a) below. On the other (b) interpretation, *it* is expletive and the clause is an extraposed subject. Expletive *it* cannot be a controller (see Exercise 1 (xi) above). Here *move* is intransitive, and (ii) is equivalent to *Moving is impossible*.

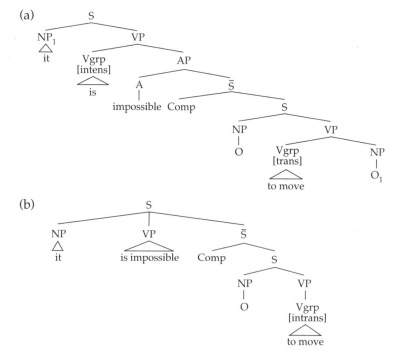

3. Type I: *mean, understand, want, imagine.*
Type II: *tell, order, warn.*

4.(i)

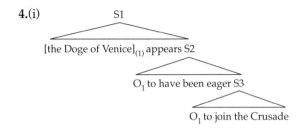

S1: Finite, main.
S2: Non-finite (*to*-infinitive), complement of Vgrp (*appears*).
S3: Non-finite (*to*-infinitive), complement to A (*eager*).

(ii)

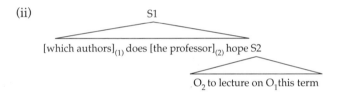

S1: Finite Wh-interrogative, main.
S2: Non-finite (*to*-infinitive), complement of Vgrp (*does ... hope*).

(iii)

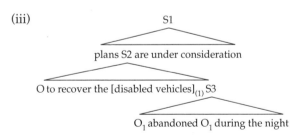

S1: Finite, main.
S2: Non-finite (*to*-infinitive), complement to N (*plans*).
S3: Non-finite (passive participle) relative, modifier of NOM (*disabled vehicles*).

(iv)

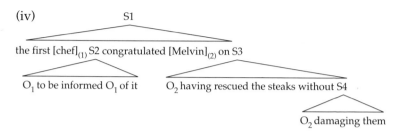

the first [chef]$_{(1)}$ S2 congratulated [Melvin]$_{(2)}$ on S3

O$_1$ to be informed O$_1$ of it   O$_2$ having rescued the steaks without S4

O$_2$ damaging them

> S1: Finite, main.
> S2: Non-finite (*to*-infinitive) relative, modifier of NOM (*chef*).
> S3: Non-finite (*-ing* participle), complement of P (*on*).
> S4: Non-finite (*-ing* participle), complement of P (*without*).

(v)

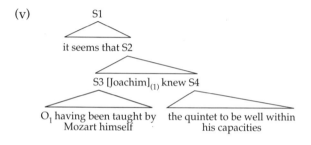

it seems that S2

S3 [Joachim]$_{(1)}$ knew S4

O$_1$ having been taught by   the quintet to be well within
Mozart himself   his capacities

> S1: Finite, main.
> S2: Finite, extraposed subject.
> S3: Non-finite (*-ing* participle), adverbial.
> S4: Non-finite (*to*-infinitive), complement of Vgrp (*knew*).

(vi)

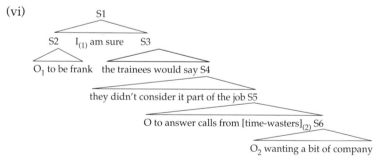

S2   I$_{(1)}$ am sure   S3

O$_1$ to be frank   the trainees would say S4

they didn't consider it part of the job S5

O to answer calls from [time-wasters]$_{(2)}$ S6

O$_2$ wanting a bit of company

> S1: Finite, main.
> S2: Non-finite (*to*-infinitive), S-adverbial.
> S3: Finite, complement of A (*sure*).

S4: Finite, complement of Vgrp (*would say*).

S5: Non-finite (*to*-infinitive), extraposed Vgrp-complement (note expletive *it* in S4). See Chapter 8, Further Exercise 7.

S6: Non-finite (*-ing* participle) relative, modifier of NOM (*time-wasters*).

Further exercises

1. Draw Abbreviated Clausal Analyses (with the information asked for in Exercise 4 above) for the following. The last is ridiculously complex, but it *is* the last.

(a) Who did Sarah try to tell what to say?

(b) Tutors can decide whether to insist on the distinctions being respected at this point. (ambiguous)

(c) Malingering is pretending to be ill with the intention of avoiding work.

(d) Virginia is reluctant to ask any of the players which court it made them most nervous playing on.

(e) Don't you remember suggesting that any circus staff caught allowing animals on the trapeze should be fired?

(f) The invitation to attend the ball sent to Cinderella at her stepmother's address was intercepted by her ugly sisters, who were anxious not to be outshone in beauty while dancing and (more prosaically) to have the washing-up done in their absence.

Note: Readers who feel confident with the material in this chapter and who have lots of paper to spare can amuse themselves by drawing *complete* phrase-markers for (a)–(e). (f) will be more difficult.

2. Draw phrase-markers for each of the interpretations of the following ambiguous sentences. In (d) and (e), the differences are a matter of indexing only.

(a) Richard has plans to leave.

(b) I saw the boy studying in the library. (three possibilities)

(c) Flying planes can be dangerous.

(d) The chicken is ready to eat.

(e) Max thought Jim too old to play.

Note. In respect of (e), assume there are three levels of AP structure: AP, ADJ, and A, (parallel to NP, NOM, and N) and that *too* premodifies ADJ (*old to play*).

3.   Explain the ungrammaticality of **John is impossible to sleep.*

4.   Draw phrase-markers for the following, paying special attention to indexing. To bring out the intricate differences between the examples, assign indexes to all NPs, including the pronoun. Where *them* cannot be co-indexed with another NP, can you explain why it cannot? It will help if you consider what small change would be required to allow that object NP to be co-indexed with another NP.

(a)   I wonder who the men expected to see.
(b)   I wonder who the men expected to see them.
(c)   I wonder how the men expected to see them.

In connection with (b) and (c), notice that the only typographical difference between them is that the letter *w* is the eighth letter in (b) but the tenth letter in (c). There is a further discussion of the more general implications of this in Chapter 11.

5.   Discuss the relations (drawing phrase-markers with indices if helpful) between the following three sentences.

(a)   To taste this wine might amuse you.
(b)   It might amuse you to taste this wine.
(c)   You might be amused to taste this wine.

Two analyses of (c) are possible, one of them suggested by the relation between (b) and (c), the other (adopted in this book) suggested by the possibility of modifying *amused* by *very* or *rather*.

6.   The difference between Type I and Type II verbs manifests itself in more ways than were discussed in the text. Compare, for example, the following three (a)–(b) pairs. Discuss precisely how the difference in interpretation (and acceptability) between the (a)s and (b)s further illustrates the distinction. Try this out with other verbs.

(1a) (i) Sarah believed Dr. Fernandez to have treated Paul.
     (ii) Sarah believed Paul to have been treated by Dr. Fernandez.
(1b) (i) Sarah persuaded Dr. Fernandez to treat Paul.
     (ii) Sarah persuaded Paul to be treated by Dr. Fernandez.

(2a) (i) She wanted her colleagues to trust Paul.
     (ii) She wanted Paul to be trusted by her colleagues.
(2b) (i) She encouraged her colleagues to trust Paul.
     (ii) ?She encouraged Paul to be trusted by her colleagues.

(3a) (i) She expected all trainees to crush the garlic really well.
     (ii) She expected the garlic to be crushed really well by all trainees.
(3b) (i) She reminded all trainees to crush the garlic really well.
     (ii) !?She reminded the garlic to be crushed really well by all trainees.

Chapter 11

Languages, Sentences, and Grammars

This concluding chapter is concerned with the general background to, and ultimate purpose of, the kind of analysis you have encountered in previous chapters, rather than with extending that analysis.

Languages

I will begin by considering a very general question:

[1]   What is a language?

How do you begin to think about this? The question seems so general as to be almost empty of content. How one goes about answering such a question depends very much on one's reasons for asking it in the first place. It would not be far from the truth to say that one could really understand the question only in the light of particular answers to it. Different thinkers about language have answered it in their different ways and, in doing so, have given the question a different significance.

A natural answer often given is

[2]   A language is a system of communication.

Expanding that answer (deciding e.g. what we meant by 'system' and 'communication', and what it is about the system that permits communication) and exploring its implications would open up one avenue of thought about language, and a perfectly valid one. But other answers are possible. My purpose in considering the question in [1] is to raise certain questions about the kind of analysis you have encountered in previous chapters, and to put that analysis into a general context. In order to do this, I will consider the following answer:

[3]   A language is a set of sentences.

It would be understandable if at this stage you felt that this was a rather dry, unappealing answer to our question, one that fails to do justice to any sense of the wonder of language. I hope by the end of this chapter to show that this answer – when its implications are properly teased out – does indeed do full justice to the wonder of language. It was Noam Chomsky, Professor of Linguistics at the Massachusetts Institute of Technology, who early in his career suggested that thinking of a language in this way (as a set of sentences) opened up an interesting and fruitful avenue of thought on the nature of language, more interesting and accurate than any other idea around at the time. Taken alone and out of context it makes little sense. But answers like that are just beginnings: we have to ask what it means to say [3], what its implications are for how languages are to be described, what further questions it raises. In fact, the further questions raised by [3] have had a profound effect on the development of language study over the last forty years or so.

Before considering these, however, we need to compare this account with what is perhaps a more common idea of what a language is. If a language really is a set of sentences, it follows that **different languages are distinguished by being made up of different sets of sentences**. Two people will speak exactly the same language if (and only if) the set of sentences in each of their languages are exactly the same. A consequence of this is that, almost certainly, no two people speak exactly the same language.

By way of illustration of this, consider again [4]

[4]   Max put the car in the garage and Bill did so in the lay-by.

If I had inadvertently said this, I would consider it a mistake on my part and, given the opportunity, I would want to correct myself. So, for me, [4] is not a (grammatical) sentence of my language, even though it is perfectly understandable to me. In fact, there is a measure of agreement among English speakers that [4] is not a sentence of their language. But suppose we do find someone who could use [4] without any feeling that there is something wrong with it. Then, for that person, [4] *is* a sentence of his or her language. Now, if a language is a set of sentences, that person and I must be said to speak slightly different languages, different to the extent that the set of (grammatical) sentences that constitutes his or her language includes [4] whereas the set of sentences that constitutes my language excludes [4].

When I say that this other speaker and I speak 'slightly' different languages, I am assuming for the purposes of the discussion that she and I agree about the other sentences mentioned in this book, disagreeing only about this sentence [4]. But wait a moment. If all the (grammatical) sentences mentioned in this book are sentences of this other speaker's language, doesn't that mean that this other speaker speaks what is known as *English*? And don't I, as author of this book, speak English too? And English, after all, is a language. Surely, then, we speak the same language: English.

This conclusion appears to contradict the idea that a language is a set of sentences and that particular languages are distinguished by consisting of different sets of sentences. English is normally regarded as a language, yet by the definition of a language given in [3], speakers of English are characterised as speaking more or less different languages. Do speakers of English speak the same language or don't they?

This last question is really a matter for us to decide, because it amounts to this: should we use the expression 'a language' in a way that allows us to say that English is a language, the common language of its speakers (this is a decision to abandon [3]), or should we use that expression in a way that obliges us to say that strictly speaking, English is not a language itself, but a gigantic collection of largely overlapping languages? Answer [3] encourages this second use – and is arguably closer to the facts of the matter.

There is nothing to stop us using the expression 'a language' in both of these ways. In fact, we normally do use it in both ways. It depends on the context in which one is using it. Clearly, by comparison with French (or, the gigantic collection of overlapping languages that go to make up what is known as French) English is an identifiable language (in the first sense above), absolutely distinct from the French language. But within what is known as English, you know as well as I that there are differences. Geordies, Glaswegians, Londoners, Californians, Belfastians, Jamaicans, Canberrans, Sidneysiders speak differently. And this is not simply a matter of accent. Each and every Geordie, Glaswegian, Californian (etc.) has a language and each of these languages can be described as a set of sentences. These sets are known to differ to a greater or lesser degree. I'll give just two small examples. [5] is a grammatical sentence of the language spoken by most Geordies:

[5] You can't do it, can't you not?

but not of the languages spoken by, for example, Jamaicans, Californians, or Glaswegians. Conversely, [6]

[6]   Did you eat yet?

is a grammatical sentence of the language of Californians (and most U.S. languages) but not, for example, of Geordies, Jamaicans, or Londoners.

The discussion so far suggests that it is not in fact such a calamity to conclude that, **in one useful sense of the expression 'a language', English is not a language (but a collection of overlapping languages).**

Indeed, there is almost no limit to the variety within English we may recognise if it suits our purpose. I have mentioned general variation associated with geographical differences. I could also have mentioned variation associated with age differences, educational, social, and political differences, and I would still have said nothing about linguistic variation across time, variation caused by the fact that languages change through the centuries. In one perfectly good sense of 'a language', we, Shakespeare, Chaucer, and the Gawain poet have different languages. In another perfectly good sense, it is all the same language. Amid all the variety, we cannot lose sight of the common ground, the overlap between the varieties. It is this overlap that justifies the label 'the English language' (and the use of the word 'English' in the title of this book) and it is this that enables its speakers, with more or less success, to communicate with each other.

Linguistic variation, however, is a study in its own right (sometimes called socio-linguistics, or dialectology) and is not the topic of this book. I shall continue to assume, safely I believe, that the sentences and structures analysed in this book fall within the common ground, forming a central part of the language of its readers. Let us now consider some more specific consequences of [3] for the description of languages.

Describing languages

If a language is a set of sentences, then the job of describing a language consists in indicating, for every sequence of words,

whether or not that sequence counts as a grammatical sentence of the language.

The idea that a language is a set of sentences suggests to many people encountering it for the first time that you should be able to gather all the sentences of a language together, make a list of them, and say 'This is the complete language'. And certainly, if you could make a list of all the sentences of a language, [3] suggests a very easy way to go about *describing* a language: to give a fully explicit and comprehensive description of a language, all that is required is to draw up such a list, one that includes all the word sequences that are grammatical sentences of the language and excludes all word sequences that are not.

Imagine, if you can, a language in which there are just ten sentences. We could call this language 'Justen'. If a language is a set of sentences, we have only to list those ten sentences in order to have an explicit and comprehensive description of Justen. By consulting that list we would be able to tell immediately what was, and what was not, Justen.

How realistic is this? Can you really imagine a proper language in which you could say just ten things? I doubt whether such a 'language' properly deserves the name. 'Code' would perhaps be a more appropriate description. So, that account of what a language is works well enough for Justen, but Justen is altogether unreal. Should we, then, reject that account?

Well, if you share the feeling that [3], as a definition of what a language is, makes it appear as though all languages are as simple as Justen, then you probably do want to reject it. This is probably because the definition suggests to you that a language has to be a fairly small set of sentences, small enough at least to make a list of and put a number on. But there is nothing in the idea that a language is a set of sentences to suggest that it has to have any limit on it. A set of things can be indefinitely large. Indeed, there is no reason why a set of things should even be finite. For example, numbers form a set of things, and this set is infinite: there is no largest number. What about the set of sentences that form a language?

We have agreed that Justen is unreal. But how unreal is it? If your language does not contain just ten sentences, how many does it contain? Five hundred? Five thousand? Five million … ? Could you, in fact, put a number on it?

In asking this question, I am not asking how many sentences you have actually used and understood so far in your life. Nor am I asking how many you will have used and understood by the time you die. These are questions, not about your *language as such*, but about your *use of language*. We are concerned with your language, not the use you happen to make of it. So **the question concerns the number of word sequences that you would accept as being sentences of your language, available for your use whether or not you actually get to make use of them**. Now, if what we are concerned with is not the number you will actually use in your lifetime but the number that are in principle *available* for use, we come closest to the truth in saying that there is no finite number of sentences in your language. **You speak an infinite language**.

There are well-known ways of demonstrating this. Consider, for example, a single word of your language, the word *and*. We can be perfectly confident that Justen does not include any word having the same function as *and*. How can we be so sure of this? Well, if Justen included this word it would, quite simply, be an infinite language. Adding this one word to that ten-sentence language changes it, at a stroke, into an infinite language. One of the functions of *and* is to join any two or more sentences together to form another, co-ordinate, sentence. Say we number the sentences of the original Justen, S1 to S10. With the addition of *and* a whole new language opens up, one that includes the following four sentences:

(i) [S1 and S2]
(ii) [S1, S2 and S3]
(iii) [[S1 and S2] and S5]
(iv) [[S1 and S2], [S6 and S3], and S8]

and an infinity of further sentences.

Your language includes *and*. There is no sentence of which you could say 'This is the longest sentence in my language'. For any sentence that you care to think of, however long, it is always possible to create another, longer, sentence by co-ordinating a further clause within it.

And is not the only device that allows you to elaborate the length and complexity of your sentences. Another, encountered in Chapter 9, is the relative clause. Think of the nursery rhyme 'This is the house that Jack built'. Here's the last sentence: *This is*

*the farmer sowing his corn that kept the cock that crowed in the morn
that woke the priest all shaven and shorn that married the man all tat-
tered and torn that kissed the maiden all forlorn that milked the cow
with the crumpled horn that tossed the dog that chased the cat that
killed the rat that ate the malt that lay in the house that Jack built.*

Each new sentence of the rhyme is created by subordinating
the previous sentence as a relative clause functioning as a modifier in a newly-introduced NP. This could go on for ever. The fact
that it doesn't go on longer has nothing to do with the language
itself but with factors affecting the *use* of language: boredom,
exhaustion, hunger and, finally, mortality.

Before I continue, let me summarise the last two most important points. (1) In contrast to the artificial example of Justen,
natural languages (the languages which, in the words of the
phrase, we learn at our mother's knee) are *infinite*. (2) The infinity
of natural languages does not in any way conflict with the idea
that a language is a set of sentences; sets can be infinite and a language can be defined as an infinite set of sentences.

Describing infinite languages

But now we have a new question and it is this:

[7]   How do you describe an infinite set of sentences (an infin-
       ite language)?

Clearly, we must abandon the idea of listing. Just as you cannot
list an infinity of numbers, so you cannot list an infinity of sentences. [7] is perhaps *the* most important question raised by [3].
By suggesting we think of a language as a set of *sentences*,
Chomsky was implicitly questioning an influential view of language proposed in the late nineteenth century by the great Swiss
linguist Ferdinand de Saussure. Saussure readily recognised it
was impossible to list the sentences of a person's language. He
therefore limited the notion of language (*langue*) to those expressions that *could* be finitely listed – morphemes, words, fixed
phrases, idioms. Sentences were excluded as pertaining, not to
the language as such, but to a person's particular use of language
(*parole*). Chomsky, in focusing on sentences, encourages us to see
the enterprise of describing a person's language as the enterprise
of describing and explaining a mental *capacity*, the capacity to

utter/understand an infinity of sentences (which he calls linguistic 'competence') – something Saussure, for all his insights, had less to say about. It is in this sense – by forcing us to concentrate on a person's capacity to speak an infinite language and how that capacity is acquired – that [3] does seem to address the real wonder of language. [3] forces us to state explicitly which are the grammatical sentences of the language and which are not, and do this for an infinity of sentences and non-sentences. Since listing is out, [3] encourages us to find an alternative principle on which to base our description.

I shall approach the alternative by comparing the two artificial languages considered above, Justen and the language that consists of the ten sentences of Justen augmented by *and*. We can call this second language 'Justenand'. I have shown that nothing is easier than the complete description of Justen: because it is a finite language, we merely list its ten sentences. But we can't do this for Justenand. Before reading further, ask yourself whether it is possible to give a complete description of Justenand and, if so, how you would go about doing so. Remember, in asking for a complete description of Justenand, I want to know categorically, for any sequence I care to think of, whether it is a sentence of the language or not.

If you have thought about this, you will have realised that Justenand, infinite though it is, is still a very rudimentary language. It is not only possible to describe this language in its entirety, it is not even very difficult. The description will fall into two parts. The first part must be the original list of ten sentences. To account for the infinity of other sentences which have become possibilities because of the addition of *and*, something different is required. What we need, for the second part, is an *explicit statement* to the effect that **a sentence of Justenand may consist of any other two or more sentences of Justenand joined by *and***. This statement tell us that, given that S1, S2 and S3 are sentences of Justenand, (i) and (ii) above are also sentences, having the form

And, since S(i) has just been admitted as a sentence of Justenand (and S5 is listed) we know by the same token that (iii) is one too:

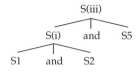

and so on *ad infinitum*. Notice that, from the explicit statement in bold above, not only do we derive the information that (iii) is indeed a sentence of Justenand, but simultaneously we are given a clue as to how to analyse that sentence. The statement automatically implies a partial description of S(iii).

By means of the statement in the second part of the description, we have given a complete description of Justenand without resorting to an infinite and hence uncompletable list. We have, in fact, provided a finite description of an infinite set of sentences. Although a list is included in the full description (and it is this list that makes Justenand hardly less artificial than Justen), that list has been supplemented by something quite different, namely a *rule*. For that is what the above statement is, a rule for forming the infinity of Justenand sentences. **It is by means of *rules* that we can give *finite* descriptions of *infinite* sets of sentences**.

This difference between List and Rule is of central importance in language study. The very idea of 'sentence' as you and I understand it is bound up with the notion of 'rule'. To see this, think about Justen again. This toy language is probably more different from your own language than you realise. In particular, it is not even clear that what we have been calling its 'sentences' bear any relation at all to the things that you call sentences in your language.

In explanation of this, remember that, since Justen is a finite 'language', it is actually possible to identify its 'sentences' by numbers. Indeed, the speakers of this so-called language could themselves identify their ten sentences by number. The only problem with this idea is that whereas the numbers are infinite, Justen has only ten sentences. But, if it is unlikely that numbers would be used, there is nothing to prevent these speakers having *names* for their ten sentences. S1 could be *Oink*, S2 *Woops*, S3 *Umph*, S4 *Whack* and so on.

Now do you see how different Justen is from your language? Names are *simple* words. They do not have syntactic structure. In other words, a language that could consist of names alone has no need of, indeed cannot be said to have, hierarchical structure, syntactic categories, or syntactic functions. In a word, it would have no syntax. Even the distinction between 'sentence' and 'word' would be meaningless. Rules would have no part to play in the description of such a language. Not only can we list the 'sentences' of this language, we must list them if we want to describe it.

By contrast, sentence-listing plays no part either in the description of your language or in the way you use that language. You do not have a list of ready-made sentences in your head. If you did, the language would have to be finite; your head, after all, has a finite capacity. Furthermore, if you could hold them all in your head, as prepackaged sentences, there would be no need for them to be complex, i.e. there would be no need for them to have structure. If knowing a natural language could be a matter of remembering sentences as such, why bother with *complex* things like sentences at all? It would be easier to remember simple names, and more efficient.[1]

Instead, you have to construct your sentences as and when the need arises. And it is the fact that you do construct sentences on the spot that enables you to utter any of an infinite number of sentences, appropriate to an infinite variety of situations. Knowing a natural language, then, does not consist in having an inventory of sentences in your head, but in knowing *how* to construct the sentences. But, and this is the important point, in order to know how to construct the grammatical sentences of a natural language, you have to know in very general terms what counts as a grammatical sentence of the language.

When it comes to describing languages, we can take our cue from this. Our ultimate task in describing a language is still to specify what the grammatical sentences of the language are. But we cannot expect to do this directly. What we can and must do is specify what it is that makes a sequence of words grammatical or ungrammatical. This amounts to saying that, **in order to describe a particular language, you have to give a general definition of the concept 'grammatical sentence' for that language**. It is by reference to this general definition that we can state, for each of an infinity of word-sequences, whether it is a grammatical

---

1. Jorge Luis Borges, in 'Funes the Memorious' (*Labyrinths*, Penguin) has written an interesting story on the effects of an infallible memory on a person's language.

sentence or not. This will be done, not by consulting a sentence-list, but by *prediction*. The general definition forces us to make predictions about word-sequences we had never even thought about or encountered before. This in turn means that, in describing an infinite language, we cannot say that a particular sequence of words is not a grammatical sentence of the language without simultaneously explaining why it isn't.

This was not done for Justen. In just listing the 'grammatical sentences' of Justen, we did not define what it was for something to be a Justen sentence. This, as we saw, was not necessary. In fact, it is not even possible. The idea of 'knowing how to construct a sentence' is completely inappropriate in the context of Justen. In the first place, you can only *construct* something if that thing is *complex*, has structure. But the sentences of Justen are perfectly simple. In the second place, you can only 'know how to construct' the things in a set by knowing general principles that apply to them. And this entails knowing not only what distinguishes them from each other but what they have in common. But only complex things (things that have parts) can have something in common and yet be different. Totally simple things can only be absolutely the same (identical) or absolutely different.

If an English-speaking 'speaker' of Justen were to point out that we had overlooked the existence of an eleventh 'sentence', all we could do would be to shrug our shoulders and add it to the list. We would have learnt nothing more about what it was to be a Justen sentence. There is no way we could have predicted or explained its existence because we have no general idea (no general definition) of what counts as a Justen sentence in the first place.

We have a better general idea of what counts as a Justenand sentence, though, and this is expressed in the general statement (the rule) that formed the second part of its description. That rule gives a partial definition of what it is for something to be a grammatical sentence of Justenand. It is only partial, since we still don't have any definition that covers the original ten sentences.

Grammars

At the risk of repetitiveness, I shall summarise what seems to have emerged so far. The discussion of Justen is neatly and more generally summarised in the following statement:

[8]   A finite language is its own grammar.

I have not used the term 'grammar' before in this chapter. Instead, I have talked about language description. But this is what a grammar is, the description of a language. In the terms established so far, then, **the function of the grammar of a language is to specify which word sequences are, and which are not, in the infinite set of its sentences**.

Justen illustrates [8] as follows: If a language is a set of sentences, then Justen *is* exactly those ten 'sentences'. A grammar describes a language. But, as we have seen, the grammar of Justen *is* the list of those ten sentences. The ten sentences of Justen, then, constitute both the grammar itself and the language itself. It is in this sense that Justen, being a finite language, is its own grammar.

It's an odd sort of grammar, though, that doesn't specify any kind of syntax for its language – one far removed from our ordinary conception of what a grammar is. And this is pretty well what is said in [8]. Essentially, there is no real grammar of Justen. In view of our conclusion that Justen cannot seriously be considered as a language, this is not surprising.

By contrast, the discussion of natural languages and their grammars can be summarised as follows.

(a)   A natural language is an *infinite* set of sentences.

(b)   The description of a language (the *grammar* of a language) states which are, and which are not, in the infinite set of its sentences.

(c)   It is the *complexity* of natural language sentences (the fact that they have structure) that makes it possible to construct an *infinity* of sentences, and it is the infinity of natural languages that makes a *general definition* of 'sentence' necessary in order to achieve what is described in (b) above.

(d)   Equally, it is the fact that the sentences of a natural language are complex that allows each different sentence to have more or less *in common with* every other different sentence.

(e)   And it is the fact that the sentences of a language do have more or less in common with every other different sentence that makes it possible to state *general principles* (to *formulate rules*) about them.

(f)   The *complexity* of natural language sentences, then, makes a general definition of 'sentence' both possible and necessary.

(g) In conclusion, the ideal envisioned here is that a grammar is the description of a language by means of a general definition of 'sentence' in that language. The definition takes the form of a set of rules. It has two interrelated functions: (i) it admits (or defines) as a sentence whatever conforms to the rules, excluding whatever does not, and (ii) gives a structural description of whatever it admits as a sentence. These are connected, for the grammar admits a sentence only in virtue of assigning a structural description to it. Furthermore, by reference to the general definition of sentence embodied in the grammar, we can expect to derive explanations of the ungrammaticality of non-sentences.

I alluded earlier to the idea that the enterprise of describing a language is the enterprise of describing *a mental capacity*. Chomsky's suggestion is that this internal capacity is constituted by a grammar. In 'knowing' (or having) a language, a speaker 'knows' (or has) an internal grammar, a set of rules constituting the definition of 'sentence' in that language. And when we, as linguists, attempt to describe a language, we are attempting to model the speaker's knowledge of language by formulating a grammar that corresponds as closely as possible to the mind-internal grammar of the speaker of that language. (It is actually slightly misleading to talk just of '*speakers* of a language' here. '*Possessors* of a language' would be better, since it is possible – and in fact not uncommon – to have a language without being able actually to speak it. Stroke victims and victims of total paralysis are an example.)

The main thrust behind Chomsky's thinking here is that language (and thus the notion of 'sentence' defined by the grammar) is a wholly mental (internal) phenomenon. It does not exist externally to or independently of internal 'knowledge' of it. This is all very abstract, so I shall give a concrete illustration of what is at issue here. Further Exercise 4 of Chapter 10 invited the reader to consider the differences between three sentences, two of which I represent here.

[9] I wonder who the men expected to see them.
[10] I wonder how the men expected to see them.

The two sentences are radically different. You can get an idea of the difference by asking yourself whether *them* can refer to *the men* or not. Having satisfied yourself as to the differences, reflect on this. This book has been concerned with what is involved in the analysis of sentences. Now, a common view of sentences is that they are the sort of (mind-external) thing you can actually see on the page (a view implied by regarding sentences as things that begin with a capital letter and end with a full stop). As a possessor of the language, you know just how different the relevant sentences are. But look at [9] and [10] again. What difference between [9] and [10] is actually there to be *SEEN*? Hardly anything. Simply, the letter *w* has hopped over the *h* and the *o*. That simple visible difference can hardly be held responsible for the intricate interpretative differences between the two sentences. The linguistic difference does not consist in the difference in position of the letter *w*. Someone capable only of identifying that typographical difference could stare at those letter sequences for ever without forming the merest idea of the *linguistic* (grammatical) differences so important to you as a possessor of the language.

The point I am drawing your attention to here is simply this. The external, visible, difference between [9] and [10] is exhaustively described by saying that the letter *w* is the eighth letter in [9] but the tenth letter in [10]. Since this statement, although entirely accurate, completely fails even to touch on the crucial *linguistic* differences beween two sentences of your language, we must conclude that in analysing linguistic expressions such as sentences, we are not analysing anything that is there to be seen on the page. Indeed, we are not analysing anything that is external to your mentally constituted possession of the language. In considering the *linguistic* differences, you looked inwards and consulted your mentally constituted grammar.

Two caveats are in order here. The first is this: bear in mind that, when Chomsky suggests that language does not exist externally to or independently of internal 'knowledge' of it, he is emphatically *not* saying that language (or linguistic expressions such as sentences) is in any sense unreal. Quite the contrary. Linguistic expressions (the grammars in terms of which they are defined) are real enough, believe me: the linguistic difference (i.e. the internally constituted 'knowledge' of the difference) between *Flick the switch or the bomb will explode* and *Flick the switch and the bomb will explode* might one day have the very real effect of saving your life. The second caveat concerns something you may (and, in my view, should) have been worrying about in connection with [9] and [10]. I *hope* you were persuaded by my discussion of these that language (the notion of sentence) as such is not there to be seen on the page but is inside your head. Nevertheless, even if you were persuaded, it would still be reasonable to ask: what is the *connection* between the mentally constituted language (including the relevant two sentences, the differences between them) and the visible strings of letters which I have labelled '[9]' and '[10]' above? For they clearly are connected: I succeeded in making you look inside yourself to consider the relevant sentences and the differences between them only by presenting you with those two visible letter sequences. In my view, this is an interesting and important question. So interesting is it, I don't propose to answer it here (though I have my views). It is a highly controversial question – in linguistics, philosophy, and cognitive science – and its discussion would take us too far afield here. All I can say is that, if you were thinking about this, keep thinking about it. It is important.

Grammars and sentence analysis

How do these very general considerations relate to the analyses discussed in previous chapters? You might be forgiven if at some point in your reading of those chapters you had asked yourself whether phrase-markers were the be-all and end-all of syntax. You might be forgiven for thinking 'OK, so now I know how to draw a plausible phrase-marker. Where do we go from here?'

We have seen what phrase-markers can do. They provide explicit descriptions of sentences in terms of category, function, and constituency. Descriptions of sentences, whether given in the form of phrase-markers or some equivalent notation (e.g. labelled brackets), are an important part of language-description. They are not by any means the whole story. Your reading of this chapter should have given you an idea of what phrase-markers, in themselves, cannot do.

For example, you know that [11] does not represent a (grammatical) sentence of your language.

[11] *Stream a beside sunbathed Sam.

Nothing I have said so far in this book, however, prevents us assigning it a phrase-marker, [12] for example:

[12]

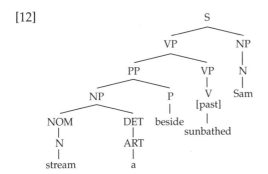

Indeed, there is nothing that obliges us to give it that phrase-marker even.

I have suggested that, to describe a natural language, a definition is required of what it is to be a (grammatical) sentence of the language. And I have suggested that such a definition would, automatically and simultaneously, predict which are the grammatical sentences and which are not, describe the grammatical sentences, and explain the non-sentences. In other words, if you wish to predict that [11] does not represent a grammatical S in your language, nor *Stream a beside sunbathed* a grammatical VP, nor *stream a beside* a grammatical PP, nor *stream a* a grammatical NP, you must explain why not, and, in order to explain why not, you must describe (by means of rules) what does count as a grammatical S, VP, PP, NP … in your language.

While phrase-markers *describe* sentences, they do not, in themselves, give an indication of what it is to be a sentence; hence they do not, in themselves, make any *predictions*, or give any *explanations*.

Ultimately, then, we must make the connection between the phrase-markers on the one hand and, on the other, the rules that constitute the definition of what it is to be a grammatical sentence.

This is a natural connection to make. It is clear from the discussion of this chapter that the rules of the grammar must be expressed in terms of syntactic categories and how they are structured into sentences. After all, it is the complexity of natural language sentences (i.e. all that we understand by their having structure) that makes such rules both possible and necessary. And the descriptions given in previous chapters are expressed in phrase-markers in just these terms. This suggests that the rules should be formulated in such a way that they, in some sense, create phrase-markers as their descriptions of sentences, so that, in admitting a sequence of words as a grammatical sentence, the rules assign it a descriptive phrase-marker.

Phrase-markers, in themselves, then, are just a beginning. A variety of questions now present themselves. The most general and obvious one is: What are the rules governing the construction of phrase-markers? But there are others, among them: What are the best rules? And what counts as 'best' in this context? Given that the rules will be formulated in terms of syntactic categories, what syntactic categories do we need to recognise? Can everything we want to say about sentences be expressed in phrase-markers? Can everything we want to say about each sentence be expressed in a single phrase-marker?

Of course, it will have occurred to you that, although no explicit mention was made of rules in the preceding chapters, the analyses suggested there are not just arbitrary; in suggesting them, I have been guided *implicitly* by general principles. In asking 'What are the rules?' then, we are concerned with laying bare those general principles, with making them fully *explicit*, and with whether those are the best general principles available.

Such questions, and the thinking that leads up to them, open up the prospect of a rich and extremely ambitious method of language description. When a grammar is conceived of in the terms outlined in this chapter, it is called a generative grammar. In giving a general definition of 'sentence' for a language, the grammar is said to 'generate' the sentences of that language. In the section on Further Reading that follows, I briefly discuss more detailed introductions to the enterprise of generative grammar. Here I have been concerned to give an idea of the kind of thinking that gives rise to that enterprise, and to place the phrase-marker descriptions within a more general context. Of course, a conclusion that consists of questions like those above is something of a cliff-hanger. If you feel this, I have at least succeeded in whetting your appetite.

Finally, why bother? Why is it so important to formulate the rules of natural languages in a fully explicit manner? After all, we all speak one language or another without bother. Why not leave it at that?

There are two related answers to this. The first takes us back to comments made in the introduction. It is precisely the fact that we all speak (and, more mysteriously, acquire) a language without bother that gives this enterprise its interest and importance. There is a sense in which you know the rules of your language. This must be so, since you are capable of making an infinite number of judgements as to what is and what is not a grammatical sentence of your language. But the sense in which you know these rules is different from the sense in which you know the rules of chess, know how to read music, make zabaglione, or drive a car. You know (and acquired) the rules of your language *implicitly*, as if by instinct. The job of the generative grammarian of a language is to describe what its speakers implicitly and instinctively know about that language, in other words, to make *explicit* what it is that speakers know in knowing their language.

Secondly, the discussion above might have given the impression that the grammarian first of all decides what the most appropriate descriptions of sentences are and then goes to work on the rules that govern the construction of those descriptions. It is not quite like this, however. There is no guarantee that, when we attempt to state the rules in the best possible way and as explicitly as possible, we will not want to revise our ideas as to what the best descriptions are. If anything is guaranteed, the opposite of this is: it is by attempting to formulate a systematic and fully explicit set of rules for a language that we can expect to gain new insights into its structure, new insights, that is, into what it is that a speaker knows in knowing that language.

Further Reading

There are many texts available on both linguistics and descriptive English grammar. The following is a brief discussion of a small selection of those appropriate as further reading in connection with the present text, which has been influenced both by a descriptive English grammar tradition and by the theoretical perspective of generative grammar.

Quirk, Greenbaum, Leech, and Svartvik's *A Comprehensive Grammar of the English Language* (CGE) is the contemporary standard reference work on English grammar, offering a wealth of detail on the structures mentioned here and lots more besides. The description given here is in part based on that in CGE – in particular, the verb sub-categorisation of Chapter 4 is that of CGE. **Quirk and Greenbaum's** *A Student's Grammar of the English Language* (SGE) is a very condensed version of that. I refer to these collectively as 'the Grammars'.

There are differences, however. Most generally, the present text emphasises constituency and its representation; in the Grammars there is little discussion of constituency. On a detailed level, the Grammars allow for obligatory adverbials, whereas in the present text it is part of the definition of 'adverbial' that adverbials are optional. There are some minor differences in terminology, too, the most salient being the use of the term 'Verb Phrase'. In the Grammars, 'Verb Phrase' is used to refer to what in the present text is called the 'Verb Group'; and what in the present text is called 'Verb Phrase' is called 'Predicate' in the Grammars.

The reader might consult the Grammars for constructions not dealt with in the present text (or mentioned only in passing). (i) Nominal relative clauses (also known as Free relative clauses). (ii) Apposition. (iii) Gerunds (also known as Gerundive Nominalisations). (iv) Imperatives (mentioned here in Chapter 3, Further Exercise 4) – in CGE they are called 'Commands'. (v) Existential (*there*) sentences (mentioned here in Chapter 10).

Particularly appropriate as further reading in connection with the present text is **Huddleston's** *Introduction to the Grammar of English*, which offers more wide-ranging and detailed discussion of English structures. Descriptive complexities ignored or merely alluded to here are there given more attention. There is a useful bibliography of items that should be accessible to intermediate students.

Apart from my assumption of some correlation between constituent structure and meaning, little has been said about meaning. This was particularly marked in the discussion of verbs. **Leech's** *Meaning and the English Verb* is an excellent short introduction. **Palmer's** *The English Verb* is more comprehensive.

The other influence on this text is that of generative grammar (mentioned in Chapter 11). In this connection two books should be mentioned: **Radford's** *Transformational Grammar: a first course* and **Haegemann's** *An introduction to Government and Binding*. Both of these take constituency and its representation as the leading idea in syntax. Haegemann starts from a position that will be familiar to readers of *Analysing Sentences*. Having read the present text, students should have little difficulty in tackling these. See also **Cook and Newson's** *Chomsky's Universal Grammar*.

More generally, I can recommend **Pinker's** *The Language Instinct* and **Smith's** *The Twitter Machine*, both of which are entertaining and intriguing. **Salkie's** *The Chomsky Update* is a readable introduction to Chomsky's philosophy of language and mind – and to his politics. Of **Chomsky's** own work, *Language and Problems of Knowledge: The Managua Lectures* is the most accessible.

All these books fall within the framework of a particular theory of generative grammar, transformational (generative) grammar. The central claim of transformational grammar is that, in describing a language, it is impossible to express everything that needs to be expressed about each sentence within a single phrase-marker. The claim is that several phrase-markers are required, the phrase-markers being linked by transformational (movement) rules. I have made use of this idea of movement in several places in the present text. Other ways of doing this have been contemplated. A theory of generative grammar that rejects the idea of movement is Head-Driven Phrase Structure Grammar (HPSG). The standard introduction here is **Pollard and Sag's** *Head-driven Phrase Structure Grammar*.

CHOMSKY, N. (1988) *Language and Problems of Knowledge: The Managua Lectures*. M.I.T. Press.

COOK, V. and M. NEWSON (1996) *Chomsky's Universal Grammar: an introduction*. Blackwell.

HAEGEMANN, L. (1994) *An Introduction to Government and Binding*. 2nd Edition. Blackwells.

HUDDLESTON, R. (1984) *Introduction to the Grammar of English*. Cambridge University Press.

LEECH, G. (1971) *Meaning and the English Verb*. Longman.

PALMER, F. (1974) *The English Verb*. Longman.

PINKER, S. (1994) *The Language Instinct*. Penguin.

POLLARD, C. and I. SAG (1994) *Head-driven Phrase Structure Grammar*. University of Chicago Press.

QUIRK, R. and S. GREENBAUM (1990) *A Student's Grammar of the English Language*. Longman.

QUIRK, R., S. GREENBAUM, G. LEECH, and J. SVARTVIK (1985) *A Comprehensive Grammar of the English Language*. Longman.

RADFORD, A. (1988) *Transformational Grammar: a first course*. Cambridge University Press.

SALKIE, R. (1990) *The Chomsky Update*. Unwin Hyman.

SMITH, N. (1989) *The Twitter Machine: reflections on language*. Blackwells.

Index